A Communion of Communions:
One Eucharistic Fellowship

A COMMUNION OF COMMUNIONS: ONE EUCHARISTIC FELLOWSHIP

The Detroit Report and Papers of the
Triennial Ecumenical Study
of the Episcopal Church, 1976–1979

Edited by J. ROBERT WRIGHT

A Crossroad Book • The Seabury Press • New York

1979 • The Seabury Press • 815 Second Avenue • New York, N.Y. 10017

Library of Congress Cataloging in Publication Data

Main entry under title:
A Communion of communions: one Eucharistic fellowship.

"A Crossroad book."
Includes index.
1. Protestant Episcopal Church in the U.S.A.—Relations—Addresses,
essays, lectures. I. Wright, John Robert, 1936–
BX5926.C65   283'.73   79-65999   ISBN 0-8164-2008-4

To Peter Day,
Distinguished Layman,
Upon Retirement as Ecumenical Officer
of the Episcopal Church

From Many Friends
Who Have Helped Make this Publication Possible,
Some of Whose Names are Inscribed
at the Close of this Volume

Contents

Foreword

[Editor's note—The following was written by the Ecumenical Officer of the Episcopal Church, Peter Day, to accompany this volume before he learned that it would be dedicated to him.]

Assumptions and opinions formed in previous years may no longer be descriptive of contemporary church life, including the life of the Episcopal Church. The Standing Commission on Ecumenical Relations and the ecumenical office of Executive Council have long been aware of the need for an overview of their work and developing new plans for the future. The need was plainly seen, but the resources in personnel and finances had yet to be found.

With the support of Presiding Bishop John M. Allin, we requested the Episcopal Church Foundation to grant us a substantial sum for the cost of a major consultation process. The Foundation granted the Commission $9,000, reported to us by Executive Vice President Frederick L. Redpath. This news made the impossible possible. It makes me ponder how often the Foundation has made impossibilities possible, enriching the Church's life over the years.

The other impossible possibility for the success of our Consultation was William A. Norgren, former executive director of the Faith and Order Commission of the National Council of Churches. A priest of the Episcopal Church, he accepted the post of assistant ecumenical officer in 1975 and, with his experience in small meetings and large, was the ideal planner for the National Ecumenical Consultation. My own contribution to the Consultation I count as my bringing Bill Norgren to the Episcopal Church Center staff.

It was decided early that the book should be edited by J. Robert Wright, author of other important books and articles on ecumenical and theological subjects and a member of the Standing Commission on Ecumenical Relations.

EDEO—the Episcopal Diocesan Ecumenical Officers—was led in its formative years by John H. Bonner of Chattanooga, who has been followed by the able new chairman, William B. Lawson of Lynn, Massachusetts. Under their leadership, the ecumenical officers of the dioceses conducted provincial ecumenical meetings in all eight domestic provinces, gathering data on the present ecumenical outlook of the Episcopal Church across the nation for report to the Consultation.

Others must be mentioned: Bishop John H. Burt, chairman of the Standing Commission on Ecumenical Relations and his co-workers on the Ecumenical Commission; and Anna Quillen, indefatigable secretary of the ecumenical office.

So it all happened, and the Standing Commission will bring its proposed ecumenical resolutions to the 1979 General Convention for debate and action. The people of the Church are the ones who must understand themselves to be members of the whole Body of Christ, and hear their own call to the ministry, clerical or lay, the ministry of reconciliation for which our Lord lived and died and rose again as the living Shepherd and Bishop of our souls.

Votes of Convention are important and agreements between churches are important, but to give them their deepest significance we must all follow those demanding words of St. Paul in I Corinthians 13:4–7: "Love is patient and kind; love is not arrogant or rude. Love does not insist on its own way; it is not irritable or resentful; it does not rejoice at wrong, but rejoices in the right. Love bears all things, believes all things, endures all things." Christian love must find its own opportunities for expression in the unplanned personal encounters of daily life.

Christ's high-priestly prayer in John 17 also stresses the theme of Christian love—the perfect love between the Father and the Son— ". . . that the love with which thou hast loved me may be in them [his disciples]." Earlier in the prayer he says ". . . that they may be perfectly one, that the world may know that thou hast sent me." The ecumenical task is to make Christ known to the world and to make the relationships of the churches a visible sign of the one Church which is His Body.

Peter Day

Introduction

In the present movement for the unity of the churches, as they attempt to follow Jesus' command "that they may all be one . . . so that the world may believe" (John 17), the question may be asked: Where does the Episcopal Church now stand and what are its goals? That is the theme of this book.

"We do not counsel patience" was a concern frequently expressed in the deliberations of the National Ecumenical Consultation of the Episcopal Church when it met at the Mercy Center, Farmington Hills (near Detroit), from 5 to 9 November 1978. That this concern was not just a call for action without sufficient theological forethought was evident from the more modest but hopeful way in which the very sentence of the Detroit Report containing this phrase reached its conclusion: "We do not counsel patience . . . for steps (toward unity) can be taken here and now by each Christian and each church." This was not a call for some cataclysmic revolution, therefore, but rather it was one way of stating a principle heard frequently at the same consultation, that in ecumenical matters "the goal and the way belong together." The kind of final unity God wills for his church, that is, can not be discerned in a vacuum apart from individual steps ventured along the way, any more than the church's unity can be envisioned in isolation from its mission or than the unity of the church can be conceived apart from the unity of humankind. Partnership in mission, spiritual ecumenism, and doctrinal consensus are all necessary if the expressed goal of visible unity in one faith, in "one eucharistic fellowship, a communion of communions," is to be achieved.

The Detroit Report, which culminated this three-year study process, should obviously be read in its entirety below, but its description of the goal and the way should be noted here. It proposes to the Episcopal Church at this stage of history a goal of visible unity as well as an outline of the path to follow in order to reach it. The goal is "one eucharistic fellowship, a communion of communions, based upon mutual recognition of catholicity." The elements of this catholicity are spelled out as mutual recognition of members and ministers, sharing in the one Eucharist, acknowledgement of each other as "belonging to the body of Christ at all places and at all times," proclaiming the

Gospel with "one mind and purpose," and serving "the needs of humankind with mutual trust and dedication." For these ends the churches "will plan and decide together in assemblies constituted by authorized representatives whenever this is required." The goal statement also mentions matters on which further clarification is needed, such as "the shape of the collegiality, conciliarity, authority, and primacy which need to be present and active" in parishes and dioceses as well as "nationally, regionally, and universally." Also requiring clarification are ways in which "the particular traditions of each of the communions will be maintained and developed" and how the church will be "shaped by the particular histories and cultures within which she is called to fulfill her mission." As part of this process along the way towards becoming "a communion of communions," moreover, the report urges especially the need for a renewal of eucharistic life and practice as well as doctrinal consensus about the Eucharist, in order that the full meaning and relevance of the goal of "one eucharistic fellowship," as distinct from organizational and governmental merger, can emerge. Such a vision, it should be added, is only the preamble, albeit also the central theme, for the many detailed proposals that the entire process of study called forth.

The pages that follow, therefore, constitute not just one more popular-level paperback Anglican book on ecumenism, of which the number is already legion. Rather, they represent the most extensive and thorough study the Episcopal Church has yet undertaken of all its ecumenical relations, and they reflect the hope of the nearly five hundred persons directly involved that this study will offer some guidelines, recommendations, and agenda for every agency and level of the Episcopal Church by the time of the 1979 General Convention and beyond. The situation which the study addresses is nothing less than an expansion of the meaning and content of the word "ecumenical" itself, as it has gradually come to include virtually everything done together with other churches or fellow Christians at every level of the church's life, from the careful work of scholars in joint theological studies, to problems over mixed marriages, to cooperation in many areas of mission and service and the sharing of prayers and worship in local congregations and world assemblies. As the ecumenical agenda has grown, however, the goal and coordination of these many activities has become less clear, and a major purpose of the triennial study process has been an attempt to define common goals, to make recommendations, and to shape the rough outlines of a path to follow.

The 1976 General Convention of the Episcopal Church mandated this Triennial Ecumenical Study with the following resolution:

> *Resolved,* that the Commission on Ecumenical Relations under-
> take, through the convening of regional meetings culminating in
> a special national conference or other appropriate ways, to assess
> this Church's present ecumenical posture and involvement, to
> suggest restatement, where necessary, of those essentials to which
> the Episcopal Church is committed, and to formulate those priori-
> ties and goals which can guide our ecumenical activities in the
> future;
> *And be it further resolved,* that a complete report of this study, to-
> gether with any recommendations, be prepared for and presented
> to the 1979 General Convention.

The study was commended to all bishops and diocesan ecumenical
officers by the Presiding Bishop, the Rt. Rev. John M. Allin, in a letter
dated 20 June 1977. Cooperating in the study were the Executive
Council of the Episcopal Church, the organization of Episcopal Diocesan Ecumenical Officers, and the Standing Commission on Ecumenical Relations. General oversight was given by the Standing Commission
under the leadership of its chair, the Rt. Rev. John M. Burt, Bishop of
Ohio, and the study process was coordinated by the Ecumenical Office
of the Episcopal Church under the service of Dr. Peter Day and the
Rev. William A. Norgren. Over the 1976–79 triennium every diocese
of the Episcopal Church, as well as nearly every agency and congregation, was invited to describe and evaluate its ecumenical involvement
and commitments as part of the study process.

As will be obvious from the outline of the contents of this book, the
study as a whole had three basic objectives: 1) to assess the Episcopal
Church's general ecumenical posture (here numbered as Chapter 2
under the question "Where are we now?"); 2) to articulate those ecumenical goals toward which we intend to move (here numbered as
Chapter 1 under the question "Toward what goals should we move?");
and 3) to restate those essentials to which we are committed (here
numbered as Chapter 3 under the question "To what are we already
committed?"). The contents of this book display some of the ways in
which each of these objectives was met.

Three final reports from the study process, collected here in Chapter 1, answer the question "Toward what goals should we move?" The
National Ecumenical Consultation (made possible through a generous
subsidy from the Episcopal Church Foundation) was obviously the
central event in this entire process, and the Detroit Report drew together its findings and recommendations. Of the nearly 70 persons
who took part in this five-day meeting (a list follows the text of the
report) Bishop Burt from the chair observed that it was the first time
so many Episcopalians working in so many different contexts for the

cause of unity, as well as some leading ecumenists from the Roman
Catholic, Lutheran, Presbyterian, Methodist, and other churches, had
all been brought together and given "both voice and vote in helping to
frame the ecumenical policy of our church." The Detroit Report's 57
recommendations are now before the church at large. Even more
extensive than the national consultation, however, was the local process that fed it, and that process is summarized in the Report of the
Episcopal Diocesan Ecumenical Officers. Some 200 persons representing 76 of the 92 domestic dioceses of the Episcopal Church gathered
in eight provincial consultations to collate and analyze the ecumenical
profiles of their own dioceses, using diocesan questionnaires as well as
position statements from the bishops and materials from the Anglican
Consultative Council and elsewhere. Participating in these provincial
consultations were bishops, diocesan ecumenical officers, laity and
clergy, partners from other churches, and theological consultants.
The posture descriptions from each province were not the sort of
material that could easily be reproduced for inclusion in this book, but
it should be noted that they have already been published fully in the
Ecumenical Bulletin (no. 29, May–June 1978) and that the preparatory
questionnaires, checklists, and study outlines were published in earlier
issues of the same *Bulletin* (nos. 24 and 25, July–August and
September–October 1977). The final EDEO Report, adopted at Tulsa
in April 1978 and printed here, is therefore only the most succinct
summary of what was really a very thorough nationwide study process. Moving, finally, from the local to the national arena, the last
report presented here comes from the Executive Council and represents its contribution to the triennial study. Prepared in conjunction
with the council's Standing Committee on National and World Mission, this report is an analysis of the Episcopal Church's official involvement (indeed, of its historic leadership) in national and global
ecumenical structures. The appended Resolutions of Implementation,
based upon the report and prepared by a Committee of Conference
appointed by the Presiding Bishop from the standing committees of
the Executive Council and adopted by the council as amended at its
meeting of September 1978, constitute the Executive Council's recommended guidelines and resolutions for the ecumenical objectives
of the general church program budget over the next three years. All
three of these reports, therefore, attempt to articulate goals. They try
to answer the question "Toward what goals should we move?" (It
should be added that, because each of these reports has already been
amended and adopted by a church body, very little attempt has been
made to edit them further for publication.)

A second question of the study was "Where are we now?" Although something of an answer to this question is already comprised in the four reports that constitute the first chapter of this book, the second chapter tries to assess our present ecumenical posture with specific reference to the other churches with whom the Episcopal Church has especially close relationships, and it presents papers commissioned by the Standing Ecumenical Commission on this question. First, there is a careful and penetrating theological analysis of the four major national ecumenical dialogues in which the Episcopal Church is officially engaged, prepared by a team of five theologians who have compiled, reviewed, and evaluated critically the results and findings of each bilateral or consultation. Following upon similar analyses already completed by Roman Catholic and Lutheran theologians on behalf of their churches in the U.S.A., this part of the study brings needed theological cross-perspective to the Episcopal Church's current ecumenical conversations and at the same time points the way to a continuing service that theologians can and should render to the cause of church unity. Next there follow papers setting forth the vision of visible unity held by each of these four ecumenical partners, with particular reference to the Episcopal Church and the Anglican Communion. Here a concerted effort has been made to hear from the others, as the Standing Commission decided to invite an outstanding theologian from each to be an author and to participate in the Detroit Consultation: from the Roman Catholics, the Rev. Herbert J. Ryan, S.J., professor of religious studies at Loyola Marymount University in Los Angeles, a member of the Anglican–Roman Catholic Consultation in the U.S.A. and of the Anglican–Roman Catholic International Commission; from the Lutherans, the Rev. William G. Rusch, director of Fortress Press in Philadelphia and formerly associate executive director of the Division of Theological Studies of the Lutheran Council in the U.S.A.; from the Consultation on Church Union, the Rev. Gerald F. Moede, its general secretary; and from the Orthodox, the Very Rev. Protopresbyter Stanley S. Harakas, dean of Holy Cross Greek Orthodox Theological School, Brookline, Massachusetts. This chapter concludes, finally, with an analysis and survey of a significant but less well known aspect of the Episcopal Church's official ecumenical relationships, the concordats and the Wider Episcopal Fellowship, by the Rev. William A. Norgren, assistant ecumenical officer. A number of other papers, it should be added, were also commissioned by the Standing Ecumenical Commission for this study but are not included here for lack of space. Peter Day, the Episcopal Church's courageous and indefatigable ecumenical officer (the fruits of whose patient leader-

ship are in effect summarized by this very study), called the entire
Detroit Consultation "back to the basics" with a presentation of
"Church Unity in the New Testament." Robert G. Torbet, former
ecumenical liaison officer of the American Baptist Churches, offered
the background for a decentralized but promising dialogue which the
Standing Ecumenical Commission is currently initiating in a paper
entitled "Consensus and Divergence on Visible Unity among Baptists,
with Particular Reference to the Episcopal Church." Still two other
papers, prepared for other occasions and already printed elsewhere,
were considered carefully in the study process: J. Robert Nelson, a
leading Methodist and professor of systematic theology at Boston
University School of Theology, on "Conciliarity/Conciliar Fellowship"
(printed in *Midstream* 17:2 (April 1978) 97–117); and Robert T.
Handy, leading Baptist and professor of church history at Union
Theological Seminary in New York City, on "Issues of Religious Freedom and Christian Unity That Relate to Our Pluralism" (partially
printed in *Midstream* 15:4 [October 1976] 354–365).

The final chapter of this book is entitled "To What Are We Already
Committed?" Here again there is a certain and inevitable degree of
overlapping from the previous two chapters, especially from the Detroit Report, the Ecumenical Report of the Executive Council, the
Theological Analysis of the Dialogues, and the Concordat paper. This
final chapter, however, subtitled "The Episcopal Church's Vision of
Visible Unity: Changing and Unchanging," is composed of a collection
of some 126 documents drawn from the official decisions of Lambeth
Conferences and General Conventions. It represents a first attempt,
however imperfect and inadequate, to gather the textual evidence for
the way in which the Episcopal/Anglican ecumenical position has developed over the years up to the present. Whether these documents in
their entirety comprise a "restatement of essentials" is of course ques-
tionable, but, on the other hand, whatever essential statements the
Episcopal Church and the Anglican Communion have made on ecumenical matters are surely to be found within this collection. Of
paramount importance, for both historical and theological reasons, is
the Chicago-Lambeth Quadrilateral of 1886–88 (below, pp. 230–33;
PBCP pp. 876–78), of which a contemporary reaffirmation is proposed
in the Detroit Report (below, pp. 3–29). Further consideration of all
these documents, which have been specially collected for the purpose of
the Triennial Ecumenical Study, will undoubtedly yield deeper knowledge of what should be considered essential as well as some indication
of any restatements that may be desirable. That the whole study points
to the need for still further analysis, sifting, coordination, and re-

statement, is obvious. The Episcopal Church's preeminent role in the movement for church unity, it may be added, makes it even more imperative that the principles upon which its own unity rests should also be more clearly defined.

This Triennial Ecumenical Study of 1976–79, drawn from the roots and springs of the Episcopal Church, is now the property of the Episcopal Church as a whole. Thus far its component parts carry the authority only of those who have compiled or endorsed them, but a call for some more official ratification and implementation is obviously implied. There is no need for any further introduction or summary of its components here, as each must be allowed to speak for itself.

General Theological Seminary   *J. Robert Wright*
New York City
1 February 1979

· I ·

TOWARD WHAT GOALS SHOULD WE MOVE?

Final Reports from the Study Process

The Detroit Report:
National Ecumenical Consultation of the Episcopal Church, Farmington Hills, Michigan (Detroit), 5–9 November 1978

Our Lord continues to call us to make visible the unity He has given the Church. His prayer is "that they may all be one; even as thou, Father, art in me, and I in thee, that they also may be in us, so that the world may believe."[1] We hear this call in Holy Scripture and the tradition of the Church, through the needs of humankind, and through the good things happening in the ecumenical movement. The call comes with increased urgency because of forces of disunity and destruction at work today in the churches and in society.

I. *The Visible Unity We Seek*

The Episcopal Church, with other churches of the Anglican Communion, is committed to the ecumenical movement and, in particular, to the goal of the visible unity of the Church.[2] As long ago as 1897 the Lambeth Conference resolved "that every opportunity be taken to emphasize the Divine purpose of visible unity amongst Christians, as a fact of revelation."[3] It is always the Church's task to express and renew this unity. "The mission of the Church is to restore all people to unity with God and each other in Christ."[4] The following two paragraphs summarize the consensus we have reached:

> The visible unity we seek is one eucharistic fellowship, a communion of communions, based upon mutual recognition of catholicity. In this communion the churches will all recognize each other's members and ministries; "they will share the bread and the cup of their Lord; they will acknowledge each other as belonging to the body of Christ at all places and at all times; they will proclaim the Gospel to the world with one mind and purpose; they will serve the needs of humankind with mutual trust and dedication. And for these ends they will plan and decide together in assemblies constituted by authorized representatives whenever this is required."[5]
>
> We do not yet see the shape of the collegiality, conciliarity, authority, and primacy which need to be present and active in the diocese with its parishes as well as nationally, regionally,

universally. We do not yet know how the particular traditions of each of the communions will be maintained and developed for the enrichment of the whole Church. We do not yet see how the Church will be shaped by the particular histories and cultures within which she is called to fulfill her mission.

In recent years, Anglicans have sought ways to express more fully among themselves the Biblical principle of mutual responsibility and interdependence. We believe ways can now be found to express this principle in a communion of the churches in the body of Christ. As the churches become partners in mission they will move from present interrelatedness to interdependence.

Within this situation, moreover, Episcopalians are called to the creative recovery of their own rich heritage of ecumenical leadership. We are challenged to understand anew the dynamic tension among the apostolic, catholic, and reformed aspects of our Anglican character. We are confronted with the necessity of demonstrating the seriousness of our life and doctrine as these are grounded in the sacramental character of our worship. With all other Christians, we have been promised the aid of the Holy Spirit in meeting such a call, and the ecumenical challenge of our age is to pursue this renewal in concert with others.

The visible unity we seek will require long and steady growth as well as various steps. We do not counsel patience, however, for steps can be taken here and now by each Christian and each church to exercise a ministry of reconciliation.

Call to Action

We call the Episcopal Church through its local ecumenical officers, its diocesan commissions, its seminaries, its Standing Commission on Ecumenical Relations, to discover the ways in which this Report to the Episcopal Church can be of value for (a) theological reflection, (b) the life of prayer and worship, and (c) the apostolate to the world.

A. Doctrinal Consensus: Theological Reflection

The above statement of the visible unity we seek, together with the statement of principles for unity and the analysis of each conversation in Section II below, provides a structure for theological reflection in order that the people of God may enter more deeply into the mystery of God and his Church. We must ask ourselves, at the deepest theological level, why we are called to be one in Christ. For this purpose we urge that there be serious study of the statements from our conversations by dioceses, parishes, theological seminaries, and those groups within the Church who are called to common prayer and study.

Again, the Episcopal Church is one of more than a hundred member churches of the World Council of Churches reflecting on the Faith and Order Commission's three statements on Baptism, Eucharist, and Ministry.[6] These documents reflect the fruits of the direct national and international conversations between world families of churches like our own and should also be studied seriously.

The National Council of Churches is now redefining its identity and purpose on Biblical and theological grounds. This process is paralleled by its own Faith and Order Commission's study of conciliar fellowship, a commission composed of Orthodox, Roman Catholic, Anglican, Lutheran, Reformed, Baptist, Methodist, Disciples, and conservative evangelical members.

In the dioceses, where more direct encounter with Christians of other traditions occurs, Episcopalians are increasingly drawn into delicate theological issues related to human rights, sexuality, justice for the poor and suffering, and stewardship of the environment.

At all of these levels, therefore, for the promotion of theological reflection and the process of doctrinal consensus, we offer the following recommendations.

RECOMMENDATIONS

1. *Whereas,* the three Agreed Statements of the Anglican–Roman Catholic International Commission have greatly advanced the understanding of each other shared by Anglican and Roman Catholic Churches, and

   Whereas, the Common Declaration signed in Rome on April 29, 1977 by the Pope and the Archbishop of Canterbury reminds us that "the moment will shortly come when the respective authorities (of both churches) must evaluate the conclusions" (referring to the three Agreed Statements) and recommends that this work "be pursued through procedures appropriate to our respective communions, so that both of them may be led along the path towards unity"; and

   Whereas, the preface of the Twelve-Year Report of the Anglican–Roman Catholic Consultation in the U.S.A. speaks of "a unity which demands visible expression and testimony now"; and

   Whereas, the report of the provincial consultations held by the Episcopal Diocesan Ecumenical Officers reflects such an overwhelming "interest in and dialogue toward visible unity . . . mainly with the Roman Catholics" and shows "a preference for visible unity with the Roman Catholic Church"; therefore, be it

   Resolved, that the National Ecumenical Consultation request the Standing Commission on Ecumenical Relations to take steps to initiate a conference of Episcopal and Roman Catholic leaders in the United States to consider the practical implications of these statements and what can be done to implement them in the life of the Church as the next step in the process toward visible unity.

2. *Whereas,* out of discussions at the National Ecumenical Consultation there surfaced the need to relate ecumenical priorities more directly to the General Convention and its preparations; therefore, be it

   Resolved, that this Consultation request the Standing Commission on Ecumenical Relations to

   a. urge the presidents of the Episcopal Diocesan Ecumenical Officers and the National Association of Diocesan Ecumenical Officers to have prepared an introduction to the basic documents on Anglican–Roman Catholic relations in a simple form and style of language for the information and use of Bishops and Deputies to General Convention;

   b. prepare and urge diocesan ecumenical officers to meet with and inform the deputations of each diocese to the General Convention of the ecumenical concerns and issues;

   c. provide each Deputy to General Convention with a copy of the booklet *The Three Agreed Statements;*

   d. request from the proper authorities of General Convention a time and place for an open hearing on ecumenical issues to come before Convention and prepare for this open hearing in conjunction with the executive committee of the Episcopal Diocesan Ecumenical Officers;

   e. prepare resolutions on the Anglican–Roman Catholic International Commission and Anglican–Roman Catholic Consultation documents moving beyond the usual "commitment to study," and indicating that official acceptances of the documents will represent forward steps in the process of establishing visible unity; and

   f. request that officially appointed representatives of the Roman Catholic Church be seated with voice in the meetings of the ecumenical committees of both Houses of Convention.

3. The Consultation recommends to the Executive Council that the "Use Guides" under preparation for the new Church's Teaching Series include references to the Episcopal Church's understanding of Christian unity, set forth our present ecumenical relationships, and offer suggested resources for further study.

4. The Consultation requests the Standing Commission on Ecumenical Relations to prepare guidelines and, if necessary, legislation

for General Convention to facilitate an appropriate official response from this Church to agreed statements resulting from bilateral conversations. We suggest that appropriate elements would include (1) agreed procedures for evaluation, (2) agreed procedures for ratification of statements by General Convention upon the recommendation of the Standing Commission (with or without qualifying conditions and clarifications), and (3) agreed procedures for implementation of the statements in the life of the Church through the Executive Council or other appropriate agencies. We emphasize the need to assure necessary funding and administrative accountability so that we may pass from the stage of dialogue, negotiation, and ratification to the stage of implementation and application.

5. *Whereas,* those who work for the unity of God's Church are eager to support all others who work toward the same end, and
   Whereas, many work in diverse places and areas of concern; therefore, be it
   Resolved, that the Consultation request the Ecumenical Office to ensure all documents regarding ecumenical affairs, when issued and before distributing, be labeled with author or origin, intended purpose, authorization, and date of issue.

6. *Whereas,* we live in a pluralistic society that involves increasing numbers of ecumenical marriages; and
   Whereas, clergy and laity in many places seek guidelines for ministry to the faithful especially in Anglican–Roman Catholic marriages; and
   Whereas, a special international commission of Anglicans and Roman Catholics has issued a *Final Report on the Theology of Marriage and Its Application to Mixed Marriages* (1975); therefore, be it
   Resolved, that the Consultation request the Anglican–Roman Catholic Consultation in the U.S.A. to consider this report and produce a document addressing the concerns of the faithful in Anglican–Roman Catholic marriages, both for the consideration of our two churches in the U.S.A. and for transmission to the Anglican–Roman Catholic International Commission for possible incorporation into a new international statement on this subject.

7. *Whereas,* the Anglican–Roman Catholic International Commission has produced Agreed Statements on Eucharist, Ministry, and Authority, and of these the Windsor Statement on Eucharist is nearing its final revised form; and
   Whereas, the Anglican–Roman Catholic Consultation in the U.S.A. has produced a statement on *The Purpose or Mission of the Church*

drawn from eucharistic texts of our two Churches; and,
Whereas, the Episcopal Church has already studied these documents in some depth; therefore, be it
Resolved, that the Consultation request the Standing Commission on Ecumenical Relations to present to the General Convention in 1979 a resolution to accept the Windsor Statement as a statement of the eucharistic faith received and held by this Church and the statement on *The Purpose or Mission of the Church* as a description of the mandate this church has received to proclaim the Gospel of our Lord Jesus Christ.

8. The Consultation proposes as a model process for reception of the emerging ecumenical consensus that the 1979 General Convention urge the study of the 1979 version of *In Quest of a Church of Christ Uniting* in theological schools, diocesan ecumenical commissions, and selected parishes during a period of two years. Findings from this study would be received and collated by the Ecumenical Office and the Standing Commission on Ecumenical Relations with recommendations to the 1982 General Convention for an official response, so that other churches in the Consultation on Church Union may learn how the process of ecumenical consensus-building places upon the Episcopal Church the responsibility to give account of its faith in an ecumenically significant manner. Experience with this process (and the education generated thereby) may in turn suggest a procedure for responding to the emerging theological consensus in bilateral conversations with the Orthodox, Roman Catholic, and Lutheran Churches.

9. The Consultation commends the Standing Commission on Ecumenical Relations for beginning the dialogue with Southern Baptists and looks forward to this developing fellowship.

10. The Consultation calls on the Standing Commission on Ecumenical Relations to strengthen the Wider Episcopal Fellowship, especially by keeping the churches of this Fellowship informed on the progress of the dialogues and working to bring them into these dialogues.

11. The Consultation requests the Episcopal Diocesan Ecumenical Officers and the Standing Commission on Ecumenical Relations to draft for the Church's consideration such canonical changes as may be needed effectively to implement the "Toward a Mutual Recognition of Members" from the Consultation on Church Union.

12. The Consultation requests the Episcopal Diocesan Ecumenical Officers to take counsel on the possibility of establishing an ecu-

menical "flying squad" to help dioceses or parishes in their ecumenical planning.[7]

13. The Consultation recommends wider circulation by the Ecumenical Office of the Moscow Statement of the Anglican-Orthodox
Joint Doctrinal Commission for serious study as a way by which
our understanding of the theology of the Church can be enlarged
and deepened.

14. We recommend the Standing Commission on Ecumenical Relations initiate negotiations with the Consultation on Church
Union on the subject of the reconciliation of ordained ministries
in view of the convergence of the document "In Quest of a
Church of Christ Uniting" with the Lambeth Quadrilateral.

B. Spiritual Ecumenism: The Life of Prayer and Worship

Lex orandi, lex credendi est ("The rule of prayer is the rule of belief").[8]
Ecumenical agreements reached by our Church's representatives
must be explored and tested also in a context of prayer to see if the
agreements reached in them are consistent with the development and
nurture offered by Anglican spirituality. This task of spiritual discernment requires knowledge and appreciation of how the churches
reaching such an agreement "school" their members in the life of
prayer through public worship and private devotion. Therefore we
urge each of the dialogues to treat the question of prayer and spiritual
life so that they can express in a brief statement how the churches in
dialogue view each Christian's relation to God in prayer. In this way
we can appreciate and experience the spiritual treasures of other
Christian traditions by testing the theological agreements in this
deeper context.

The term "spiritual ecumenism" signifies a "change of heart" toward Christians of other traditions. It is manifested in the search for
holiness of life, public and private prayer for Christian unity, celebrat-
ing in worship what Christians have in common, and appropriation in
humility of gifts which God has revealed to other traditions. The Holy
Spirit may prompt us to receive from each other such treasures as
Biblical interpretation, liturgies, prayers, hymns, spiritual exercises,
and saintly lives which truly belong to us all. Spiritual ecumenism
requires a minimum of formal authorization and is therefore a logical
priority in ecumenical development.

The urgency of spiritual ecumenism may be seen in the growing
evidence of the failure of a merely secularist view of life with its legacy
of superficiality, emptiness, and restlessness, manifest among other
ways in the increase of violence, sexual anarchy, abuse of alcohol and

drugs, and compulsion to acquire more things. While the many churches individually may have the Gospel with which to address the ultimate spiritual longing of humankind, some more urgent and immediate needs are emerging among Christians which cannot be met adequately by any one church without resources from the other Christian traditions. Such crises call for Christians to draw together in a more vigorous proclamation of faith and hope, and the unity discerned in this process can give urgency to the search for removal of barriers to eucharistic sharing.

One major focus of spiritual ecumenism is prayer, and Anglican liturgical language assumes that there is but one Church. It conspicuously lacks denominational references. This assumption, we believe, should be reflected more adequately in the life of the Episcopal Church. Furthermore, the liturgical movement itself has led to a remarkable consensus in prayer among churches which calls for visible expression through some common rites.

PERCEPTIONS

- Much spiritual ecumenism is spontaneous and unplanned.
- The most dynamic form of spiritual ecumenism today may be charismatic renewal, although this can represent both a promise and a danger.
- A growing number of Cursillo events, prayer groups, retreats, etc. are ecumenical.
- Leaders in spiritual renewal move freely across denominational lines.
- The hunger for Bible study is widespread and cuts straight across the old denominational lines.
- Much spiritual ecumenism takes place in covenanting parishes (Anglican–Roman Catholic) and events of Interim Eucharistic Fellowship and Generating Communities (Consultation on Church Union).
- The mobility of our society often makes "pilgrims out of tourists," who may thereby discover and experience the spiritual heritage of churches other than their own.

RECOMMENDATIONS

1. Message of Greetings and Goodwill to the Polish National Catholic Church: We are grateful to the Most Rev. Francis C. Rowinski, Prime Bishop, for sending his representative, the Rev. Edward J. Sobolewski, to this National Ecumenical Consultation of the Episcopal Church. We look forward to deepening the relationship be-

tween our two churches as together we move into ever wider dialogue with other Christians. We hope and long for the day when we can recover the Intercommunion which our two Churches have shared for thirty years.

2. *Resolved,* that the following outline be proposed to the Standing Commission on Ecumenical Relations as the basis for a statement to be developed by the Commission for use in the Episcopal Church:

STATEMENT ON EUCHARISTIC PRACTICE

a. Fundamental Understandings
Eucharistic celebration by God's people—his will
Real Presence—Christ's Body, not ours
Importance of *koinonia*
Discipline in sacraments—a legitimate function of the Christian community

b. Holy Communion within a Divided Church
Normative practice—unity of faith and order
Unquestioned exceptional cases—pastoral situations
Special circumstances
By whom regulated
Concordats of full communion
Inter-church *koinonia* (e.g., ecumenical, Cursillos, covenanted parishes, Interim Eucharistic Fellowship)
Guests at the table of a different family
Mixed marriages—weddings and after
Relation to ongoing church membership
Respect for the discipline of another church

c. Regulations and the Practice of Hospitality
Who may participate
The nature of the invitation
Limitations in duration
Conscience—the ultimate guide
Episcopalians in other churches

d. The Pain of Broken Communion
An experience of the cross in a sinful world
Spiritual communion while others communicate
Incentives for reconciling and healing

3. Recommendation to the Standing Commission on Ecumenical Relations, for transmission to General Convention:
Statement on Individuals Receiving Communion at the Lord's Table Where Intercommunion between Churches Does Not Exist
The Holy Communion must be seen in its proper context of the

fellowship of committed Christians in the household of the Apostolic faith, to which we are admitted by Baptism. In the Apostolic tradition which the Episcopal Church maintains and practices the normative condition of the church is a union in one fellowship of faith, of hearing and proclaiming the Word, of sacramental practice, of personal relations, and of church order.

Since the General Convention of 1967 adopted a Statement on Communion Discipline, from which the above paragraph has been drawn, several developments have occurred that affect the practice in this church of admitting members of other churches to partake of the Lord's Supper at altars in the Episcopal Church:

a. The admission of children not yet confirmed has put the focus on Baptism within our communion of faith as the sole sacramental prerequisite for receiving Holy Communion.

b. The Proposed Book of Common Prayer locates the Eucharist in a central place in the life of the Christian family. All rites in the new book are placed in the context of the Eucharist.

c. The overwhelming positive response to the Anglican–Roman Catholic International Commission's Agreed Statement on the Eucharist (Windsor, 1971) undergirds the strong agreement in this church on the Eucharist as a mystery offered by God to his gathered church, and the recognition of Christ's real presence in this sacrament.

d. Ecumenical practice increasingly calls for mutual participation in the sacrament of the Lord's Supper as a means to unity and not just a sign of unity.

e. Inasmuch as the sharing in Christ's Body and Blood is a sign of and a means toward a growing unity in Him, a certain openness to eucharistic sharing with those of other communions should be maintained. This stance, however, requires a real sensitivity to the constraints of conscience on those whose churches officially do not approve of this sacramental participation.

In view of the above, therefore, it is proposed that the following standard be adopted for those of other churches who desire to receive the Holy Communion in Episcopal Churches:

a. They shall have been baptized with water in the name of the Father, and of the Son, and of the Holy Spirit, and shall have previously been admitted to the Holy Communion within the church to which they belong.

b. They shall examine their lives, repent of their sins, and be in love and charity with all people, as this church in its catechism (PBCP, p. 860) says is required of all those who come to the Eucharist.

c. They shall approach the Holy Communion as an expression of the real presence of Jesus Christ whose sacrifice once upon the cross was sufficient for all mankind.

d. They shall find in this Communion the means to strengthen their life within the Christian family.

4. Recommendation especially for the Episcopal Diocesan Ecumenical Officers:

The number of opportunities for spiritual ecumenism needs to be increased (e.g. covenanting parishes, Interim Eucharistic Fellowship, Generating Communities), particularly between Episcopalians and Orthodox.

C. Partnership: The Apostolate to the World

To be a Christian is to be called to serve the world in the Name of Christ. The Episcopal Church and those other churches with whom we are in dialogue must discover ways in which their service to the world arises, not from expediency nor from accident but from a common commitment to the Gospel and the leading of the Spirit.

There is ample and diverse evidence of shared Christian action in local, regional, national, and global contexts. We rejoice in such efforts as both signs of the visible unity we seek and means by which it may grow. We believe that a greater united response to human need will have to be rooted in the Baptismal Covenant which calls us to:

• proclaim by word and example the Good News of God in Christ;
• seek and serve Christ in all persons, loving one's neighbor as oneself;
• strive for justice and peace among all people, and respect the dignity of every human being.[9]

RECOMMENDATIONS

1. We commend to the Episcopal Diocesan Ecumenical Officers the following questions as a means for congregations, dioceses, and other church planning groups to examine their commitment to ecumenical partnership and service:

Do we visibly manifest our Baptismal unity with all Christians in this place?

• By recognizing that burning questions of today are too great to be addressed separately?

• By consulting and planning together in order to carry out our mission and service in the world?

• By sharing our resources for mission and service?

2. The Consultation recommends that the Episcopal Diocesan Ecumenical Officers bring to the attention of appropriate diocesan

commissions the following elements as being necessary or at least desirable for Christian action programs in ecumenical contexts:

   a. A sound theological understanding of the "why" of Christian social action and how it is more than secular service.

   b. Adherence to the "Lund Principle" as embodying, not only our understanding of God's call for witness but also the human dimension of effective stewardship in use of talents and resources.[10]

   c. Engagement in prophetic ministry in order to provide signs which point to the reality of God's continuing action in the world, thus generating *hope* and stimulating services for all or many peoples (e.g., Youngstown Ecumenical Coalition).

   d. Deep and extensive scholarly knowledge when addressing public issues. The Church's responsibility is to seek a theological basis for decision-making, encouraging a variety of just and responsible actions, both public and private.

3. The Consultation recommends that the Executive Council, the Standing Commission on Ecumenical Relations, the Episcopal Diocesan Ecumenical Officers, and other appropriate bodies:

   a. In cooperation with other communions, (1) provide programs of Bible study (in ecumenical context) on the demands that God lays upon us for Christian social action (*diakonia*) in the world, and (2) develop a kindergarten-through-adult educational program unit on the ecumenical imperative for effective Christian service.

   b. Call for a tangible recognition in our seminary curricula of the necessity for an ecumenical life-style in the ordained ministry.

   c. Challenge repeatedly our use of separate and under-utilized buildings.

   d. Initiate, expand, or utilize more fully ecumenical task forces in councils of churches and other agencies that are working on new ethical questions such as biomedical ethics and business practices of multinational corporations.

4. The Consultation requests the Standing Commission on Ecumenical Relations to consider the possible implementation in this church of the practice of the Presbyterian Church, U.S., of having representatives of other churches with seat and voice in its General Assembly, and with seat, voice, and vote in all its Standing Committees.

5. In order to receive the witness of other Christian traditions in the councils of our church, the Consultation recommends that persons from Christian bodies with whom the Episcopal Church is in

dialogue be invited to participate fully in appropriate committees of General Convention.

6. The Consultation recommends that the Executive Council, Standing Commission on Ecumenical Relations, and the Episcopal Diocesan Ecumenical Officers convene a National Ecumenical Consultation each triennium.

7. The Consultation proposes that the Executive Council of the Episcopal Church and the Standing Commission on Ecumenical Relations make an official response, when appropriate, to actions of the Central Committee of the World Council of Churches and the Governing Board of the National Council of Churches as an expression of partnership by the Episcopal Church in the development of ecumenical responsibility and decision-making.

8. Recognizing the pain and difficulty surrounding the recent establishment of the Anglican Catholic Church (formerly Anglican Church of North America) and because of our special relationships with these people, parishes, and clergy over the years, the Consultation suggests that the Standing Commission on Ecumenical Relations seek ways in which contact can be established and/or restored.

9. The Consultation requests that contact be established between the Presiding Bishop's Advisory Committee on Christian-Jewish Relations and the Episcopal Diocesan Ecumenical Officers so that grass roots communication and dialogue may develop.

II. *Principles of Unity*

The Gospel calls us to unity in God's Church. But even a partial view of the Church, conditioned by time and history, reveals to us a broken fellowship among those who confess one Lord, one Faith, one Baptism. Created and called by God to be an instrument of the saving and liberating mission of Jesus Christ in the world, this fellowship is nonetheless visibly divided, its purpose obscured, its mission impeded, and its witness weakened.

The Episcopal Church longs for and actively seeks the unity for which our Savior prayed. For almost a century that search has been guided by the bold vision of our forefathers, set forth in what we know as the Chicago-Lambeth Quadrilateral of 1886, 1888.[11] It has been the major criterion by which our ecumenical conversations have been established and pursued. Our experience challenges us now, once again, both to discern future potential and to discover new patterns of Christian unity.

We are grateful for the pioneer leadership of the Episcopal Church that has helped us enter this ecumenical age. We are also repentant for our failures to appreciate and seize earlier opportunities that could have hastened and advanced this movement. Today, however, challenges arising from growth in theological understanding as well as from wide-ranging ecumenical encounters pose urgent opportunities, and the impatience of many of our own people with the Church's reluctance to address these challenges is a source of inspiration and hope.

It is our desire to re-affirm the spirit expressed by the bishops of this church in the preamble[12] to the Chicago-Lambeth Quadrilateral as a continuing source of guidance in our quest for deeper unity. In this same spirit, now, we make bold to propose to the Standing Commission on Ecumenical Relations for transmission to General Convention new affirmations of principles for ecumenical reunion in our own day. Although deeply rooted in the Chicago-Lambeth Quadrilateral, these principles are designed to speak to issues arising out of current ecumenical dialogue.

We affirm as principles on which our own unity is established, and we propose as our principles for unity with other churches:

1. A mutual recognition that the Holy Scriptures of the Old and New Testament are the Word of God as they witness to God's action in Jesus Christ and the continuing presence of His Spirit in the Church. They are the authoritative norm for catholic faith in Jesus Christ and for the doctrinal tradition of the Gospel. Therefore we can declare that they contain all things necessary for salvation.
2. A mutual recognition that the Ancient Creeds are the form through which the Christian Church, early in its history in the world, under the guidance of the Holy Spirit, understood, interpreted, and expressed its faith in the Triune God. The continuing doctrinal tradition is the form through which the Church seeks to understand, interpret, and express its faith in continuity with the Ancient Creeds and in its awareness of the world to which the Word of God must be preached.
3. A mutual recognition that the Church is the sacrament of God's presence to the world and the sign of the Kingdom for which we hope. That presence and hope are made active and real in the Church and in Christian men and women through the preaching of the Word of God, through the Gospel sacraments of Baptism and Eucharist, and through our apostolate to the world in order that it may become the Kingdom of our God and of his Christ.
4. A mutual recognition that apostolicity is evidenced in continuity with the teaching, the ministry, and the mission of the apostles.

Apostolic *teaching* must be founded upon the Holy Scriptures and the ancient fathers and creeds, drawing its proclamation of Jesus Christ and His Gospel for each new age from these sources, not merely reproducing them in a transmission of verbal identity. Apostolic *ministry* exists to promote, safeguard, and serve apostolic teaching. All Christians are called into this ministry by their Baptism. In order to serve, lead, and enable this ministry, some are set apart and ordained in the historic orders of Bishop, Presbyter, and Deacon. We understand the historic episcopate as central to this apostolic ministry and to the reunion of Christendom. Apostolic *mission* is itself a succession of apostolic teaching and ministry inherited from the past and carried into the present and future. Bishops in apostolic succession are, therefore, the focus and personal symbols of this inheritance and mission as they preach and teach the Gospel and summon the people of God to their mission of worship and service.

The Conversations: Analyses and Recommendations

A. Consultation on Church Union

1. Affirmations
a. We receive with gratitude the document *In Quest of a Church of Christ Uniting*. It represents amazing theological consensus among ten churches, appears completely to satisfy the concerns of the Chicago-Lambeth Quadrilateral, and constitutes in a way a compendium of American ecumenical theology for our day. We urge that it be received and widely studied, that a response be given to it by the Episcopal Church (bishops, clergy, seminaries), and that our delegates to the Consultation on Church Union be informed of this response by the Standing Commission on Ecumenical Relations and the Episcopal Diocesan Ecumenical Officers under the guidance of the ecumenical officer of this church.

As work continues on this emerging theological consensus, we would urge further consideration and conscious incorporation of two additional concepts:

(1) the concept of "conciliar fellowship," which appears to be a useful expression of a goal and a method by which the separated churches may grow into unity, both locally and universally. We note that both the Anglican Consultative Council and the World Council of Churches have commended this concept as a natural

elaboration of the World Council's New Delhi statement, which stresses the imperative that all in each place be one.

(2) the notion of the "apostolicity of the Church." As we move toward the one Church Christ prayed for, we have become aware that each of the churches in the Consultation has elements of this apostolicity which can be shared with, and enrich the understanding of, the others. We believe this notion can enhance a process of complementarity.

b. We also commend the Consultation as the primary place in which Episcopalians are called upon and enabled to dialogue seriously with neighboring Christian communions, both black and white, in the pluralistic American scene.

We also appreciate the existence of the Consultation as a forum where some of the major ethical issues that influence our ecclesiastical life (such as racism and sexism) can be discussed and treated at first hand.

2. Reservations and Concerns

a. After the publication of the 1970 *Plan* of the Consultation, the member churches in their study process made clear that they did not accept the structure proposed in that plan. It appeared to envisage the loss of treasures and traditions, and to allow absorption into a monolithic structure, neither of which would be acceptable to the Episcopal Church. We urge that the Consultation take very seriously the fact that this part of the first *Plan* failed to win approval.

b. The Episcopal Church affirms the vision of the Lambeth Appeal of 1920 in which it was said that God's purpose is to manifest Christian fellowship in "an outward, visible, and united society," and that the manifestation of greater unity "depends upon the readiness with which each group is prepared to make sacrifices for the sake of a common fellowship," but the Episcopal Church also urges that the Consultation envision its goal in terms of a communion in which diverse histories can continue to enrich one another.

c. Roman Catholic and Lutheran scholars have been full participants in the preparation of theological and liturgical documents of the Consultation in recent years. Though the Roman Catholic Church is not a participating member of the Consultation on Church Union, the Consultation is regarded by the Roman Catholic Church as one of the most important ecumenical endeavors of the current time. Since the Roman Catholic Church in the U.S.A. is not an autonomous national church, it relies on the Episcopal Church as its "sister church" in this country to interpret the catholic experience in the United States to the Consultation. This is an example of trust among "sister churches."

Even though this relationship of trust may commend the Episcopal Church to continue in the Consultation, this is not the primary reason for the Episcopal Church to remain a member, for the Episcopal Church as a nationally structured church in the catholic tradition brings to the Consultation its own unique contribution.

3. Models of Growing Together

Since 1973 the churches in the Consultation have stressed the importance of "living their way toward union." This process is experienced in several ways: (a) Interim Eucharistic Fellowships (15 in number, most of which include Episcopalians), which have brought the local churches together in common prayer and sacramental sharing. (b) Generating Communities (5), which are somewhat similar to the Anglican–Roman Catholic covenanting parishes, but also have a eucharistic dimension. These communities have devised common programs for education and social ministries as well. (c) Clusters of local churches, most of which include not only the churches of the Consultation but others who share the still undefined vision of a Church of Christ Uniting.

We commend these approaches to unity to the Episcopal Church at both parish and diocesan levels within the guidelines authorized by the General Convention, and we urge further Episcopalian participation (both clergy and laity) in these manifestations of the ecumenical mission of Christ's Church.

4. Elements of the Pilgrimage

The Anglican Consultative Council as well as many worldwide communions and ecumenical bodies, has commended the goal of "conciliarity" in national and local settings. This concept involves mutual recognition of members and interchangeability of ministries.

The Consultation on Church Union, likewise, has prepared for the American context an affirmation of mutual recognition of members, and each of its ten churches (the Episcopal Church among them) has now officially accepted the baptisms of members of the others. In 1979 the Consultation will pose several questions to each of its member churches arising out of this study, since the initial responses indicated that this affirmation meant different things to different churches. Inasmuch as this process is compatible with the recommendation of the Anglican Consultative Council, we urge that careful consideration be given to these questions by the 1979 General Convention. We also recommend consideration of the use of a universal baptismal certificate.

The Consultation itself has future agenda concerns identifying the elements involved in the mutual recognition of ministries among its member churches. It is hoped that by 1981 a revised theological treatment of ordained ministry will be ready for study and discussion. Moreover, the Consultation's Commission on Worship, which has Roman Catholic participation, later will prepare a service which could be used as a form and order for the reconciliation of ministries, when the churches are ready for this step. The purpose of this process would be to make interchangeability of ministries possible. Inasmuch as there is already Roman Catholic representation on the Commission we trust that this work will also proceed with Roman Catholic participation. We urge that this work be encouraged by the 1979 General Convention.

For other recommendations of the National Ecumenical Consultation concerning the Consultation on Church Union see Section IA on doctrinal consensus above (pp. 8–9.)

B. Anglican-Orthodox Theological Consultation

1. The long-standing conversations between the Anglican and Orthodox Churches have been affected by recent events in the Episcopal Church, and our Orthodox partners are uncertain about what they had come to feel was a "special relationship." Hence we and the Orthodox members of the Consultation are required to reassess frankly the goal and methods for continuing the dialogue and the seriousness of our commitment of personnel and time to the dialogue. In the light of that reassessment, we may need to re-examine the nature of the representation we desire for the continued dialogue.

We wish to affirm vigorously the importance of the dialogue between the Orthodox and Anglicans, not only on the international level but even more so on the national level. We recognize fully that our Orthodox partners have the same responsibility and right as we do to determine the goal of the dialogue and the terms under which it is pursued, but we wish to stress the value of the dialogue no matter what may be the precise results of that agreement.

2. *Whereas,* in the Moscow Agreed Statement (1976) the Anglican members of the Anglican-Orthodox Joint Doctrinal Commission concluded and agreed that "the *Filioque* clause should not be included in this (Nicene) Creed"; and

Whereas, the Lambeth Conference (1978) requested that "all member Churches of the Anglican Communion should consider omitting the *Filioque* from the Nicene Creed"; and

Whereas, the Moscow Statement has been presented ". . . so that it may be studied and discussed by members of our Churches . . . with the hope that the agreements . . . would be more widely shared among the faithful . . . for the promotion of the Ecumenical Movement and Christian Unity" (K. Ware and C. Davey, editors, *Anglican-Orthodox Dialogue,* London: SPCK, 1977, p. 94), and

Whereas, we wish to respond with the utmost care and deliberation which befit a topic of such a serious nature; we, therefore,

Request the Commission on Theology of the House of Bishops and the Conference of Anglican Theologians to study the theological issues involved and to give the Standing Commission on Ecumenical Relations their counsel for an appropriate response to the Moscow agreement and the Lambeth request. The counsel and advice of the Primates Committee and the Anglican Consultative Council as well as of the Consultation on Church Union, the Anglican–Roman Catholic Consultation, and the Lutheran-Episcopal Dialogue should also be requested. In preparing their counsel and advice for the Standing Commission on Ecumenical Relations, we would desire examination of the Moscow Statement and also an answer to the question whether it is proper to conclude that the *Filioque* is an example of the possibility that "the same mystery can sometimes be conveyed more effectively by different formulas in different cultural contexts" as was affirmed in the statement on "Doctrinal Agreement and Christian Unity" of the Anglican–Roman Catholic Consultation, 1972. It is hoped that a serious and responsible recommendation about the *Filioque* can be formulated for presentation to the 1982 General Convention. At the appropriate point, the Episcopal Diocesan Ecumenical Officers should be called upon to assist in preparing all levels of this church for an informed and careful response to this most important matter.

3. We recall and are encouraged by the mutual understanding of tradition reflected in the Moscow Agreed Statement. We believe, however, that our U.S.A. dialogue must press on with continued examination of the subject of tradition, considering whether and how development or explication of the tradition can occur and how the authenticity of the process can be tested. The topic is particularly significant in this country because of the pluralism (both religious and cultural) which prevails here, and because of challenges posed by new medical techniques and scientific discoveries and by the rapid changes in contemporary society. In the United States, both Orthodox and Anglican Christians are confronted by the question of tradition in a fashion which is especially intense.

4. We urge our participants in the Anglican-Orthodox Theological Consultation to request inclusion in its agenda of some evaluation of

the documents produced or forthcoming in our other ecumenical dialogues with Roman Catholics, Lutherans, the Consultation on Church Union, etc. The insights of the Orthodox may enrich our share in the other dialogues, while at the same time stimulating and deepening the discussion between Anglicans and Orthodox themselves.

We feel disappointed that to date the Anglican-Orthodox Theological Consultation in the U.S.A. has not made known for the benefit of other dialogue groups the unique insights characteristic of Orthodoxy. There are some convictions, in addition, shared jointly by Anglicans and Orthodox which could be more effectively presented in the other dialogues if set forth as a united witness.

5. We ask the Episcopal Diocesan Ecumenical Officers as well as the Standing Commission on Ecumenical Relations to implement the Lambeth resolution for local contacts between Orthodox and Anglicans to discuss issues which unite or divide us, using the Moscow Agreed Statement as a primary resource. These local contacts might reveal other concerns and opportunities which should be brought to the attention of participants in the international doctrinal discussions.

For other recommendations of the National Ecumenical Consultation on Anglican-Orthodox relations see Section IA on doctrinal consensus above (p. 9.)

C. Lutheran-Episcopal Dialogue
1. In accord with the resolution of Lambeth 1978 on Relations with Lutheran Churches, we recommend:

a. that the Standing Commission on Ecumenical Relations study the Pullach Report of 1972 (*Lutheran-Episcopal Dialogue: A Progress Report*, pp. 139–175) and the Lutheran-Episcopal Dialogue Report (pp. 11–46) and make its judgment known on the theological basis and on all of its several recommendations to the members of the Lutheran-Episcopal Dialogue.
b. that the Standing Commission on Ecumenical Relations give special attention to our ecclesial recognition of the Lutheran churches in the Lutheran-Episcopal Dialogue on the basis of these reports and resolutions.
c. that the Standing Commission on Ecumenical Relations and the Ecumenical Office seek ways of extending hospitality and of engaging in joint mission with the Lutheran Churches in the Lutheran-Episcopal Dialogue.
d. that the Standing Commission on Ecumenical Relations be asked to give a judgment upon the comparative methodology followed in

the Lutheran-Episcopal Dialogue, series I and II, which does not cast Anglicans in the position of a confessional church and which on the basis of our substantial commonality in Apostolic succession, sees an appropriate place for eucharistic sharing as the context for our continuing discussions and life together.

2. In the light of the present pastoral situation in which the Dioceses of Michigan and Western Michigan have acted upon our substantial commonality by officially offering and implementing the recommendations of the Lutheran-Episcopal Dialogue together with their local neighboring churches and synods in the Lutheran-Episcopal Dialogue, and who thereby extend the call "to witness boldly and persuasively to our common Faith and Membership in the body of Christ" (*Free to Share,* p. 2), we recommend the following:

a. that the Standing Commission on Ecumenical Relations, considering the documentation offered in *Free to Share* as well as that found in the reports mentioned by Lambeth 1978 and cited in (1a) above, and considering the Report of the Archbishops' Commission on Intercommunion (1968), offer its reflections and counsel to the two Michigan dioceses, to the Lutheran-Episcopal Dialogue, and to the Joint Working Group of the International Anglican-Lutheran Conversations.
b. that the Lutheran-Episcopal Dialogue be asked to explore the theological acceptability and mutual willingness to implement the recommendations of the Pullach Report and the Lutheran-Episcopal Dialogue Report concerning eucharistic sharing by means of concelebration, which mode of sharing would continue until such time as further agreement arising from the Lutheran-Episcopal Dialogue and our life together would render such a mode no longer helpful and appropriate.
c. that the Lutheran-Episcopal Dialogue be asked on the basis of the specific recommendations made in the Pullach and Lutheran-Episcopal Dialogue reports, and using the Consultation on Church Union Interim Eucharistic Fellowship guidelines as a model, to formulate the guidelines under which such eucharistic sharing should be carried out.
d. that the Standing Commission on Ecumenical Relations determine and seek such legislation as would enable such eucharistic sharing by members of the Lutheran-Episcopal Dialogue to take place.
e. that the Episcopal Diocesan Ecumenical Officers be asked to conduct a survey to determine what exchange between Lutherans and Episcopalians is currently going on, in order to commend and

suggest further ways of extending hospitality and engaging in joint ministry with the Lutheran Churches in Lutheran-Episcopal Dialogue.

3. The Pullach and Lutheran-Episcopal Dialogue reports and the survey of these discussions written for this Consultation have not made fully explicit the reasons why our participants in the Lutheran-Episcopal Dialogue find it possible for us to engage in eucharistic sharing with Lutheran Churches in the Lutheran-Episcopal Dialogue prior to their acceptance of the historic episcopate, nor how this could be done without thereby implying that the historic episcopate is for us *adiaphora* nor why such an action would not in principle be applicable to all Protestant churches of a creedal/confessional nature. We recommend therefore:

a. that the Episcopal participants be asked to prepare an unofficial statement of their reasons for so recommending, to be considered by the members of the Standing Commission on Ecumenical Relations.
b. that the statement be written in such a fashion as would fit it for wider use in the process of reception of the Lutheran-Episcopal Dialogue's work by the churches.
c. that the Lutheran participants be asked to consider doing the same with respect to their willingness to affirm that they see in the Episcopal Church a true confession of the apostolic faith despite our lack of a confessional document which serves us as the "Augustana" serves them.

D. Anglican–Roman Catholic Consultation

1. a. We affirm the Episcopal Church's commitment to official dialogue with the Roman Catholic Church. We accept the Anglican–Roman Catholic Consultation's Twelve-Year Report, and we recommend that ARC proceed with its agenda; we ask for the implementation of the task forces which it proposes. We accept the work of the Anglican–Roman Catholic International Commission and, recognizing that the Venice Agreed Statement on Authority in the Church is incomplete, we look forward to its completion.

   b. From the theological evaluation of the work of the Anglican–Roman Catholic Consultation and the Anglican–Roman Catholic International Commission we make the following observations in keeping with the 1972 Anglican–Roman Catholic Consultation statement on "Doctrinal Agreement and Christian Unity: Methodological Considerations."

The major problem between the Episcopal Church and the Roman Catholic Church is that of authority.

(a) To many Episcopalians the style or exercise of authority in the Roman Catholic Church appears to be authoritarian. Though the definiteness and clarity of the Roman Catholic Church's exercise of authority is admired by some Episcopalians, most Episcopalians see deficiencies in the Roman Catholic Church's exercise of authority. These deficiencies are
  (i) lack of discernible lay voice for proper discernment of the Spirit by and for the whole people of God;
  (ii) lack of clear synodical form of Church decision-making which would implement the collegiality of the episcopate as affirmed by the Second Vatican Council.
On the basis of Episcopalians' experience of the Church, these deficiencies give rise to a suspicion and mistrust of the decision-making process and agencies for the implementation of decisions within the Roman Catholic Church.

(b) Thus we recommend that the Anglican–Roman Catholic International Commission address this problem in the second part of the Venice Statement and that the Anglican–Roman Catholic, U.S.A. task force on the pastoral role of bishops have this problem high on its agenda. In both of these dialogues we would affirm that Episcopalians offer a particular experience of the bishop seen as "sacrament" of pastoral caring, of the Church's unity, and of Gospel proclamation and teaching amongst the people of God. These elements are more in evidence in the Episcopal tradition than those juridical functions which appear so prominently to be associated with bishops in the Roman Catholic Church.

(c) The Episcopal Church has now ordained women to the sacramental diaconate and priesthood, within the three-fold Catholic ministry. An increasing number of Episcopalians hope that this action will enable a full and continuing dialogue with Roman Catholics and other communions that moves beyond the obvious issues of tradition to a consideration of the doctrine of God and Christian anthropology which this decision illuminates. Many see this action of their church as a response to the Gospel imperatives expressed in our common Baptism; others hold the issue to be one of discipline rather than doctrine. For authentic and fruitful dialogue between Roman Catholics and Anglicans, however, there must be no limitation of the question to the realm of discipline. Only a full theological exploration can serve our common pilgrimage toward wholeness and unity.

(d) The historic gift and doctrine of the Apostolic succession has many facets, including continuity with the Rule of Faith, an enabling of all the ministries of Christ, and a personal sign of the ministry of oversight and unity reaching back to the earliest days of the Church. The Episcopal Church has for historical reasons often laid too narrow a stress on linear succession and can therefore be enriched and made more faithful in her ministry by attention to recent Roman Catholic theological reflection on the bishop's prime function as proclaimer and enabler of the proclamation of the Word. At the same time, Episcopalians may well expect that such a broadened notion of Apostolic succession will lead the Roman Catholic Church to move towards a recognition of Anglican orders. Finally, both Episcopalians and Roman Catholics treasure the gift of the symbol of apostolicity in the person of the bishop.

(e) In this time of increasing political conservatism and retrenchment from issues touching social justice, the Roman Catholic and Episcopal Churches need each other for mutual support that both may remain faithful to their common commitment to Christ's poor.

(f) We need to explore with the Roman Catholic Church differences and commonalities in the interpretation and binding authority of Scripture and tradition as regards the formation of conscience and the setting of acceptable Christian life-styles concerning human sexuality, marriage, and the family. This is a major pastoral priority.

(g) Though the Episcopal Church may broaden its understanding of Apostolic succession, this does not require that the Episcopal Church cease to offer the historic episcopate to its partners in ecumenical dialogue. The Lutheran-Episcopal Dialogue and the Episcopal Church's participation in the Consultation on Church Union are not prejudicial to the dialogues of the Anglican–Roman Catholic Consultation and the Anglican–Roman Catholic International Commission. All three dialogues are striving to promote the integral catholicity of Christ's pilgrim Church. Proper balance in the Episcopal Church's ecumenical commitment calls for dialogue with at least all three of these partners simultaneously.

(h) We anticipate that the successful conclusion of the dialogues of the Anglican–Roman Catholic International Commission and Anglican–Roman Catholic Consultation in the U.S.A. will produce a mutual statement of common faith sufficient to permit a reconciliation of Anglican and Roman Catholic ordained ministries. This mutual recognition of Orders would then make possible a full sacramental sharing between the two churches.

For other recommendations of the National Ecumenical Consultation concerning Anglican–Roman Catholic dialogue see Section IA on doctrinal consensus above (pp. 5–8.)

NOTES

1. John 17:21.
2. *Journal of the General Convention, 1967*, p. 362.
3. *The Six Lambeth Conferences 1867–1930* (London: SPCK, 1948), Lambeth Conference of 1897, Resolution 34, p. 297.
4. *Proposed Book of Common Prayer*, Catechism, p. 855.
5. "The Meaning of Conciliar Fellowship," Report of Committee I, Commission on Faith and Order, World Council of Churches, Bangalore, India, 1978.
6. *One Baptism, One Eucharist and a Mutually Recognized Ministry*, Faith and Order Paper No. 73 (Geneva: World Council of Churches, 1975).
7. Such a service corps might model itself on the national Peace Corps or the Volunteers in Mission programs which sought to centralize the response to indicated need and provide fresh energies for solving what appeared to be insurmountable problems. The Episcopal Church might establish a center for equipping ecumenical teams to be sent to ecumenically "deprived or underdeveloped" areas, regions, dioceses, or cities, either on invitation of local hosts or at the initiation of the national church. Such teams of equipped and energetic persons might then assist, for example, in conducting ecumenical workshops of general or particular nature, diocesan conferences, offer advice in shaping covenants and help with their implementation, bring suggestions and opportunities for developing ecumenical structures of all sorts, be a conduit for materials, printed and human resources. Groups, ecumenical, lay and clerical, male and female, young and old, would be selected for work in regions which have identified ecumenical "deficiencies" on the basis of skills, e.g., a team with expertise in Anglican–Roman Catholic relations would be sent to a diocese about to embark on what for that region would represent a new enterprise in dialogue with the Roman Catholic Church. Such an Ecumenical Service is limited only by human imagination and should be structured and administered in such a way as to enable it to respond to any opening which the Lord of the Church might provide.
8. This principle originated c. 435–442 A.D. in the writing of St. Prosper of Aquitaine (*Defense of St. Augustine*, ed. P. de Letter [Westminster, Md.: Newman, 1963], p. 183).
9. *Proposed Book of Common Prayer*, Baptism, p. 305.
10. *Journal of General Convention, 1976*, p. B-34.:
    Resolved, and in the spirit of the "Lund Principle" approved by our Church's delegates and others attending the World Conference on Faith and Order in 1952 and affirmed by the 1968 Lambeth Conference, that the Episcopal Church at every level of its life be urged to act together and

in concert with other churches of Jesus Christ in all matters except those in which deep differences of conviction or church order compel us to act separately.

And be it further resolved, that in all future presentations of budget and program to this General Convention, consideration be given to what efforts have been expended to secure data ecumenically and to plan ecumenically;

And be it further resolved, that the dioceses be urged to establish a similar policy of ecumenical review and planning.

11. *Proposed Book of Common Prayer,* Historical Documents of the Church, p. 877f.

12. *Proposed Book of Common Prayer,* p. 876f.

APPENDIX:
List of Participants

The Rev. Canon John Backus
The Rev. Robert D. Bee
Dr. V. Nelle Bellamy
The Rev. J. Raymond Bolger
The Rev. John H. Bonner, Jr.
The Rev. Keith Bridston
The Rev. William G. Burrill
The Rev. Robert V. Burrows
The Rt. Rev. John H. Burt, Chairman
Isabel Calkins
The Very Rev. James E. Carroll
Dr. Peter Day
Sr. Therese Dion, S.S.A.
Dr. William F. Dornemann
Patti Drapes
Alice Emery
Frank P. Foster
The Rt. Rev. Randolph O. George
The Rev. William B. Green
The Rev. James E. Griffiss, Jr.
Phebe Hoff
The Rev. John F. Hotchkin
The Rev. Thomas F. Hudson
The Rev. Canon Harold G. Hultgren
Jean Jackson

Dr. Marion Kelleran
The Rev. John E. Kitagawa
The Rt. Rev. John M. Krumm
The Rev. Lewis Lancaster
The Rev. John Langfeldt
Dr. Jorge Lara-Braud
Dr. Charles Lawrence
The Rev. William B. Lawson
The Rev. Charles Long
Dr. Eleanor McLaughlin
The Rev. Gerald Moede
James Morse
The Rev. R. C. Nevius
The Rev. William A. Norgren
The Rt. Rev. Donald J. Parsons
The Rev. David Perry
The Rev. William Petersen
Carolyn M. Pollie
The Rt. Rev. David B. Reed
The Rev. Robert E. Richardson
The Very Rev. John H. Rodgers, Jr.
The Rev. Richard C. Rowe
The Rev. William C. Rusch
The Rev. Thos. G. Russell
The Rev. Herbert J. Ryan, S.J.
The Very Rev. Elton O. Smith
The Rev. Edward Sobolewski

The Rev. C. Allen Spicer, Jr.

Sarah Steptoe

The Rt. Rev. Robert E.
Terwilliger

The Rev. Jean-Marie Tillard,
O.P.

The Rev. Thomas Tiller

The Rev. Samuel Van Culin

The Rt. Rev. Arthur A. Vogel

The Rev. William James Walker

The Rev. Paul Washington

Dr. Cynthia Wedel

The Rt. Rev. William G.
Weinhauer

The Rt. Rev. J. Stuart Wetmore

The Rev. Harry B. Whitley

Bette Winchester

The Rev. J. Robert Wright

Summary Report
of the Episcopal Diocesan
Ecumenical Officers
(Adopted, April 1978)

The triennial ecumenical study mandated by the 1976 General Convention, to report back in 1979, is being conducted through the Standing Commission on Ecumenical Relations, the Executive Council, and the Episcopal Diocesan Ecumenical Officers (EDEO). The EDEO portion of the ecumenical study involves (1) diocesan work on models of ecumenical activity and implementation of the Lund Principle and (2) provincial ecumenical consultations.

Eight provincial ecumenical consultations took place between October 1977 and February 1978, the main purpose of which was to prepare "posture descriptions" of their portions of the Episcopal Church. The primary aim of the consultations was to know "where we are" ecumenically in the Episcopal Church.

Each diocesan officer and his bishop was asked to submit in writing to the provincial consultation the answers to these questions:

1. The bishop to state his personal view of ecumenical ministries in his diocese, how he believes these are received by his people, and how he sees himself enabling ecumenical ministries.
2. What sharing of the Eucharist is happening with other churches in the diocese, authorized or unauthorized, and what is the people's response to it?
3. What are the three most significant ecumenical ministries in the diocese?
4. What two ecumenical activities cause the most difficulty in the diocese and why?
5. What are the goals for visible unity in the diocese in the next ten years?

An amazing amount of material was produced, and this was shared at the consultation so that all could see what was happening in the province. This material is available for further use in the provinces and dioceses. (See *Ecumenical Bulletin,* no. 29, May-June 1978)

The diocesan delegations were asked to address four key questions at each consultation, in light of the excerpt "Pillars of Light" from the report on Christian Unity from the 1976 meeting of the Anglican Consultative Council. These questions were the basis for drafting the posture descriptions as reports of the consultations, aimed primarily at giving an indication of directions on visible unity in the near future.

1. What kind of visible unity could you accept?
2. With what churches should we try to be united visibly?
3. What is the extent of differences in the dioceses on these questions?
4. How is work toward visible unity related to common witness and action with other churches?

In addition, each delegation filled out a "check list" of ecumenical activities within the diocese and these were collated.

The provincial consultations varied in size from 18 to 36 people with an average of 25. Of the 92 domestic dioceses of the Episcopal Church, 76 were represented. Participants included bishops and ecumenical officers, people active in ecumenical work and people not active, clergy and laity, partners from other churches, theological consultants, and the national ecumenical officers. The consultations were financed by special contributions from the dioceses.

Summary of Posture Descriptions

The following summary attempts to capture the sense of the posture descriptions of the eight provincial consultations. All the descriptions acknowledge, explicitly or implicitly, that in dealing with the questions their understanding of visible unity was not as clear as they could wish. This summary represents, therefore, a stage in a process of discovery. A large debt of gratitude is owed to the hundreds of people who participated in this work and for the progress represented in the posture descriptions.

1. *What kind of visible unity could you accept?* The visible unity we can accept will not be organizational or governmental merger; we do not envisage joining in one church body. We understand visible unity to originate in the one Lord Jesus Christ and the people which is His Body. This spiritual dimension is the source of yearning for unity, and when it is not felt or understood the movement toward unity becomes barren.

The one body of which Jesus Christ is the Head is made visible through these signs (goals quoted from "Pillars of Light"[1] with additions in parentheses):

- the confession of a common faith
- mutual recognition of membership (Baptism as the sacrament of initiation into the body)
- interchangeability of ministries (lay ministries as well as ordained ministers; at present we recognize some ordained ministries more fully than others and positions on this diverge in the provinces)
- complete eucharistic fellowship
- sharing of resources (people and property in common service and witness)
- streamlining of structures (not necessarily a sign of unity, although it may be a result)
- maintenance and development of such diversity as enriches the whole Church

This unity through reconciliation accepts diversity and glorifies God through his Son Jesus Christ in the power of the Holy Spirit, while honoring our heritage of Apostolic Faith, Ministry, and Mission.

We perceive that sharing of resources as a sign, already present in some measure, offers the greatest promise for advance in the immediate future.

2. *With what churches should we try to be united visibly?* In all provinces interest in and dialogue toward visible unity takes place mainly with the Roman Catholics. The reports show a preference for visible unity with the Roman Catholic Church. In addition, three of the provinces would seek visible unity with churches having a similar sacramental view of life to our own. Other Churches mentioned are the Lutheran (6), Orthodox (2), Presbyterian (3), United Church of Christ (2), Churches in the Methodist tradition (3), and Churches of COCU (1). There was a consensus, however, that we wish to continue dialogue and develop deeper relationships with all Christian churches. We note interest also in dialogue with other faiths.

In the reports the approach toward visible unity is seen bilaterally rather than multilaterally (as in COCU and councils of churches). There is a consensus, however, that we should be open to coalitions with all churches, and coalitions are perceived in terms of responding to human need and dignity, and bearing prophetic witness.

3. *What is the extent of differences in the dioceses on these questions?* Differences between and within the dioceses were not completely analyzed,

but it appears that some arise from the variations in church populations among regions, states, and communities. We do see general agreement in reports on questions 1 and 2 and a desire to pursue the issues more fully. Differences also arise according to the level of ecumenical leadership in dioceses and parishes and the willingness of other Churches to participate.

4. *How is work toward visible unity related to common witness and action with other churches?*

There was no uniformity in the way the posture descriptions answered this question. Efforts to state the problem are reflected in such phrases as these:

> When we share the Eucharist we must be willing to share Christ's mission to the world.

> Doing things together heightens awareness of deeper issues.

> Concern for visible unity guards against being satisfied with just common witness and action.

> There is a strong sense that common witness and action are part of the process towards visible unity and that we have not perhaps worked toward understanding and using our work in the world as a start for conversation and dialogue in the theological arena.

> We have come to acknowledge that the past, filled with projects for hunger, ministries to college campuses, outreach in times of disasters, has been a time of working toward visible unity and should be celebrated. We cannot, however, allow ourselves to become complacent with such projects of Christian social action but need to recognize that they are only beginnings. Consequently, we also come to see that our small steps into visible unity are contributions toward the goal of a common faith and are actions of common witness to Our Lord Jesus Christ with all churches. The fullness of the church's mission calls for visible unity.

> Our work towards visible unity requires keeping as a goal our Lord's High Priestly prayer that His church be one. This is achieved through the love that we have for our Lord and for one another, and this applies to churches as well as to individuals. We give witness to the love through our willingness to work together and by accepting one another. This latter witness requires doctrinal statements concerning mutual acceptance of members (baptism), holy orders, and Eucharist.

NOTE

1. *ACC-3 Trinidad,* Anglican Consultative Council, Report of Third Meeting, Trinidad, 23 March–2 April 1976, pp. 14–22.

Ecumenical Report
of the Executive Council

The General Convention in 1976 resolved that the Standing Commission on Ecumenical Relations "undertake, through the convening of regional meetings culminating in a special national conference or other appropriate ways, to assess this Church's present ecumenical posture and involvement, to suggest restatement, where necessary, of those essentials to which the Episcopal Church is committed, and to formulate those priorities and goals which can guide our ecumenical activities in the future."

The Executive Council of the Episcopal Church and the Episcopal Diocesan Ecumenical Officers (EDEO) are cooperating with the Standing Commission in this triennial ecumenical study. Each of the three bodies conducts a part of the triennial study in communication with the others, looking towards a national ecumenical consultation to assess the situation, priorities, and goals as a whole. The Standing Commission will carry out the 1976 Convention's further resolution "that a complete report of this study, together with any recommendations, be prepared for and presented to the 1979 General Convention."

Our triennial study comes at a time when many churches are reappraising their ecumenical commitments. Sensing this need, the Fifth Assembly of the World Council of Churches at Nairobi in 1975 urged:

> *A reappraisal of ecumenical commitments.* The vision of conciliar fellowship at all levels represents a challenge to the present ecumenical situation, and raises a sharp question about the extent to which our ecumenical commitments actually contribute to a resolute quest for unity. We ask the churches to review the pattern and degree of their present commitment to the ecumenical structures at local, national, regional, and global levels, and ask themselves whether these are functioning as means towards unity or as a substitute for unity.

The Assembly also drew attention to the fact that the work of councils of churches, efforts towards church union, and bilateral conversations between world families of churches "do not always assist and enrich one another but are often in tension with one another." It urged the churches to ensure that "by a concerted action these efforts support, influence and encourage one another."

Early in 1976 the former Executive Council Standing Committee on Ecumenical Relations asked for an evaluation of Council involvement in national and global ecumenical structures. This "Ecumenical Report of Executive Council" grew out of that initiative and now becomes an Executive Council contribution to the triennial study. The Report is prepared for presentation and referral to committees at the February meeting, and suggestions and criticisms will be welcomed before action at the May 1978 meeting.

1. *Historical Sketch*

Participation and leadership of the Episcopal Church in the ecumenical movement began with the movement itself. A multitude of activities and decisions—national, local, and international—constitute this participation and leadership. Some highlights of this patrimony follow.

The Episcopal Church participated in the first World Missionary Conference in 1910. The first formal proposal for a World Conference on Faith and Order was made by the General Convention in 1910. This Church participated in all World Conferences on Faith and Order and in the World Conferences on Life and Work. The General Convention in 1937 endorsed the proposal for a World Council of Churches (as outlined by the Edinburgh Conference on Faith and Order) and the Episcopal Church was a founding member in 1948.

Slower to join the Federal Council of the Churches of Christ in America, the Episcopal Church did so in 1940, and was a member of the successor National Council of the Churches of Christ in the U.S.A. from its inception in 1950. The World and National Councils of Churches were a way for this church to join Protestant, Orthodox, and Old Catholic Churches in bearing witness to their unity in Jesus Christ, seeking visible unity, and working together. Meanwhile many dioceses and parishes of the Episcopal Church joined state and city councils of churches to cooperate with other churches committed to the ecumenical movement. Many priests joined local ministerial associations.

Councils of churches were not the only way the Episcopal Church participated and led in the ecumenical movement. Earlier the House of Bishops at General Convention in 1886 adopted a platform on which it would seek visible unity with other churches, called the Lambeth Quadrilateral when adopted by the Lambeth Conference in 1888 with slight changes. Though some U.S. churches expressed interest, the fourth point—the historic episcopate—proved to be a barrier with churches that had a different form of ministry.

Efforts to reach agreements with Congregationalists, Presbyterians, and Methodists led to no concrete results in the first half of the twentieth century. In 1961 the General Convention voted to join with these and other churches to form the Consultation on Church Union, but a plan of union issued in 1970 failed to gain support. During this time theological scholars were meeting and reading across confessional lines, and bishops and other leaders were forming valuable associations and personal friendships.

Later in the turbulent 1960s, the Executive Council joined with several other churches in forming the Joint Strategy and Action Committee (JSAC) to enable national (and some regional) denominational staffs to collaborate in task forces on urban mission, church development, minority ministries, and other areas of national mission. In the same period the Executive Council joined with other denominations to form Joint Educational Development (JED) for similar collaboration in areas of education.

The Episcopal Church's ecumenical commitment was reflected in the work of numerous Episcopalians. The general program budget of this Church also reflected its commitment. In the 1970s severe reductions in the budget inevitably affected grants to ecumenical structures as well as the number of Episcopalians who could participate nationally. The same thing happened in other U.S. churches. Meanwhile state and city ecumenical structures suffered from budget restrictions in dioceses.

In this same period an increasing number of Episcopalians sought to make ecumenical commitment and action meaningful in dioceses and parishes. In 1974 the spontaneous formation of an association of Episcopal Diocesan Ecumenical Officers (EDEO) brought local ecumenical developments into focus. This vital network became a major new ingredient in the ecumenical participation and leadership of the Episcopal Church.

2. *Changing Context*

The Episcopal Church with the Anglican Communion continues to participate and lead in the ecumenical movement and in the structures that serve it. As this Church shares in the movement, it gives but it also receives. Renewal of the Episcopal Church depends in part on openness to the ecumenical movement. This Church should question itself again and again about the adequacy of its participation and leadership in the movement, and in the structures that serve it. But this Church should also question the effectiveness of the structures intended to serve the movement. How do we evaluate their work? How do we measure, in the words of the Assembly, whether they are "functioning as means towards unity or as a substitute for unity?"

Before we can deal with these questions we must take note of significant changes that affect both the Episcopal Church and the ecumenical structures. First are the seismic effects of the Vatican II Council. Not only did the Council commit the Roman Catholic Church to full participation in the ecumenical movement; it brought substantial reform to that Church and so laid a new foundation upon which dialogue with other churches could begin. Anglican, Protestant, and Orthodox Churches responded with changed attitudes and their relationships with the Roman Catholic Church have been transformed. The relationship of the Episcopal and Roman Catholic Churches in the U.S. has altered to the extent that the Anglican–Roman Catholic Consultation believes we are ready to move into new areas of collaboration while we continue to press forward in the dialogue.

A related change is the rise of official bilateral conversations between families of churches. The Roman Catholic Church, accustomed to acting universally, and other world families of churches, diverse in their ways of acting but accustomed to participation in the World Council of Churches, have formed world bilateral conversations. That these conversations should have diverse goals is not surprising. Nearly all assess the situation, mutually describe their history and characteristics, and clarify difficulties and new possibilities in interchurch relationships. Some aim at mutual understanding, others at some form of visible unity. Some develop coordination of relationships between two families of churches and encourage practical cooperation and exchange on different levels.

Diverse as their goals and functions are, the bilateral conversations are responsible for a major restructuring of ecumenical relationships. The different world families of churches, once regarded as stumbling blocks in the way of unity, are now seen in these conversations to be opening new ways to unity. The Episcopal Church has participated in bilateral conversations with the Roman Catholic, Lutheran, and Orthodox Churches globally and nationally. Dialogue should lead to action, so when proposals for practical collaboration are made, a decision will be needed in each case whether two families of churches or several will collaborate. In any case the world families of churches are a growing reality with an important potential for partnership in mission.

Another change is the growing influence of Orthodox Churches located in the socialist countries of eastern Europe. Orthodox participation is strong in the World Council of Churches, whose largest member church is the Russian Orthodox. After a long time of mutual ignorance and misunderstanding between Eastern and Western Christianity, Orthodoxy is slowly coming forward as a third force in world Christianity with an outstanding theological and spiritual contribution to make to modern theology and church life. The preparation for a "great and holy synod" of all the Orthodox Churches is renewing their synodical consciousness. Issues for the synod include the Orthodox diaspora (New York City alone has ten mutually independent Orthodox dioceses), an urgent problem because large numbers of Orthodox in the U.S. are no longer immigrant churches seeking to establish their own identity but have become integrated into the American scene, and must clarify and implement their mission. A new attempt is also being made in the synodical process to understand the traditions of other churches and to take the necessary consequences for the Orthodox Church.

A change with profound implications is the growing influence of the churches of the "third world" as they assume theological and missionary responsibility. The influence in the churches of deprived and relatively powerless people in "first world" countries such as the U.S. has also grown, sometimes producing new polarizations but also heightening awareness of legitimate diversity. Christians seem to be more aware and concerned for social justice, especially needed by those who are most abandoned, by the exploited, and by those on the margins of society. We note the special attention being paid to issues of participation and partnership of women and men in the Church and the world.

The reassertion of the validity of pluralism is a major stream of change. The more that personal awareness grows and the more consideration is given to legitimate differences, the greater grow the demands of pluralistic options. The question is how such demands can be met within the unity of faith of the ecclesial community, and how such demands can be kept within their reasonable limits.

A change with overtones of paradox is that localism has risen, not declined, in a global age. Obsession with the local sometimes leads to a loss of vision and service, but is inevitable as people use churches for a zone in which responsiveness and responsibility can be experienced. Those who care about the ecumenical movement worry about relations among local churches and then concern themselves with networks and linkages for the sake of a larger world.

Many other significant changes can be cited: almost everywhere one notes new spiritual vigor with renewed regard for prayer, Bible study, spiritual exercises, and for the action of the Holy Spirit within the Church. Significant developments occur in Biblical and liturgical studies and in dogmatic and systematic theology, so that doctrinal discussions involve re-examining questions in the light of both Biblical teaching and inherited traditions of the families of churches. Dialogue between Christians and representatives of other living faiths and ideologies evolves slowly. Charismatic renewal is a force in interchurch relationships. Differences continue in the churches between evangelical conservative groups and those whose primary concern is for social and ecumenical questions, but the former give increasing attention to social, churchly, and ecumenical questions. Within the churches there are traditionalist movements maintaining that the meaning of Scripture and tradition is not rightly transmitted in new prayers and hymns, and in preaching in many churches which is marked by the "spirit of the age."

A most significant change is the rise of a richer model of visible unity which propels the churches beyond such earlier models as cooperation in a council of churches or merger in national united churches. The emerging model, in which proper diversity is protected, is variously named "reconciled diversity," "sister churches," plurality of "types" within one communion, "communion of communions," and "conciliar fellowship." (Study of models is underway in the Standing Commission on Ecumenical Relations.)

Ecumenists formerly assumed that "confessionalism," meaning the identity of a church rooted in a creedal statement or in a particular historical experience, and the existence of churches such as the Lutheran, Baptist, Roman Catholic, or Anglican, were obstacles to be overcome by "ecumenism." Confessional differences were equated with mutual rejection. This opposition between confessionalism and ecumenism was sometimes expressed in opposition of structures—for example, the World Council vs. world families of churches or the National Council vs. denominations.

A richer model of unity in which particularities of the churches are not blended but reconciled (locally, nationally, regionally, universally) may lead to complementarity of communions in the one body of Christ. When the ecumenical movement, led by the Holy Spirit, reaches such unity in faith and sacraments between the churches that it is possible to re-establish full communion among them, ecumenical structures will cease their existence as having fulfilled their purpose. The churches will find appropriate ways and forms for their "conciliar fellowship" themselves, and their fellowship will become a normal manifestation of the fullness of the conciliar life of the One, Holy, Catholic, and Apostolic Church.

3. *Ecumenical Responsibilities in the Episcopal Church*

The Episcopal Church has ecumenical responsibilities in the U.S. and the world as "a constituent member of the Anglican Communion, a Fellowship within the One, Holy, Catholic, and Apostolic Church, in communion with the See of Canterbury, upholding and propagating the historic Faith and Order as set forth in the Book of Common Prayer" (Constitution of the Episcopal Church).

These responsibilities are carried out according to the canons by the General Convention (legislates) and its Standing Commission on Ecumenical Relations (develops policy and strategy), the Presiding Bishop of the Church (chief pastor), and the Executive Council (develops and implements program). The national Ecumenical Officer assists the Standing Commission, the Presiding Bishop, and the Executive Council to carry out their responsibilities.

The *General Convention* consists of two houses which sit and deliberate separately: the House of Bishops and the House of Deputies. Either house may originate and propose legislation but all acts of the Convention must be adopted and authenticated by both houses. Each house has a committee on Ecumenical Relations to which proposed resolutions are referred and which reports recommendations for action. Through its legislative process Convention determines ecumenical commitments, policies, and programs of the Episcopal Church.

The House of Bishops meets annually between Conventions and has certain responsibilities of its own. The bishops occasionally state the mind of the house on doctrinal or pastoral issues involved in ecumenical relations, thus setting policy as chief pastors of the dioceses. On some matters they may act as "the body known as the Bishops in Council, as an assemblage of Catholic Bishops, and considering and acting upon matters of duty or responsibility resting on them as a portion of the universal Episcopate . . ." (Rules of Order).

The *Standing Commission on Ecumenical Relations* is canonically responsible "to develop a comprehensive and coordinated policy and strategy on relations between this Church and other churches, to make recommendations to General Convention concerning interchurch cooperation and unity, and to carry out such instructions on ecumenical matters as may be given it from time to time by the General Convention. It shall also nominate persons to serve on the governing bodies of ecumenical organizations to which this Church belongs by action of the General Convention and to major conferences convened by such organizations" (Journal of General Convention, 1976).

The Standing Commission was the result of a merger in 1964 of three former Joint Commissions concerned with ecumenical matters (Co-operation with the Eastern and Old Catholic Churches, Approaches to Unity, Ecumenical Relations). The resolution to merge spelled out its tasks: "to develop a comprehensive and coordinated policy and strategy on relations with other churches, confirming, interpreting, or making fresh definitions in harmony with the faith and canons of the Protestant Episcopal Church, thus involving (a) statements on Faith and Order, (b) theological discussions with other churches, separately or in ecumenical gatherings, and (c) questions of Church law, tradition, and worship, arising in relationships with other churches" (Journal of General Convention, 1964). As early as 1949 the old Joint Commission on Ecumenical Relations was instructed "to see that the church is kept informed as to progress in this field, especially at the grass roots level, and that it be held responsible for maintaining and furthering our close fellowship and cooperation" with the World Council of Churches, "particularly with that Council's Commission on Faith and Order" and the National Council of Churches (Journal of General Convention, 1949).

Today most of the work of the Standing Commission is done through six subcommittees, each faced with a full agenda: Relations with Eastern Churches, Relations with the Roman Catholic Church, Relations with Protestant Churches and other Communities, Unity Consultations, Diocesan/Local Ecumenism and Councils, Wider Episcopal Fellowship. The Presiding Bishop and the Chairman of the House of Deputies are *ex officio* members of the Standing Commission.

The *Presiding Bishop* of the Church, as "the chief pastor thereof," is charged with responsibility for giving leadership in initiating and developing the policy and strategy of the Church "and speaks God's word to the Church and to the world, as the representative of this Church and its episcopate in its corporate capacity" (Canons of the Episcopal Church). The Presiding Bishop assures that ecumenical commitment is manifested in this Church and represents this Church through primatial visits to leaders of other churches in the U.S. and abroad and in ecumenical structures. The Presiding Bishop delegates others to represent him from time to time.

The *Executive Council* is canonically responsible "to carry out the program and policies adopted by the General Convention." It has "charge of the unification, development, and prosecution of the Missionary, Educational, and Social Work of the Church, and of such

other work as may be committed to it by the General Convention."
The Presiding Bishop is President of the Council. The Executive
Council's Standing Committee on National and World Mission was
given responsibility for ecumenical affairs in 1976, and has subsumed
the tasks of the former Standing Committee on Ecumenical Relations.
The tasks are:

(a) To keep the ecumenical dimension of the Executive Council's
    work under review and make recommendations to the Council in
    this area in accord with the policies and guidelines established by
    General Convention . . .
(b) To assist in building working relationships between the Executive
    Council's program units and the cognate units of the World
    Council of Churches, National Council of Churches and other
    ecumenical agencies . . . understanding the importance of our
    own Church's autonomy in setting its programmatic goals and
    methods while taking into account the advantages of a common
    Christian approach to many of the issues and opportunities faced
    by the Episcopal Church . . .
(c) To supervise and monitor the programmatic implementation of
    any applicable General Convention resolutions.
(d) To advise the ecumenical officer and assistant ecumenical officer
    on various aspects of their work including programs and activities
    for the study and promotion of ecumenism, service to diocesan
    ecumenical commissions, and keeping church people informed on
    ecumenical developments.
(e) To maintain liaison between the Executive Council and the Joint
    Commission on Ecumenical Relations . . . The Executive Council
    has primary responsibility for *policy execution* in the ecumenical
    programmatic areas as finally adopted by General Convention . . .

The Executive Council is accountable to General Convention and
makes a full report concerning the work with which it is charged to
each meeting of the Convention. Between sessions of General Convention the Council may initiate and develop such new work as it deems
necessary. The Council submits to each General Convention a program for the succeeding triennium, including a detailed budget for
the ensuing year and estimated total budgets for the two succeeding
years.

The position of national *Ecumenical Officer* was established by General Convention in 1961 as a special assistant to the Presiding Bishop
and (as with other Executive Council staff) to be appointed by him.

Today the Ecumenical Office is located in the National and World Mission unit of the Executive Council. The responsibilities of the Ecumenical Officer were spelled out in an appendix to the report of the then Joint Commission on Ecumenical Relations: administrative responsibilities for the Commission, day to day business with the National and World Councils of Churches, keeping the Church at large adequately informed and in touch with all phases of the ecumenical movement, education at diocesan and local levels, apprising the Presiding Bishop and Executive Council staff of matters of importance, deepening and extending the involvement of provinces and dioceses, coordinating the ecumenical activity and work of the Episcopal Church, and planning for its responsible participation in ecumenical affairs.

The Ecumenical Office plans and develops program with the executive for National and World Mission and the staff Administrative Group, under the overall guidance of the Presiding Bishop. Other units of the Executive Council also utilize ecumenical structures to carry out Episcopal Church goals and objectives. Program plans are incorporated in the general church program budget submitted by Executive Council to General Convention through the Joint Standing Committee on Program, Budget, and Finance.

The Ecumenical Office plans and develops policy and strategy, under the overall guidance of the Presiding Bishop, to assist the Standing Commission on Ecumenical Relations to carry out its responsibilities. The Office receives suggestions from various sources, particularly the Episcopal Diocesan Ecumenical Officers, and keeps the executive for National and World Mission, the Administrative Group, and others informed.

The bishops of the Episcopal Church participate with other bishops of the Anglican Communion in the *Lambeth Conference,* an historic expression of the unity of the Anglican Communion, at the invitation of the Archbishop of Canterbury. At two-year intervals between Lambeth Conferences, three clerical and lay delegates from the Episcopal Church participate in the *Anglican Consultative Council.* The Archbishop of Canterbury is president of both bodies. The Anglican Communion has no legislative authority, so the member provinces or churches must decide whether to approve conclusions reached by either body. Both deal extensively with ecumenical policy and their conclusions are influential, particularly resolutions of the Lambeth Conference. The office of the secretary general of the Anglican Consultative Council plans, on behalf of the Archbishop of Canterbury and the Anglican Communion, theological conversations and ecumenical relations with other world families of churches. The Archbishop of Canterbury's Counsellors on Foreign Relations aid the Anglican Consultative Council in this work. Episcopalians participating in the work are nominated by the Presiding Bishop and appointed by the Archbishop.

Global and national bodies, because of the very way in which Christ is manifested in His Church, are in no way a substitute for the Church in each diocese. The wider bodies afford a process to reach consensus on issues which transcend diocesan and provincial boundaries, a means to promote the life of the local churches, and an expression of unity. The Church in each diocese with its parishes responds to global and national agendas but it has an agenda of its own, an original form of ecumenism springing from the presence of Christ in its worship and life. In many cases this agenda of prayer, dialogue, and service for unity has yet to be developed in light of the particular characteristics and issues of the place where the diocese has its mission and ministry.

It was in pursuit of this form of ecumenism that the diocesan ecumenical officers formed in 1974 a national association of *Episcopal Diocesan Ecumenical Officers* (EDEO). General Convention in 1976 commended the new network and "encourages their participation in the expansion of local and diocesan ecumenical activity." EDEO responsibilities are spelled out in its bylaws: to initiate, support, and communicate ecumenical activity at the diocesan and local level, to serve as a communicator for the Standing Commission on Ecumenical Relations on national and world ecumenical activities and conversations in which the Episcopal Church and the Anglican Communion are involved, to assist in the mobilization of the church to commitment on every level to the ultimate goal of the visible unity of the Church, and to work to move the church to provide the necessary resources to achieve this goal. EDEO reports both to the Standing Commission and the Executive Council, and suggests to the Standing Commission resolutions for General Convention related to diocesan/local ecumenism. The Ecumenical Office assists in the work of EDEO.

4. *Ecumenical Policy of the Episcopal Church*

The ecumenical vocation of the Anglican Communion is to maintain a dynamic balance, to seek wholeness, to look toward visible unity in one faith and one eucharistic fellowship with all Churches—Roman Catholic, Protestant, and Orthodox. The 1967 General Convention voiced this historical vocation in a succinct policy statement:

> Our ecumenical policy is to press toward the visible unity of the whole Christian fellowship in the faith and truth of Jesus Christ,

developing and sharing in its various dialogues and consultations
in such a way that the goal be neither obscured nor compromised
and that each separate activity be a step toward the fullness of
unity for which our Savior prayed.

The ecumenical policy of the Episcopal Church is the visible unity of
the whole Church, but this has never meant that it must wait until all
churches reach full agreement before acting. The Anglican Churches
have entered into full communion with churches where there is a
sufficient unity in faith and sacraments. The Bonn Agreement has
been mutually affirmed with the Churches of the Union of Utrecht
(Old Catholic) and with the Philippine Independent, Iberian, and Mar
Thoma Churches (the case of the united churches of India, Pakistan,
and Bangladesh is somewhat different as they incorporated former
Anglican dioceses). The eucharistic fellowship of these churches and
the churches of the Anglican Communion is called the Wider Episcopal Fellowship, though it has not yet received conciliar expression
for common counsel and mutual aid.

The Episcopal Church with the Anglican Communion has meanwhile entered and deepened conversations with other major families
of churches. Conversations aimed at visible unity exist, in chronologi-
cal order, with (1) the Orthodox Churches, (2) the Methodist, Reformed, and Disciples families through the U.S. Consultation on
Church Union, and more recently with (3) the Roman Catholic
Church, and (4) the Lutheran Churches. The stance of Episcopalians in
these conversations, reaffirmed as recently as the 1976 General Convention, is that of the Lambeth Quadrilateral and related documents
(see *Ecumenical Bulletin* 26). Decentralized conversations aimed at
mutual understanding are beginning with Southern Baptists, a part of
the largest Protestant family in the U.S.

In this complex process of dialogue the Episcopal Church receives
new insights and finds new ecumenical opportunities. Since the Vatican II Council, relationships with the Roman Catholic Church have by
all accounts become the principal and most important (but not the
only) ecumenical concern of the Episcopal Church and the Anglican
Communion. Our policy on visible unity of the whole Christian fellowship, including non-Episcopal churches, should not stand in the way
of relationships with an episcopal church such as the Roman Catholic.
Another example of new perspectives is our conversation with Lutherans, a family of churches (like the Baptists) to which we have not been
formally related in the past.

Conversations with these families of churches are financed by the
General Convention budget of the Standing Commission on Ecumeni-

cal Relations. In the case of the Consultation on Church Union, while the Standing Commission is responsible for conducting and financing the conversation, the Executive Council is responsible for financing some program implementation. Relations with churches of the Wider Episcopal Fellowship are the responsibility of the Standing Commission for policy and the Executive Council for program, but in this case we deal with mission partnership within the framework of already existing visible unity, or full communion.

What ecumenical policy guides other Executive Council program? The General Convention policy statement quoted above, owing to its context, made no explicit reference to ecumenical activities beyond "dialogue and consultations," yet it seems implicit that all ecumenical participation and leadership of the Episcopal Church should in some sense "press toward the visible unity of the whole Christian fellowship in faith and truth of Jesus Christ." Here we recall the urging of the Nairobi Assembly quoted in the introduction that all ecumenical structures should function "as a means towards unity."

We confront a serious problem at this point. In the U.S. the churches have never had *both* an articulated vision of an ultimate goal of visible unity and a process or way by which unity can be experienced (though not fully) now. This is embedded in our ecumenical structures. Councils of churches had no affirmation of a goal (unlike the World Council), but they did have a process of joint activities. The Consultation on Church Union had a goal, but few experiences on the way.

Two mistaken or partial assumptions may have motivated U.S. ecumenists. The first assumption is that visible unity is a product of doing things together. The mistake is in thinking that unity can be a human achievement. Doing things together can produce new experiences and new relationships between persons, groups, and institutions, but cannot produce the unity created in Jesus Christ. Indeed, when what we do together is authentic it sometimes produces disunity, for example, in work for a just society.

The second mistaken or partial assumption is that visible unity is a matter of reaching theoretical or theological agreement which can then be legislated and the desired change produced. The mistake is in thinking that if we can achieve a consensus of leaders and take it through a legislative process we can produce a new community. Unity is not something we can produce in this way either.

If the churches continue to work in the National Council of Churches only on immediate concerns and have no vision, the churches will continue to deal with a remote goal in their work for visible unity in bilateral conversations and COCU, and in the National Council they will never give meaning to unity beyond the crises. How can vision and process be held together in our ecumenical structures and in Episcopal participation and leadership? Again we recall the urging of the Nairobi Assembly quoted in the introduction that ecumenical efforts and structures "support, influence and encourage one another."

At the 1976 General Convention the Lund Principle, first uttered by the World Conference on Faith and Order at Lund, Sweden, in 1952 and affirmed by the Lambeth Conference in 1968, was reaffirmed. The Convention resolved that "the Episcopal Church at every level of its life be urged to act together and in concert with other churches of Jesus Christ in all matters except those in which deep differences of conviction or church order compel us to act separately." Because the Lund Principle is somewhat vague, the resolution provided a specific means of implementation: "that in all future presentations of budget and program to this General Convention, reference be made to what efforts have been expended to secure data ecumenically and to plan ecumenically." Dioceses were "urged to establish a similar policy of ecumenical review and planning."

The Lund Principle thus became a part of the Episcopal Church's ecumenical policy. It is vital to recall, however, that the Lund Principle uttered in 1952 by the World Conference on Faith and Order speaks *both* of pursuing theological conversations and acting "together and in concert." Action together in obedience to the unity we have goes hand-in-hand with conversations aimed at visible unity in one faith and one eucharistic fellowship. We have not yet reached the point where we can ignore the divisions which have separated us for centuries, but even now we must act "together and in concert" and plan together.

This brief look at the Lund Principle suggests an unfinished agenda for Executive Council and its units: to work out what action together and in concert is justified, indeed required by "obedience to unity which is already given" and what action is to be separate because "deep differences of conviction or church order compel us to act separately." It is impossible to make an *a priori* definition along these lines; rather it will be necessary to work it out step by step, decision by decision.

Explicit policy on the National and World Councils of Churches is limited to membership and cooperation through them with other churches (Journal of General Convention, 1949). Because councils have no authority to commit member churches, participation or agreement in programs, statements, activities, etc. is governed by appropriate organs of the churches.

How should Executive Council make decisions to commit or not to commit? Executive Council and its units should be guided first by policies and positions adopted by General Convention on the relevant social, ethical, educational, ministerial, missional, and ecumenical issues. Since ecumenical participation is a "two-way street," planning in ecumenical structures should be fed back to Executive Council and its units to be used in the continuous process of arriving at new or revised policies and positions which may be adopted by General Convention. Similarly, decisions of Executive Council and its units on grants to ecumenical structures and use of staff and volunteer time should be made in light of Executive Council program goals and objectives. Because ecumenical participation is a "two-way street" here too, planning in ecumenical structures should be fed back to Executive Council and its units to test program goals and objectives and to help in devising future ones.

5. *Motivation*

In the foregoing description of Episcopal Church life and the structures through which its ecumenical policies are formed and carried out, warnings have been given that Christian unity is not a product of doing things together. It is not something we produce, but rather a gift of God to humankind. In a world capable of destroying itself, unity is not only a gift to the followers of Christ but potentially a gift to all nations.

St. Paul, in his letter to the Galatians, reminds his followers of this gift: "In Christ Jesus you are all sons of God through faith. For as many of you as were baptized into Christ have put on Christ. There is neither Jew nor Greek, there is neither slave nor free, there is neither male nor female; for you are all one in Christ Jesus." (Gal. 3:26–28) Whatever divides us is obliterated by the fact that God has made us one.

Baptism and Holy Communion are the foundation of our union in Christ and the source of our unity with our fellow-Christians, the pilgrim people of God. This unity is obscured by our past divisions into separate fellowships, an estrangement which has made us look upon other churches as enemies or competitors.

The task of restoring relationships is not necessarily to join in one monolithic church structure, but rather to learn to live by what we have in common—our relationship to God in Christ. Among churches this unity in relationships can be expressed and organized in diverse ways, relying on the varied gifts of the one Spirit to different churches. As Cardinal Willebrands has said, "If we are going to fossilize, common sense would seem to suggest that it is not very important whether we do so together or separately. Unity is vital only if it is a vital unity."

An old haggadic legend tells this tale: "I was walking in the mist at evening, when suddenly I saw a monster looming in the mist. As the apparition drew closer, I saw that he was a human being; and when we came face to face, I saw that he was my brother."

Christian unity is not made by man, but by the discernment given by the Spirit to recognize what we are—what God has made us in Christ.

If the Church is to fulfill its mission to mankind, it must reorder its own life so faithfully that the world may see that Christ is indeed the way, the truth, and the life. So, in his high-priestly prayer Jesus prays "that they may all be one; even as thou, Father, art in me, and I in thee, that they also may be in us, so that the world may believe that thou hast sent me" (John 17:21–23).

The greatness of the mission to which Christ calls us and the future glory of its consummation is, and ought to be, the motivation which impels us to unity with our fellow-Christians in "reconciled diversity." It is in this context that we now turn to a consideration of the Executive Council's involvement in ecumenical action through a variety of programs and agencies.

6. *Existing Executive Council Ecumenical Involvements*

Evaluation of existing Executive Council ecumenical involvements began in 1976 with a survey of staff contacts (updated periodically). The survey included use of staff time and grants, both important allocations of resources. In general, staff estimates of the value of contacts were quite positive, and there was appreciation of the opportunity to work with other churches. Satisfaction was related to task completion, however, and the inter-church relationship was not regarded as an end in itself.

Staff evaluations of contacts ranged, of course, both for their work and for the general mission of the Church, from the highest possible to nearly the lowest possible ratings. It would be hazardous to suggest any single reason for the ratings, but task completion is a key.

Staff who spent the most time at ecumenical meetings did not complain about the demands made on their time, while those who spent relatively little time complained. All staff live with heavy schedules, so the basic problem is not time, though the small staff has severe limits in this respect. The basic problem is the nature of the work in the Episcopal Church Center. Policy is for staff to focus on dioceses and not on the Episcopal Church Center. When ecumenical contacts support and enable their work, staff rate them highly and spend whatever time is necessary.

a. World Council of Churches

Fewer Executive Council staff have contacts with the World Council of Churches than before because of the greatly enlarged participation of churches from the third world and the socialist countries of eastern Europe. There are nearly 300 member churches. This lessening of contact is serious because the WCC is an important part of this Church's ecumenical participation: intercontinental, multiracial, transcultural, and interconfessional.

The Ecumenical Office works steadily to increase the number of Episcopalians who have contacts and to enable them to communicate content of meetings and conferences to others. WCC staff visits to the Episcopal Church Center are arranged to strengthen the confidence between WCC staff in Geneva and this Church. We should work with other member churches to make the U.S. Conference of the WCC an effective regional center to enable a wider participation of Episcopal leaders, including staff, alongside leaders of other churches. In some areas of program the National Council of Churches functions on behalf of the WCC.

The WCC should continue to improve communication with its member churches and pay greater attention to ecumenical needs of their local churches (dioceses/parishes). Study of relations between the WCC and the world families of churches has also begun, to see in what further ways the families can act jointly, but progress is likely to be slow. The future of the WCC is less that of an institution embodying the ecumenical movement and more that of an enabler of unity, mission, and service in the world families of churches. New flexibility within the WCC will bring fresh possibilities for increased partnership with churches not likely under present conditions to become members of the WCC—for example, the Roman Catholic Church and evangelical conservative churches, which also embody something of contemporary ecumenism.

b. National Council of the Churches of Christ in the U.S.A.

The main problem of Executive Council staff is that the style and work of some of the committees and staff in the NCCC do not fit with their functioning in Executive Council. In particular, agendas prepared by some NCCC units do not make it possible for them to be in dialogue with people from other churches. Rather than helping the member churches to develop ecumenically, there is still a desire to own programs and initiative. Executive Council staff have a high regard for inter-church coalitions and a collaborative style, but coalitions are often facilitated by avoiding the NCCC.

A related problem is that the NCCC does not take the local church (diocese/parishes) adequately into account in its planning. One consequence is that it lacks sensitivity to public opinion in the churches. The priorities of NCCC in the 1970s have been in the area of the social implications of the Gospel, yet in the process of developing policy statements and resolutions the NCCC makes little provision for their usefulness in the local churches. The results are often counterproductive because the statements have slight overall impact and much of the constituency considers NCCC irrelevant.

A third problem is that while the last 65 years and particularly the last 15 years have brought an historic ecumenical transformation in most of the churches, the NCCC has hardly changed. A successful attempt of the 1940s and 1950s to structure relationships between certain ecumenically involved churches through practical cooperation was valuable, but this structuring is outdated. The member churches have an opportunity to transform the NCCC into a forum for all churches of ecumenical good will in the U.S. which will call the churches to the goal of visible unity. At the same time it will be important not to lose functions and activities of NCCC that are of value, such as work on the social implications of the Gospel, however NCCC itself is reshaped.

As things stand, the NCCC Governing Board fails to measure up to the Nairobi Assembly's urgings, quoted in the introduction, about unity and about interdependence of ecumenical efforts. Nor does it measure up to the ecumenical policy of the Episcopal Church as described in Section 4. Composed of a limited number of ecumenically involved churches, the NCCC has lost some of its ecumenical credibility. The Governing Board's lack of serious attention to visible unity means that it lacks a comprehensive agenda for mission and ministry. Limiting itself for the most part to social, political, and economic issues, the Board has little or no oversight of divisions and commmissions that do most of the work and spend most of the budget.

The future of the NCCC in light of the transformations mentioned in Section 2 is to be reconceived and reshaped by a continuing process as a national "network" serving, but not embodying, the ecumenical movement by interrelating diversities in American pluralistic Christianity. The task of the Council is to maintain and develop networks which are strongly administrative and enabling, to link the churches.

The task of the churches through the networks is to promote the goal of visible unity (in diversity), renewal, and common witness. The network itself is to create interaction without forcing integration. A reshaped NCCC will have a revised constitution with clearly stated purposes on the basis of which member churches can evaluate effectiveness of performance. It will be a modest-sized institution with a servant relationship to the churches.

The NCCC is a significant potential point of convergence for the ecumenical aspirations and activities of Protestant, Orthodox, Anglican, and Roman Catholic Churches. Yet it remains only the servant of the ecumenical movement which has a much wider and deeper significance as it penetrates beyond the boundaries of church institutions, quickens universal fellowship among the followers of Jesus Christ, and draws its power from the indefinable presence and activity of the Holy Spirit.

c. Consultation on Church Union

The Ecumenical Office offers this evaluation. Predominant in the 1960s, COCU has less importance in the 1970s relative to other conversations of the Episcopal Church. This multilateral conversation recently produced a theological statement of interest, and continues to sponsor local experimentation through "interim eucharistic fellowship" and "generating communities." A certain ambiguity attaches to COCU and to the churches which formed it because the 1961 charter calls for a "united church truly Catholic, truly Reformed, and truly Evangelical," whereas today the earlier model of organically united national churches is widely questioned and newer models are being developed. A related problem is that COCU, unlike the parallel multilateral conversation of Faith and Order, has not been able fully to include the Roman Catholic, Lutheran, Orthodox, Baptist, and evangelical conservative Churches. Yet in another sense COCU is already too inclusive to bring the participating churches into one church organization, for it includes Protestant and Anglican, "free" and connectional, black and white, reformed and evangelical traditions.

The policy of the Episcopal Church is to work toward visible unity of all churches, but more effective ways could be found to work toward closer relations with the Reformed, Methodist, and Disciples families of churches.

The churches which formed COCU need to review its 1961 charter and purpose in light of the ecumenical transformations in the last 16 years, particularly the richer model of visible unity (see the Anglican Consultative Council's response to the WCC discussion of "conciliar fellowship"). The experience of a search for one singular model may have been only a temporary step in the pilgrimage. Much of what we have learned so far is only part of a new whole, which none of us yet can clearly see. COCU could become the core group to expand mutual recognition of members and ministries, etc. to all ecumenically involved churches. However it is refashioned and used, it is important that we not lose present functions and activities of COCU that are of value.

The National Council of Churches' constitution makes room for efforts toward unity, but does not specify visible unity in its stated purposes (as does the World Council) and has little activity aimed at this goal. All the Churches in the Consultation on Church Union are also members of the NCCC, and it appears that both ecumenical organizations lack what the other has. What steps could be taken to find ways in which these organizations could work together to demonstrate the vital relationship between unity and mission and to be of service to non-member as well as member communions?

d. Joint Educational Development

JED continues to be a viable working group for the Episcopal Church and 11 other denominations. Primarily a task-oriented organization, JED provides a good opportunity for ecumenical working relationships in religious education research and projects. The collaborative style of JED is structured in such a way that it permits members to support joint educational projects or to decline them, depending on their respective needs, goals, and objectives.

JED is presently supporting some 15 projects, five of which the Episcopal Church supports. The projects range from a variety of explorations into new concerns of education to a fully developed curriculum system. Though JED does not belong to NCCC, the two are in constant liaison with each other to facilitate coordination and prevent duplication.

e. Joint Strategy and Action Committee

JSAC causes few problems among Executive Council staff participating in its task forces. The small JSAC staff enables a large number of national (and some regional) staff from 26 denominations to collaborate for strength, using their limited separate resources in study and exploration together, normally carrying out program in parallel but sometimes together. The JSAC style permits the Southern Baptist Convention and the American Lutheran Church to be full members, relating them in mission to member churches of NCCC.

The collaborative style of JSAC should not be lost. It has considerable potential in the national mission field and complements rather than competes with NCCC. JSAC is coordinated with the NCCC Division of Church and Society, Commission on Regional and Local Ecumenism, and Research and Planning office. JSAC cannot belong to NCCC because of the membership of non-NCCC churches; on the other hand, its collaborative style is a good example for NCCC program planning.

f. Local and Regional Ecumenism
The Ecumenical Office offers this evaluation. The Episcopal Diocesan Ecumenical Officers (EDEO) receive a grant from the general program budget under this title. Since 1974 the EDEO network has worked principally to establish ecumenical officers and commissions in dioceses, report diocesan and local activity through surveys, and see that useful information is shared. In 1977 EDEO began work on its goals and objectives within the context of the triennial ecumenical study. Eight provincial ecumenical consultations are developing "posture statements," officers are working in dioceses to articulate the Lund Principle, and exchange of "working models" is continuing.

Ecumenical work of the Church in each diocese is obviously in the early stages of development and is one of the most important components of this Church's ecumenical program. In some parts of the church the ecumenical movement is still a recent importation, and in all dioceses new generations must be involved for future leadership and commitment. EDEO will be identifying its future work in such areas as: (1) continuing education of diocesan ecumenical officers and commissions under the leadership of the Bishop, and education of the whole *laos* (clergy and laity); (2) processes for dioceses and their parishes to respond to ecumenical agreed statements, not only with theological analysis but with reappraisal and renewal of diocesan and parish life.

7. *Future Executive Council Involvements*

a. Strategies
Limitations of a small staff and the Executive Council policy to focus on service to dioceses are identified in Section 6. We now turn to financial limitations. If present national economic conditions continue, we should anticipate continuing reduction in the new triennium in what available dollars will buy. It is therefore essential that Executive Council have an ecumenical strategy, a shared vision of what we expect of ecumenical structures and of what we have the capacity to fund.

Over the years the churches have accumulated a large investment in ecumenical structures, but lately they have not been able to meet all the demands that arise and to maintain all the structures at the same level. Choices, admittedly hard, have had to be made. At the same time, people who are proclaiming the Christian Gospel must sometimes, even at great cost, work together. "Bear one another's burdens" (Gal. 6:2). Concentration of our resources is the way through this predicament, to maximize the impact of the dollars and hours that we have to spend. We have asked for an ecumenical strategy, which suggests practical things to be done:

(1) National, world, and local ecumenical structures have diminished institutionally, and we should accept that fact. We should not try to defend ecumenical institutions, for they do not own the ecumenical movement. On the other hand, if we try to proclaim ecumenism as a movement, as vision, as a process with real involvement, we shall have some success.

It is essential that dioceses and their parishes take initiative to relate to other local churches for unity, witness, and service—so that ecumenical involvement of the Episcopal Church increases and resources are released where they are. Ecumenical structures that support this purpose should receive support. Episcopal Church policy should be developed nationally in the light of local experience.

(2) Ecumenism, with its emphasis on visible unity, is an essential part of the whole mission of the Church. "The mission of the Church is to restore all people to unity with God and each other in Christ" (Proposed Book of Common Prayer). The unity we have enables us to help strengthen Christians of other churches in their mission and be helped in return. A serious problem is that linkages between the churches are still weak. If we ask what should be different about the Episcopal Church's relations with other churches in the U.S. and throughout the world in future, the answer is networks.

It is essential to maintain and develop national, regional, world, and local ecumenical networks among families of churches (a) through existing ecumenical structures and, where they cannot or will not do the job, (b) through direct church-to-church relationships, so that "sustained and sustaining" relationships may increase. Churches may not delegate ecumenism to their ecumenical structures or to programs owned by those structures. The future task of the ecumenical structures is rather to enable conversation, planning, and communication among the churches.

How are decisions to be made for the 1980–83 triennium following this strategy? First we should distinguish between two kinds of "ecumenical money" in the general church program budget. One kind is identified as "ecumenical." The second kind is not so identified and is dispersed through the program budget. The financial officers have arranged to identify this second kind of money beginning in 1977 so that it will be possible to be informed on all ecumenical spending and to relate it to ecumenical policy and strategy. It will also help Executive Council to report to General Convention in 1979 about implementation of the 1976 resolution of the Lund Principle.

As responsible participants Executive Council contributes to the central budgets of ecumenical structures, but also to selected programs. Who is responsible for planning of ecumenical budgets? We recommend the following:

(1) Executive Council program units to fund ecumenical programs and projects in their own areas of responsibility because:

(a) They have the best judgment on which programs or projects carry out the goals and objectives of the Episcopal Church effectively.
(b) The staff person who influences funding will inevitably have greater influence in the decision-making process within the program unit of an ecumenical structure.
(c) The decision will be made on the basis that it carries out the goals and objectives of the Episcopal Church, not only because it is inter-church.
(d) Constituency support will be developed for ecumenical items.

(2) The Ecumenical Office to fund the ecumenical networks and the supervising and planning structures which make possible a variety of program collaboration. (Note: Some programs are made possible by support of central budgets without special funding or meetings.)

Following the ecumenical strategy, these guidelines are recommended to those responsible for decisions related to the 1980–83 triennium:

(1) In order to concentrate resources and to stimulate ecumenical involvement of the Episcopal Church and the Anglican Communion, fund ecumenical networks, modest in size, for enabling and planning.
(2) In order to support diocesan initiatives and planning, fund programs nationally and internationally when they have a bearing on the dioceses and their parishes and when they support Episcopal Church goals and objectives.

(3) Normally expect committees, programs, task forces, etc. which are supported to evaluate their work yearly as a condition of the next year's budget.

Ecumenical structures are remarkably resourceful in developing funding requests. This creates a situation which the supporting churches increasingly resent, of supporting a budget, but then receiving further intermediate appeals for additional amounts. We have recommended that decisions on program grants be made in appropriate program units in accordance with goals and objectives of the Episcopal Church. Nevertheless ecumenical policy and strategy are also valid criteria for evaluation of funding requests. The Ecumenical Office and the Standing Commission on Ecumenical Relations should stand ready to consult with Executive Council units on requests.

b. Points of Development
There will be continuous and continuing need for dialogue, cooperation, and a forum for the churches. What is needed is an institutional form that makes these debates, agreements, and realities manageable on a continuing basis. Together but independent would seem to fit the needs of all the factors—interaction without integration.

In the 1950s and early 1960s there may have been too much homogeneity in the ecumenical movement, complicated by an integrative bureaucratic style, but today there are new appreciations of cultural diversity, theological expression, "roots," etc. Ecumenism now admits much pluralism, much diversity, and therefore much dialectical tension. There is only one ecumenical movement, but that movement is neither a monolithic entity nor a univocal process.

The institutional form that best fits these needs is the network of communications, each church being autonomous but providing representation on a continuing basis. Institutionalized locally, nationally, regionally, and universally, the networks can be used by the churches to elaborate strategies to meet various needs of the area and of the individual churches.

A long-term fruitful situation in which the communions can work together will not be served by considering the Roman Catholic and evangelical conservative churches as non-existent. There will be continuing interactions among all communions and among people of the local churches, so institutional platforms should be developed on which issues can be resolved and unity promoted.

Linkages have to be institutionalized if they are to do any good. Institutional linkages within the Episcopal Church need to be developed. The national Ecumenical Office and the Standing Commission

on Ecumenical Relations need closer linkage with program committees of Executive Council. The Standing Commission needs closer
linkage with the dioceses and parishes through the Episcopal Diocesan Ecumenical Officers. The Standing Commission, Ecumenical
Office, and Executive Council all need closer linkage with the
seminaries. Wherever the linkage is weak, the strength of our ecumenical policy is affected.

Institutional linkage between the Episcopal Church and other
churches nationally and internationally exists at present in three different forms, all of which need to be developed:

(1) *The Wider Episcopal Fellowship,* comprising the churches of the
Anglican Communion and 14 other churches having more than
90 dioceses, is one in faith and sacraments and diverse in theological and liturgical expression. Expression of this unity through
"conciliar fellowship" and partnership in mission has barely begun
and is a major item on the agenda, offering a "working model" of
unity.

(2) *Councils of Churches and Consortia* already function as networks in
some respects (particularly consortia) but should intentionally develop this capacity. Yet they are made up of the same limited
group of churches, with some extension in the case of JSAC and
the National Council's Commission on Faith and Order. When
NCCC was restructured in the early 1970s, an ecumenical convocation of all Christian churches in America was proposed. This
should be implemented now. NCCC could also serve the churches
by forming a network with the Roman Catholic Church for ecumenical planning. The Episcopal Church should offer a strong
lead to NCCC and other agencies on functions we need and expect from them.

Efforts are underway through the Anglican Consultative Council
to explore partnership in mission with other world families of
churches, with WCC enabling the process.

(3) *Conversations with Roman Catholics, COCU, Orthodox, and Lutherans*
are conducted in diverse ways, and are being studied by the Standing Commission on Ecumenical Relations. Networks linking the
Episcopal Church with some of these churches are becoming necessary for partnership in mission in at least some respects. An
organized network (oriented to church union) has been in operation with the COCU churches. What emerges as new from the last
15 years of ecumenical experience and participation is a large
network of theological conversations with the Roman Catholic

Church. It has become clearer that these relationships cannot be conducted and developed through the medium of the NCCC and WCC, so new institutional linkage should be developed.

(a) *National* networks for theological conversations with Roman Catholic, Orthodox, COCU, and Lutheran churches are operating (regional networks with Southern Baptists are developing). Networks for pastoral/practical collaboration can be developed with some (linkage committees or task forces), particularly the Roman Catholic Church.

(b) *International* networks for theological conversations are in operation with the Roman Catholic and Orthodox Churches, with participation from the Episcopal Church. An Anglican–Roman Catholic liaison committee and an Anglican-Lutheran joint working group also exist, but participation is mainly from the Church of England. Episcopal Church participation in the latter networks should be developed through the Anglican Consultative Council.

Against a background of changing international conditions, there is reason to believe that strengthening international networks is most important. Primatial and other ecumenical exchanges with churches in the socialist countries of Eastern Europe, relations with centers such as the Vatican, ecumenical patriarchate, and the ecumenical center in Geneva, are in this category. Because of the great importance that attaches to relations between the U.S. and the U.S.S.R., the bilateral conversation between the Episcopal Church and the Russian Orthodox is in this category. These networks can pay attention, not only to issues of Faith and Order, but also to building bridges for friendship, peace with justice, and human dignity.

As we do not expect other Christians to be absorbed into Anglicanism or to be absorbed ourselves, our desire is that all should strive in their own traditions to deepen the fullness of their faith in a fully churchly life. No church is asked to uproot itself, to cut itself off from its theological, liturgical, spiritual, and cultural heritage, or lose its distinctive character. Rather, each is to contribute to the enrichment of all. For this reason, the ecumenical movement at its best places emphasis on prayer and fidelity, new life-styles in the Spirit, and the importance of personal contact. Where this is not so, ecumenism sometimes presents a rather barren appearance. Thus the spiritual dimension of continuous prayer, fasting, and meditation should have increased prominence in the ecumenical program of the Episcopal Church on a par with study and reflection on the problems that need to be resolved on the way to unity and cooperation of the churches in helping humanity solve the problems that confront it today.

New processes are needed for education. The Episcopal Church must develop ecumenical leaders, those who understand and articulate the vision, work it out practically, and put themselves on the line. At the same time, the ecumenical movement must not be restricted to specialists and committee elitists, but must be a process seen as a mission for everybody. The healthy influx of new participants implies that while constantly renewing itself, the ecumenical movement must serve as a seminar where people learn from each other the same things that their predecessors learned. True ecumenical learning comes from personal encounter and confrontation, not only from studying materials produced after past encounters. Finally a new patience is needed with those who have fears. To hear criticism from those who stand apart from the ecumenical movement is an important part of ecumenical education.

APPENDIX:
Resolutions of Implementation
(Reported by the Committee of Conference in May 1978 and adopted by the Executive Council in September 1978)

I. *Resolution Receiving Report*
Resolved, that Executive Council receives the Ecumenical Report.

II. *Resolution on Ecumenical Objectives*
The objectives below are based on sections of the Ecumenical Report. Explanations in parentheses are not part of the objectives. The resolution is intended to implement the findings of the Report through the general church program budget for the next triennium.
Resolved, that the ecumenical objectives of the general church program budget for the next triennium be the following, with the understanding that they are subject to further editing:

A. To participate and lead in the ecumenical movement of the churches with primary emphasis on support for diocesan and local ecumenism, and on support for national and world ecumenical structures to enable conversation, planning, and communication among the Churches nationally and world families of Churches internationally.

(Explanation: The local church is not merely an incomplete or subsidiary part of the universal Church, but is the fullness of the Church made present in a particular place. The local church is therefore the primary subject and object of ecumenical work. Our aim is to stimulate local and diocesan movement. National and world ecumenical structures can be resource centers and advocates of local ecumenism.)

(National ecumenical structures should shift from staffing program activities to ecumenizing the Churches. It is an implication of the Lund Principle that ecumenical structures should enable work "among" the Churches rather than exclusively "in" councils of churches.)

BY 1. promoting local ecumenism through support of national meetings of the Episcopal Diocesan Ecumenical Officers and promoting funding of programs of national and world ecumenical structures when they have a bearing on the dioceses and their parishes.

2. participating in and funding world and national ecumenical structures for communication, consultation, and planning among the Churches.

3. funding specific ecumenical programs when they are consistent with Episcopal Church mission, education, and social goals and objectives.

4. maintaining and strengthening theological dialogue nationally and internationally with the Roman Catholic, Orthodox, and Lutheran Churches, and the Consultation on Church Union nationally, through staff service to the Standing Commission on Ecumenical Relations and projects of the Anglican Consultative Council, to develop ecumenical policy and strategy.

(The Church participates in international bilateral dialogues and linkage with other world families of Churches through the Anglican Consultative Council, and Standing Commission on Ecumenical Relations nationally. Because of the special relationship between the two countries and particularly the two Churches, there is a bilateral dialogue between the Episcopal Church and the Russian Orthodox Church.

5. developing, locally, regionally, nationally, networks for pastoral and practical collaboration with other Churches, particularly the Roman Catholic Church.

(The National Council of Churches and Consultation on Church Union are significant networks for involvement with a particular group of Churches, but our involvement extends to other Churches. The large network of theological conversations, primarily with the Roman Catholic Church, prepares the way for greater partnership, calling for increased linkage through task forces, linkage committees, diocesan and parish covenants, etc. See the 12-Year Report of the Anglican–Roman Catholic Consultation. The key is friendly relations between leaders in the Churches as a prelude to problem solving. Ecumenical officers can facilitate collaboration between networks of Churches for hunger, etc.)

6. developing resources and processes involving laity in ecumenical education and action, to include the spiritual dimensions of ecumenism.

7. participating in the U.S. Conference for the World Council of Churches involving Churches of the North American region.

(Leaders of the Episcopal Church could benefit from relations with those of other North American Churches—U.S., Canada, Caribbean—around world agenda through a renewed U.S. Conference.)

8. communicating ecumenical thought and action throughout the Church.

B. To express the relationship of full communion among Churches of the Wider Episcopal Fellowship through partnership in mission and conciliar links (Anglican Churches, Old Catholic Churches, Polish National Catholic Church—unless communion is broken, Philippine Independent Church, Mar Thoma Church, United Churches of South India, North India, Pakistan, and Bangladesh).

(Expression of eucharistic fellowship through partnership in mission and conciliar relationship lags. In the period ahead, we can learn from the experience of fulfilling the concordat model of visible unity.)

BY 1. joint planning with non-Anglican Churches of this larger episcopal unity.

a. exploring avenues of partnership with the Old Catholic Churches in Europe.

b. initiating partnership through the Intercommunion Commission with the Polish National Catholic Church.

c. continuing collaboration with the Philippine Independent Church through the Joint Council PIC/PEC.

d. relating to the Mar Thoma Church and the United Churches of India and their joint council.

2. grants for estimated program and personnel needs to the Joint Council of PIC/PEC and other Churches.

III. *Further Resolutions*

These resolutions are based on the Ecumenical Report and the above objectives.

A. Budget

Resolved, that the division of responsibility for ecumenical budgets recommended in the Ecumenical Report be approved, whereby the ecumenical budget funds basic ecumenical structures for planning and administration, and program unit budgets fund selected ecumenical projects and programs within their areas of responsibility.

B. Accountability

Resolved, that the recommendation of the Ecumenical Report be adopted that the Executive Council annually review ecumenical structures funded by the ecumenical budget, through the administrative staff and ecumenical office;

And be it further resolved, that Executive Council annually evaluate projects and programs funded by program units, through those units;

And be it further resolved, that Executive Council request ecumenical agencies to provide adequate information on budget support by April for the following year, and strongly discourage further intermediate appeals for additional amounts.

C. National Council of Churches

Whereas, the Episcopal Church reaffirms its commitment to ecumenical participation and leadership; and

Whereas, the Episcopal Church is committed to primary emphasis on diocesan and local ecumenism; and

Whereas, the Lund Principle calls for consultation, planning, and communication among the Churches working on a collaborative model; and

Whereas, the Churches are called to visible unity in one faith and one eucharistic fellowship and the search for such visible unity should be a function of a National Council; and

Whereas, there have been many changes in the ecumenical movement since the National Council of Churches was established; and

Whereas, the Episcopal Church is committed to dialogue and working with the Roman Catholic Church and other Churches not in the National Council, it therefore records its commitment to work for a more fully ecumenical Conference of Churches; therefore be it

Resolved, that representatives of the Episcopal Church on National Council boards and committees participate with these goals and objectives in view; and be it further

Resolved, that the Episcopal Church and the National Council together re-examine National Council memberships and functions, through a dialogue between representatives of the National Council and representatives of the Episcopal Church.

D. Consultation on Church Union

Whereas, the Episcopal Church has participated in the Consultation in Church Union for seventeen years and has learned from this experience; and

Whereas, the Executive Council is involved in the development of program and budget; therefore be it

Resolved, that our representatives to the Consultation on Church Union be requested to reassess with representatives of other member Churches the 1961 charter and purpose of the Consultation on Church Union in light of recent exploration of models of unity, in particular the Anglican Consultative Council report "Pillars of Light" and the Roman Catholic/Presbyterian-Reformed statement "The Unity We Seek";

And be it further resolved, that our representatives be requested to discuss whether the Consultation and the National Council of Churches can collaborate in efforts for unity and mission.

E. Christian, North American Conference

Whereas, the Seton Hall ecumenical conference sponsored by the Consultation on Church Union and Seton Hall University proposed the organization of a Christian, North American ecumenical conference, and

Whereas, an ecumenical convocation of all Christian Churches in America was proposed when the National Council of Churches was last restructured in the early 1970s; therefore be it

Resolved, that the Executive Council of the Episcopal Church favors further exploration of a Christian, North American conference as an expression of the wider ecumenical fellowship, with as wide a sponsorship as possible.

· II ·

WHERE ARE WE NOW?

The Major Ecumenical Dialogues
of the Episcopal Church

The Concordat Relationships

Theological Analysis

by James E. Griffiss, chair;
Richard A. Norris; John H. Rodgers, Jr.;
J. Robert Wright; and William A. Norgren

Introduction

Although Anglicans have been involved in ecumenical conversations with other churches for years and years—it has been said that "the Anglican is by nature an ecumenical animal"—it is only in the last few years that it has seemed meet and right to undertake an evaluation of such conversations from some slight distance. Roman Catholics in the U.S.A. published a comprehensive and critical analysis of all their dialogues in 1972 and a second survey of this sort is now nearing completion. The Lutherans in the U.S.A. undertook a similar critique which was published in 1977. A synoptic description and assessment of all major bilateral dialogues over the world, both national and international, sponsored by the Conference of Secretaries of World Confessional Families in cooperation with the Faith and Order Secretariat of the World Council of Churches, was published in 1972 with a third edition appearing in 1975. An extensive *Workbook of Bibliographies for the Study of Interchurch Dialogues* has just been published (1978) by the Graymoor Friars of the Centro Pro Unione in Rome. And the first of a projected three forums to take an overview of all bilateral conversations has recently been sponsored by the WCC and the Conference of World Confessional Families at Bossey.

Truly, a time for reassessment seems at hand, and the questions asked in these other surveys are upon us now. What have the ecumenical conversations sponsored by the Episcopal Church found, or accomplished? Are they on the right track? What have been their procedures and goals? What new tensions have they exposed, what old disagreements have they laid to rest, what doctrinal shifts do they reveal? How successfully have they maintained a consistent Anglican position in the encounter of different viewpoints? Have they been responsible to the official authorities, to the rank and file, and to theological truth? What significance, what impact, have they had upon the life and work of the Episcopal Church and the other churches? And what, in particular, is to be said about the Consultation on Church Union, in which the commitment of the Episcopal Church has been not merely to a "dialogue" but to explore possibilities of a "Plan of Union" for the institutional and organizational merger of a particular group of churches?

Questions such as these led the General Convention of 1976 and the Standing Commission on Ecumenical Relations in 1977 to call for a theological review and critique of the Episcopal Church's four major ecumenical consultations with other churches as part of the Triennial Ecumenical Study, and this report follows. It is based primarily upon the official reports and agreed statements of these four, using position papers, minutes, and personal recollection only when needed for clarification. Its focus is upon the four *national* consultations which the Episcopal Church has sponsored through its Standing Commission on Ecumenical Relations: the Anglican-Orthodox Theological Consultation (AOTC), Anglican–Roman Catholic Consultation (ARC), Consultation on Church Union (COCU), and Lutheran-Episcopal Dialogue (LED). Official reports and agreed statements of the three *international* conversations in which the Episcopal Church is represented are noted only if they have been specifically dealt with by the national consultations. These three are: the Anglican-Lutheran Conversations (ALC), Anglican-Orthodox Joint Doctrinal Commission (AOJDC), and Anglican–Roman Catholic International Commission (ARCIC). Current participants from the Episcopal Church in the first four of these are listed in Appendix A in this section.

A task force of five theologians has worked for several months in the preparation of this report. The following specific areas of responsibility for initial analysis, evaluation, and drafting were undertaken by the five members as follows: LED by John H. Rodgers, Jr., Dean of Trinity Episcopal School for Ministry and a member of LED and ALC; COCU by Richard A. Norris, Jr., professor of church history at Union Theological Seminary and a representative of the Episcopal Church to COCU; ARC by J. Robert Wright, professor of church history at General Theological Seminary and a member of ARC; AOTC by William A. Norgren, assistant ecumenical officer of the Episcopal Church, co-secretary of AOTC, and a consultant to AOJDC; general conclusions by James E. Griffiss, professor of theology at Nashotah House, who has served as chairman of the task force. Although this was the division of labor, the entire report has been reviewed and adopted by the entire task force. While this report is tentative in the sense that all things are, the task force believes it has presented an overall view of the Episcopal Church's ecumenical conversations that is both critical and fair. It has, nonetheless, become aware in the course of its work that what follows is only a first step, and that much more needs to be done in detailed cross-analysis and comparison of the way in which particular topics (such as authority, or apostolicity, or ministry) are treated in the several dialogues.

1. *Anglican-Orthodox Consultation*

Procedures
The Anglican-Orthodox Theological Consultation ("theological" was added in 1974) began in 1962 and continues to the present, having had 21 meetings. Participants are appointed by the Standing Commission on Ecumenical Relations of the General Convention of the Episcopal Church and the Ecumenical Commission of the Standing Conference of Canonical Orthodox Bishops in the Americas. Statements published by the Consultation are "Guidelines on Anglican-Orthodox Relations," "A Reaction to the Proposed Ordination of Women," "Common Statement of Purpose," and "Statement on the Ordination of Women."

The AOTC was inaugurated by Presiding Bishop Arthur Lichtenberger of the Episcopal Church and Archbishop Iakovos, president of the Standing Conference of Canonical Orthodox Bishops. The first 12 meetings, held between 1962 and 1969, had both a theological and pastoral purpose, so theologians and pastors participated in equal numbers with two bishops as co-chairmen. The mixed purpose was indicated because only in North America do Anglicans and Orthodox live in the same society in which neither is the majority church and where they are exposed to similar challenges and needs. The meetings proceeded with participants and occasionally guests preparing papers on topics related to the overall theme chosen for each meeting. Points of agreement and disagreement were noted for future attention, but formal minutes were not kept.

During this first period, the AOTC considered information about meetings with implications for the two churches such as the Second Vatican Council, Consultation on Church Union, Pan-Orthodox Conferences, the Lambeth Conference, and the World Council of Churches assembly. Themes of the meetings, which afforded opportunity for mutual explanation, fall into three categories:

Doctrine: Nature of the Church
                The Eucharist
                The "Theotokos" in Anglican Thought
                Ikons
                Patriarch Meletios and His Recognition of Anglican
                   Orders
                The Holy Spirit and the Church
                Secularism in Orthodox Lands and the West
                Anglican Theology Today

Pastoral
Relations: Hindrances and Helps in the Progress towards Unity,
                   Especially at the Parish Level
                Survey of Popular Ideas of Anglican-Orthodox
                   Relations
                Adoption of Guidelines for Ecumenical Relations

Principles
of Unity: The Goal of the Consultation
                Principles of Unity
                Crisis and Promise in the Ecumenical Movement
                Orthodoxy and Ecumenism in Europe and America
                Christian Unity, Anglican and Orthodox Ecumenical
                   Commitments

The brevity of the meetings did not allow for the sustained grappling with these issues which might have eventuated in statements of agreement, save for the statement "Guidelines on Anglican-Orthodox Relations."

In 1970 the thirteenth and fourteenth meetings of the AOTC reviewed its purposes and membership and projected a theme for the next four meetings. The purposes adopted were (1) to inform and stimulate the then developing international Anglican-Orthodox dialogue from the point of view of the American experience of the two churches and (2) to strengthen mutual understanding and theological renewal in the two churches in the United States as a contribution toward the day of full union. The AOTC decided on a theme directly related to the common experience of the two churches, to clarify the mission of the Church through consideration of urgent and difficult questions that arise as a result of their interaction with American culture. Later, within this context, the doctrinal questions of unity raised in the international dialogue would be taken up. The assumption was that, as the two churches have a degree of unity (communion) now, they should manifest it now in such ways as are possible. The period of separation had been long, but the two churches might be on the threshold of a new unity—not organizational or communion in the Eucharist, but a unity around vision and program, the beginning of an alternative basis for living and struggling together. The AOTC also sensed that there is a limit to the value of mutual explanation and that it should aim wherever possible at consensus statements, stating differences only when they prove to be intractable.

The four meetings through 1973 considered the theme of mission with these topics:

> The Mission of the Church in Contemporary Society
> The Social Ethos of the Orthodox Church
> Church and World in the Orthodox Tradition
> Anglican Evangelicalism and Christian Social Ethics
> The Gospel Kerygma and the Mission of the Church

Emphasis fell on the issue of the Church as an instrument for social change. Informal consensus was reached that social action is a responsibility of all members of the Church but it is not the responsibility of the Church in its character as an institution. This agreement was to have been expanded and published with the papers and discussion on the theme as a resource for local church dialogue on renewal in mission and unity. The plan failed because of the unevenness of the papers, some of which were published elsewhere, but discussion at the meetings showed the fruitfulness of the approach and the enterprise as a whole was a qualified success. During this period, however, the issue of the proposed ordination of women arose in the Episcopal Church. A paper on the subject from the Orthodox perspective appeared on the agenda in 1972, and in 1973 the Orthodox asked for time on the agenda to prepare an Orthodox statement on the proposed ordination of women, to which the Episcopalians responded.

In 1974 the nineteenth meeting of the AOTC considered the roles of Anglicanism and Orthodoxy in the ecumenical movement, the sociological and cultural conditioning factors in Anglican-Orthodox relations, and a survey of Episcopal dioceses on Orthodox relations. A "Common Statement of Purpose" was adopted and a theme for the next period was outlined. The AOTC would (1) assess the progress achieved in Anglican-Orthodox relations over the past century in its bearing on current relations, (2) serve as a forum for reporting the achievements of other Anglican as well as Orthodox dialogues, and (3) relate its theological work more directly to the life and witness of the two churches, for example, by calling their attention from time to time to problems to which their common Christian tradition speaks.

The theme projected for the next period was tradition and the historical-critical method, with sub-themes of secularism or the relation of the Church, Kingdom, and world, and the practical meaning of the Eucharist. The intent was to examine the question of tradition and its interpretation in the light of the living experience of the two communions rather than as an abstraction. This theme was deferred when, once again, the proposed ordination of women to the priesthood demanded attention. At the twentieth meeting, held in 1976, the "Statement on the Ordination of Women" was produced by the AOTC after discussion of multiple papers. Partly a common statement, it included separate sections in which Anglicans upheld both positive and negative opinions and the Orthodox were unanimously negative.

When later in 1976 the General Convention of the Episcopal Church voted to remove canonical obstacles to the ordination of women to the priesthood and episcopate, the meeting of the AOTC scheduled for late 1976 was postponed at the request of the Orthodox and the delegations met separately to assess the new situation. The Anglican meeting sent a message to the Orthodox urging that the Consultation look at the underlying issues of tradition, pointing out that the departure from traditional practice "does not create a new ground of division" but was rather "an expression of more fundamental differences which lie at the root of our long-sustained and unhappy separation—consequently we believe that the decision of the Episcopal Church in regard to the ordination of women presents an opportunity for those concerned about the relations between our churches to probe more deeply the fundamental causes of our division."

Goal

When the AOTC was initiated by Presiding Bishop Lichtenberger and Archbishop Iakovos, the objective was "to identify things held in common, to analyze the nature of differences, and to seek recommendations for presentation to the respective Church authorities, with a view to mutual recognition of common faith and thereby to make a contribution toward the achievement of the goal of some form of expressed unity between the Anglican and Orthodox communions" (*Journal of General Convention,* 1964, p. 454).

In 1974 the AOTC agreed in its "Common Statement of Purpose" that "the ultimate purpose of the Consultation is the full union of the two communions" and the "proximate purpose is the encouragement of this end through the consideration of the many serious differences still existing between the two bodies, and the many internal problems with which both must contend."

Findings

Anglican-Orthodox dialogue preceded by almost half a century the rise of the modern ecumenical movement, leaving a residue of statements and minutes, both common and separate, that have not been fully evaluated in any major study. The international Anglican-Orthodox Joint Doctrinal Commission is currently adding significantly to the deposit. Formal findings from the U.S. AOTC, however, are few: a set of guidelines for Episcopalians and Orthodox approved by the House of Bishops of the Episcopal Church in 1966 and by the Standing Conference of Canonical Orthodox Bishops, a declaration of purpose for the Consultation, and two successive statements on differences over the ordination of women.

Evaluation

Seniority in the current program of ecumenical dialogues conducted by the Standing Commission on Ecumenical Relations is accorded to the Orthodox, partly because of a long history of relations going back to the establishment of a Russo-Greek Committee by the Episcopal Church in 1862. Anglicans have viewed Eastern Orthodoxy as a communion of Christians in living contact with the primitive faith and order to which they themselves appeal. They have also seen in Eastern Orthodox a more acceptable model of the Church than the Roman Catholic Communion as it existed between the Council of Trent and the Second Vatican Council.

The dialogue in the U.S. has helped to promote understanding and friendship but has not produced agreed statements contributing toward "mutual recognition of common faith" and "full union." One reason is that both Anglicans and Orthodox have to a certain extent been absorbed in changes in their internal life and challenges to the Gospel from the society. A second reason is that both Anglicans and Orthodox are internally divided. A third reason is that the "Eastern" of Eastern Orthodox is more than a convenient title: it is a reminder that the later Roman and medieval periods, the Renaissance, the Reformation, and the Enlightenment are not parts of its heritage. Understandably, Orthodox sometimes find dialogue with their "Western" neighbors frustrating and difficult. Anglicans show little indication of a true grasp of the reality of Eastern Orthodoxy. The reverse is, of course, also true.

Despite the difficulties of understanding, the AOTC is in reality an association of churches which seems to take differing forms at different times. It does not have the limited objectives of COCU and the ARC and LED dialogues; rather its agenda grows out of historical circumstances. There is a sense of belonging to one another as brothers and sisters in Christ, so the purpose of AOTC is to be together and to stay together. The reason why the ordination of women brought AOTC to an acute crisis is precisely that the Orthodox reaction was emotional as well as theological. They felt themselves to be rejected. Anglicans have to respond with love and, in particular, help Orthodox to understand historical-critical scholarship in the West. Orthodox attitudes towards authority and towards the past are being severely tested today, as are those of other churches. As the Orthodox experience pluralistic America, they face the question of what it means to be the Orthodox Church in the West, where Constantinian securities have passed away.

The Lambeth Conference of 1978 recognized that the international Anglican-Orthodox Joint Doctrinal Commission has produced the first fruits of a theological consensus in the Moscow Agreed Statement of 1976. Lambeth requested that the Commission continue to explore the fundamental questions of doctrinal agreement and disagreement between our churches, and to promote regional groups for theological dialogue which would bring to the Commission not only reactions to their work, but also theological issues arising out of local experience. The latter task was indeed performed by the AOTC in the case of ordination of women, for the international Commission's 1978 Athens statement on the subject made use of material from the AOTC's earlier statement.

The future of the AOTC is to press on with the agenda on tradition already projected, at the same time participating in terms of local experience and outlook in the work of the international Commission so that the result of its work may be adhered to. Within this theme, a further topic could be a study of Anglican and Orthodox statements on ordination of women as an instance of different interpretations of Scripture and tradition, intending to discover common ground which experience of the separate traditions occupies or is meant to occupy. The U.S. Consultation should soon add to its agenda the restoration of the Nicene Creed by the omission of the *Filioque,* as proposed by the international Commission. In all AOTC work, efforts to increase the quality of theological work should continue and progress should be recorded in published findings. The people of the Episcopal Church would be stimulated by the particular Orthodox witness to the universal tradition of the Resurrection and the Eucharist.

Christophe Dumont has often made the point that the separations of the sixteenth century would not have occurred if the Orthodox and Roman Catholic Churches had not already been separated for centuries. The dialogue between Orthodox and Roman Catholic Churches has, therefore, a specific importance in the ecumenical movement, a dimension which only a dialogue between those two churches can provide. The Anglican Church, in its dialogues with the Orthodox and Roman Catholic Churches, as well as other denominations that derive from the Reformation, also has a specific importance in the ecumenical movement. It is called to contribute, in the Western tradition, a wealth of views which are in a way parallel to those of the Orthodox, a less total contribution, but nonetheless real. It is also called to contribute to the Eastern tradition riches of Western tradition, though again it is a less total contribution than that of the Roman Catholic Church.

Meanwhile, recognition should be accorded by all concerned to the fact that issues between Eastern and Western Christianity are the deepest of all in the ecumenical movement, that their resolution will require immense patience and much time, and that even after a century or more of Anglican-Orthodox relations we are still in the *first* of the three stages outlined by the 1969 meeting in Jerusalem of the Anglican delegation to the international Commission:

1. The stage of "deepening mutual knowledge and understanding, in which we are at present"
2. The stage in which "our churches might formally recognize each other as sister Churches, loving and respecting one another in Christ, even before complete unity and full communion;" the possibility of "constant collaboration in practical matters, regular mutual consultation and support, and mutual commemoration and prayer in the Holy Liturgy"
3. The stage of "full union in faith and love, and the coming together in the common chalice of our one Lord."

2. Anglican–Roman Catholic Consultation

Procedures

Established in 1965, the Anglican–Roman Catholic Consultation in the U.S.A. (ARC) has held 20 meetings as of March 1978, with the next scheduled for January of 1979. ARC is independent of, yet closely related to, the Anglican–Roman Catholic International Commission (ARCIC), which was established in 1969 as the successor to a

similar "preparatory commission" founded in 1966. ARC is, furthermore, only one of several national Anglican–Roman Catholic
dialogues that have come to exist in Australia, Belgium, Canada, East
Africa, England, France, Ireland, Japan, Latin America, Malawi, New
Zealand, Papua New Guinea, the Philippines, Scotland, South Africa,
the South Pacific, and Wales. The operational procedure of ARC/USA
has been to meet once or twice in every year with about 18 members,
the two churches being represented in equal numbers. The co-
chairmen have always been bishops. Roman Catholic participants are
appointed by the Bishops' Committee on Ecumenical and Interreligious Affairs of the National Conference of Catholic Bishops of the
U.S.A., and Episcopalians by the Standing (formerly "Joint") Commission on Ecumenical Relations of General Convention. The Episcopal
Church has tended to divide its nine-member representation equally
among bishops, priests, and lay persons, with concern for geographical
spread, diversity of theological stance, and representation of women.
The Roman Catholic membership has tended to reflect a concern for
balance between pastoral experience and theological expertise.

Papers have been prepared to address major questions in the
dialogue, and from time to time agreed statements have been issued.
Procedurally, such statements are based more upon an examination of
the official documents and formularies of both churches than upon
the personal opinions of individual theologians or other writers.
These statements, like those of ARCIC, are conceived as "only recommendations, not decisions," as statements *to* the churches, not yet
statements *of* the churches, and they bear the official authority only of
their signatories and not of the churches themselves. In form and
content, the agreed statements of ARC are somewhat similar to those
of ARCIC, in that their approach is simple and pastoral; they are less
"academically theological" in tone than the U.S.A. Lutheran–Roman
Catholic agreed statements, for example, and they are published
without accompanying documentation, position papers, descriptions
of the process, or separate remarks addressed to each church. Perhaps
partly because of this, the brief statements of ARC (and of ARCIC)
have been widely printed and publicized in the press and in journals,
as well as in the semi-official series of booklets known as "ARC-DOC,"
and they have met with a widespread, popular, positive response. In
recent years ARC has tended to prefer such statements as its only
"official" means of communication, although in its earlier years it encouraged a greater degree of press coverage and publicity for each of
its meetings.

Another procedural aspect of the Anglican–Roman Catholic
dialogue in the USA is what ARC has called "diffusion," and it needs

to be noted here because ARC itself has officially encouraged it—both in its ARC VII pastoral statement on promoting local and spiritual ecumenism and in its frequent calls for local study and response to the national and international agreed statements. Since the close of the Second Vatican Council and the establishment of ARC/USA, both in 1965, there is little question that dialogue with Roman Catholics has been the most popular ecumenical activity of the Episcopal Church and continues so to the present day. Several surveys of the Episcopal Diocesan Ecumenical Officers have shown that this dialogue has top priority in an overwhelming majority of the dioceses, and such a conclusion has been confirmed by the most recent survey of the representatives from the eight provinces. It has also been estimated that there are some 100 Episcopal/Roman Catholic parish covenants, some seven such diocesan covenants, two such seminary covenants, and one covenant of religious orders. There is at least one joint A/RC parish. Joint Anglican/Roman Catholic conferences for clergy and laity have been held in over 150 cities. Many joint study groups have been formed, especially during the Week of Prayer for Christian Unity in January. Joint social action has been taken, joint retreats and pilgrimages have been held, resources have been shared, and observers have been exchanged for almost every conceivable church function. A number of pairs of Episcopal and Roman Catholic dioceses have their own "ARC" committees, and joint pastoral letters have been issued by many pairs of A/RC bishops. There is an international fellowship dedicated to pray and work for the organic reunion of Anglicans and Roman Catholics, the Fellowship of Sts. Gregory and Augustine, with a number of bishops from both churches as patrons and a large number of members now in the U.S.A. A great many books, booklets, study guides, cassettes, and even prayer cards have been published and sold. Even the "official" dialogue, therefore, is quite diffused.

So overwhelming has the popular movement of Anglican–Roman Catholic ecumenism been, in fact, that ARC could not actively "sponsor" all this if it had wished to do so, and instead it has preferred officially to "encourage" it, and to leave participation in such activities up to the time and inclination of its individual members. Without doubt, however, the popular movement has fed the official dialogue and *vice versa,* so that to a large extent the success of each has depended upon the procedure of the other.

Goals

The specific goals of ARC/USA have tended to fluctuate from time to time depending upon the ever-changing composition of the group's membership, the concurrent agenda of the International Commission, and the tenor of the times. The fullest official expression of its goal has come from the ARC VII statement of 1969, in which the members declared: "We see the goal as to realize full communion of the Roman Catholic Church with the Episcopal Church and the other Churches of the Anglican Communion." ARC then proposed three stages in the goal of restoration of full communion: "Re-encounter through personal exchange and dialogue," "Growing together: interim steps," and "Toward Full Communion and Organic Unity." Admitting that the terms "full communion" and "organic unity" needed further definition, ARC VII nevertheless asserted that as a common goal both terms together signified "an intention to arrive at the oneness for which Christ prayed in his high priestly prayer: a unity which shows forth the relationship between the Father and the Son in the Spirit, so that the world may see the glory of God revealed in the relationship of His disciples with one another."

ARC VII went on to note: "Full communion must not be interpreted as an agreement to disagree while sharing in the Eucharistic gifts, nor may organic unity be understood as a juridical concept implying a particular form of Church government. Such a unity is hard to visualize, but would include a common profession of faith and would mean a sufficient compatibility of polity to make possible a united mission to the human family. Whatever structural forms emerge, it is hoped that cultural and liturgical variety will remain so that the values of both the Roman and the Anglican ethos will survive and develop."

Four other brief indications of ARC's own self-understanding of its goal can be found in its agreed statements of more recent date. In its statement on "Doctrinal Agreement and Christian Unity: Methodological Considerations" in January of 1972, ARC indicated that it was seeking "to promote the cause of full mutual recognition and full ecclesiastical communion." In its October 1975 agreed statement on the church's purpose or mission, the members of ARC said they had been "charged by our churches to explore the possibility that there is a fundamental unity between us on the deepest levels of Christian faith and life." In its agreed statement on the ordination of women, finalized at the same meeting in October of 1975, ARC affirmed that its constant goal since 1969 had been "to help the two churches to arrive at full communion and organic unity." In its Twelve-Year Report of December 1976, finally, ARC said that the purpose of its official consultations was "to aid both Churches in realizing together that unity for which Christ prayed."

Underlying all these statements of ARC/USA, it should be added, has been the intention expressed by Pope Paul VI and Archbishop Michael Ramsey in their *Common Declaration* of March 1966 "to inaugurate between the Roman Catholic Church and the Anglican Communion a serious dialogue which, founded on the Gospels and on the ancient common traditions, may lead to that unity in truth for which Christ prayed."

All the above indications of goals, it will be noted, are rather general in nature, and for specific goals one can only look to the actual roster of what has been done at each of the several meetings.[1] Summarizing these, it is possible to say that ARC has considered three topics also treated by ARCIC (Eucharist, Ministry, Authority), and also issued statements on several other topics not so treated (Pastoral Ecumenism, Doctrinal Methodology, the Church's Purpose or Mission, Ordination of Women, Future Proposals). The relationships between ARC and ARCIC do not seem to have been at all contradictory in terms of goal, and three members of the one are also members of the other. Nonetheless, a certain merging of ARC's goals into those of ARCIC has been inevitable whenever the agenda of the International Commission seemed—in the opinion of ARC itself—to call for it.

Findings

Well in advance of the International Commission's Windsor Statement, ARC/USA in May of 1967 issued its Agreed Statement on the Eucharistic Sacrifice, affirming, on the basis of official documentation, the "substantial identity" of both churches in this area of Eucharistic doctrine, and in December of 1969 it released its pastoral statement on goals and the promotion of local and spiritual ecumenism which has already been discussed above.

ARC has also made formal public responses to the three major agreed statements of ARCIC. To the Windsor Statement on the Eucharist (September 1971), which affirmed "substantial agreement" on the Eucharistic doctrines of sacrifice and real presence, ARC gave its "warm approval," at the same time noting the reservations of some of its members who felt that the statement should have more clearly affirmed the Eucharist to be a sacrifice and others who felt that the Eucharistic presence should have been presented in a more dynamic or spiritual way. To the Canterbury Statement on Ministry (December 1973), in which ARCIC announced its "consensus on essential matters where it considers that doctrine admits no divergence," ARC recorded its "substantial agreement," seeing in it "our own faith and the faith of our separate churches" while at the same time calling for a number of "minor" clarifications. To the Venice Statement on Authority (released in January of 1976), in which ARCIC presented a "consensus" on basic principles of primacy qualified by certain Anglican difficulties, believing nonetheless that the statement represented "a significant convergence with far-reaching consequences," ARC issued two responses. The first response, brief and immediate because the Venice release happened to coincide with a previously scheduled meeting of ARC, noted that Venice (unlike Windsor and Canterbury) was more concerned with an ideal theory than with actual practice, and that it treated of *episcope* and primacy more fully than of "certain other expressions of authority more directly involving laity and clergy." The second response expanded considerably upon these points, urged that the eucharistic and ministerial references in Venice be read in the light of Windsor and Canterbury, and offered a list of related books and articles. Unlike its responses to Windsor and Canterbury, ARC did not record its "warm approval" or even "substantial agreement" with Venice. Nor did it invite the membership of both churches to the thoughtful and prayerful study of Venice, as it had for Windsor and Canterbury, although such an invitation may be inferred from the lengthy size of its second Venice response and the reading list appended thereto.

Still four other agreed statements have been released by ARC/USA. Its statement on "Doctrinal Agreement and Christian Unity: Methodological Considerations," approved in January of 1972, will be discussed below for reasons to be given then. In the fall of 1975, ARC completed its agreed statement on the Purpose or Mission of the Church, which had been in preparation for nearly three years. Convinced that "the prayer of the Church is the most intense expression of our faith in God and commitment to his purposes for the world," ARC decided to write its common belief about the church's purpose or mission in a context interwoven with parallel prayers from the contemporary Eucharistic liturgies of each church. Asserting, in the core of the statement, that the church's purpose or mission is basically a threefold one of proclamation, worship, and service, ARC concluded that it had found "substantial agreement" between the two churches on this topic and "no essential point on which we differ." And the church's purpose, it noted, would be served by the restoration of its unity. In this way, a context was set for much of the other work of the dialogue.

Another topic of particular timely interest that occupied a good portion of ARC's time was the ordination of women. In a joint statement also issued from its meeting of October 1975, ARC noted that it had given "careful consideration" to the scholarly papers from a special consultation on the same subject, convoked earlier in June by the authorities of both churches,[2] and expressed its agreement with the conclusion of that consultation, that "any decision, whether for or against the ordination of women, will in fact require the church to explain or develop its essential Tradition in an unprecedented way." The ARC members also affirmed in the October statement their conviction that, if one of the two churches should proceed to ordain women, "this difference would not lead to ARC's termination or to the abandonment of its declared goal." ARC said that its own contribution would not be "to propose what either church should do," but rather to place the question within the context of the agreed statements already issued. Speaking to the women's ordination question in the light of the Windsor and Canterbury statements on Eucharist and Ministry, then, it observed that "Though disagreement exists on the answer, the question is based on a common understanding of the issues involved and the meaning of terms common to both churches. We are talking about the same Eucharist and the same three-fold ministry; we share the same fundamental sources of doctrine in Scripture and Tradition . . .". Towards the end of this statement, finally, ARC raised again "the question of [the effect of ordination of women] upon the goal of full communion and organic unity." "If this goal is thought of as requiring uniformity in doctrine and discipline concerning candidates for ordination, the problem would indeed be a serious one," ARC replied, but then it concluded—citing the principles of "doctrinal pluralism" and "emphatic evaluation" from its 1972 agreed statement on Ecumenical Methodology that will be discussed below—"However, there is a development in theological thought about Church unity toward accepting diversity as a gift of the Holy Spirit who endows churches as well as individuals with varied gifts. . . . The ecumenical task is to inquire whether one church can fully recognize another in the midst of differences. . . . Even the things we do not agree with in each other's traditions may have something to teach us about God's will for his people." In sum, it would seem that this statement tried to strike a balance in presenting the opinions of both sides in both churches, and perhaps for that reason it did not get the publicity it might otherwise have enjoyed.

The latest official statement to appear from ARC by the time of the present writing is its Twelve-Year Report entitled "Where We Are: A Challenge for the Future," issued in December 1977 and recapitulating, in a way, the "first series" of eighteen ARC meetings since 1965. The summary in its introduction is especially worthy of note: "After 12 years of study ARC contends that the Episcopal Church and the

Roman Catholic Church agree at the level of faith on such topics as the Holy Eucharist, Priesthood and Ordination, and the nature and mission of the Church. There is also a common understanding between us of the theological methodology necessary for ecumenical dialogue. Yet agreement even at the level of faith is not always evident in visible expression. The Episcopal and the Roman Catholic Churches differ in their forms of worship, their traditions of spirituality, their styles of theological reflection, and in some of their organizational structures of church life. Despite these historically conditioned differences, however, ARC finds after 19 joint consultations that the Episcopal and Roman Catholic Churches share so profound an agreement on the level of faith that these Churches are in fact 'sister Churches' in the one *Communio* which is the Church of Christ."

The report then discourses over a number of areas of agreement and concern. In worship, ARC found a large area of convergence between the two churches. In the approach to scripture, it found a common agreement. In "articulation of the faith" it found a "very great body of fundamental doctrine that our churches have inherited in common and still share with little or no divergence." Enumerating the "doctrines of Trinity, Christology, sacraments, ecclesiology, and eschatology," ARC judged that any differences between the two churches in these areas are "less important than what our Churches hold in common" and therefore that "substantial agreement does exist between us at the level of faith and doctrine." On questions of authority, the papacy, and the relations of bishops to the worldwide church, ARC noted that at the time of the Reformation each church had placed differing emphases upon the expression and interpretation of the ministry of *episcope,* but that in more recent years deeper understandings and fresh perspectives have led many in both churches to suspect that perhaps they are not so far apart as one would imagine and that perhaps they are even growing closer together on these questions. On the "ethics of the Christian community," ARC asserted that both churches agree "on the primacy given to the corporate witness of the Christian life-style, . . . a responsibility of compassionate service to the whole of humankind," and that "both Episcopalians and Roman Catholics hold that the ultimate subjective norm of morality is the properly informed individual conscience and therefore share the same solution to many moral problems." Nevertheless, it found that "apparent discrepancies" do exist between the two churches as to "how the individual Christian appropriates to himself or herself what the Church proposes as the Christian life-style." As both churches "grapple separately to find what is the proper Christian response" to new questions in the areas of human sexuality, marriage, and the family, ARC found that the answers being given in each church "are not in agreement with one another," and it even went so far as to label this a "new area of growing disagreement." On the question of "Personal Life in Christ," finally, ARC found common agreement.

The Twelve-Year Report concluded with a number of "Pastoral Recommendations" offered to the sponsoring bodies. First there were four proposals for future agenda, submitted as possible areas for further investigation: authority and papal ministry, the community of women and men in the church and the world, the relationship between normative tradition and individual conscience, and the degree of unity as a necessary prerequisite to sacramental sharing. In addition, there were five proposals for possible action now through joint task forces: world hunger, evangelization, prayer and spirituality, survey of ARC covenants, and the pastoral role of bishops.

In addition to all the above, and entirely separate from ARC and ARCIC, there has also been an officially appointed "Anglican–Roman Catholic International Commission on the Theology of Marriage and its Application to Mixed Marriages," established in 1967, which submitted its "final report" in 1975. Since ARC/USA has published no comment on this report, it will not be considered here.

Evaluation

We turn now to an evaluation of this dialogue, and the first thing to be said is that for such a wide area of convergence and substantial agreement to be reached between Anglicans and Roman Catholics in the course of less than 15 years seems truly remarkable. If more has been accomplished in the U.S.A. than in England or by the International Commission, it may well be only because Americans are less conscious of past history and because the two churches in this country have been less accustomed to hurl invective at each other. And yet this, in a way, makes the three agreed statements of the International Commission all the more remarkable, in that such significant agreements as Windsor, Canterbury, and even Venice have been reached in a group dominated by the English and representing most shades of opinion in both worldwide churches from liberal to conservative and from Anglo-Catholic to Evangelical. The old disagreements about Eucharist and Ministry, at least, seem now laid to rest. There seems to be a new spirit at work in both churches, a fresh determination to understand and appreciate each other, and this in turn has been fed by the renewal of "biblical teaching and the tradition of our common inheritance" upon which Pope Paul and Archbishop Ramsey founded the international dialogue in 1966.

ARC/USA seems to have been faithful in its attempt to represent the positions of the two churches primarily from their own official formularies and documentation rather than from private opinions, and the footnotes annotating its statements on the church's purpose or mission and its Twelve-Year Report bear this out. ARC also seems to have a healthy relationship to the International Commission, both feeding it and also responding to its statements. ARC likewise seems to have been responsible both in reporting to its sponsoring bodies in this country and also in attempting to assist and encourage a mature pastoral response at the various "local" levels. Its co-chairmen seem to have been particularly diligent in keeping the group on its course. Its work seems to have been consistent with its professed goal, although the goal itself might benefit from some further exploration and delineation. ARC has been responsive to the call of the moment, such as in its statement on women's ordination, and it has also considered more long-range and theoretical issues such as the theological methodology for ecumenical dialogue.

The statement last mentioned, "Doctrinal Agreement and Christian Unity: Methodological Considerations," has not been treated above under "Findings" and will be discussed now instead, because it does not deal with any particular point at issue between Anglicans and Roman Catholics and is rather—as the survey sponsored by the WCC described it—"a set of principles which deserves the attention of all ecumenical dialogue groups as a guide in appraising doctrinal diversity and change."[3] Approved by ARC in January of 1972, this agreed statement sets forth a series of six "operative principles" by which each church in ecumenical dialogue can seek to evaluate and understand more fully the doctrinal positions of the other. These principles represent fairly the methodology that ARC has consistently used in its own discussions, and are as follows: (1) Paradoxical tension: No human theological language ever adequately reflects the reality of God to which it refers, because there is always a paradoxical tension between the language and the reality. (2) Contextual transfer: Past doctrinal utterances were made in cultural situations that are not our own, and hence they need contextual transfer if they are to be vital today. (3) Relative emphasis: Some important doctrinal definitions of the past may no longer seem of crucial importance in relationship to salvation today. (4) Doctrinal pluralism: Even within a single church, the same mystery may be conveyed more effectively by a plurality of formulas in different cultural contexts, and even the same doctrinal formula may receive a plurality of theological interpretations. (5) Empathetic evaluation: Each church should listen empathetically to the other, placing the best possible interpretation on doctrinal formulas that at first may be unfamiliar. (6) Responsive listening: Each church should consider whether its own doctrinal formulations from the past may be better expressed in contemporary statements that are less offensive to others.

In the long run, as the WCC survey in effect hinted, this particular statement on ecumenical methodology may prove to be ARC/USA's most significant evaluation of and contribution to the entire ecumenical movement. Although it received less publicity than most of the other ARC and ARCIC statements, probably because it is more abstract and does not treat particular questions of disagreement, it may eventually serve both to open new channels among all churches and at the same time allow Anglicans and Roman Catholics to realize the hope of legitimate diversity expressed by Paul VI in 1970: "There will be no seeking to lessen the legitimate prestige and the worthy patrimony of piety and usage proper to the Anglican Church when the Roman Catholic Church—this humble 'Servant of the servants of God'—is able to embrace her ever beloved sister in the one authentic Communion of the family of Christ."

From a specifically Anglican viewpoint, finally, the agreements reached by the ARC seem entirely consistent with official Anglican documents both classical and recent that are in the contemporary "working vocabulary" of the Episcopal Church, in particular the Book of Common Prayer, the Chicago-Lambeth Quadrilateral of 1886–88, the Lambeth Appeal of 1920, and the Faith and Order Statement from the report to the General Convention of 1949. Yet the statements of ARC have also been realistic in their admission of difficulties that Anglicans still generally find in some classical Roman Catholic positions. The reservations about the papacy expressed by the Anglicans of ARCIC in paragraph 24 of the Venice Statement are no doubt partly behind ARC's own very limited response to the way that church authority (especially of laity and clergy) was expressed in that statement, and such reservations were again expressed, a bit more hopefully, in the Twelve-Year Report. The ARC statement on the ordination of women appears to be an honest statement of the two churches' positions as of 1975, although in retrospect some might wish that the Anglican side of ARC had raised this question to the level of official discussion one or two years earlier. The question of disagreements in ethics (human sexuality, marriage, the family; the relationship between normative tradition and individual conscience) is treated frankly—if briefly—in the Twelve-Year Report, which is quite forth-right in setting out this and other hard questions for future agenda. Certain older areas of "classical" disagreement, however, are not prominent in ARC's or ARCIC's statements, notably the questions of Justification, Anglican Orders, and Mariology, presumably because they are generally regarded to have been set in different or wider contexts today: the first by modern soteriology, the second by new understandings of the doctrine of ordained ministry, and the third by an increasingly Christological interpretation of Marian dogmas. ARC's principles of ecumenical methodology are pertinent here. As to whether the affirmations of ARCIC in the Canterbury Statement about ministry and apostolicity, with which ARC found itself in sub-stantial agreement, and the affirmations of ARCIC about authority and papal primacy in the Venice Statement, are theologically consis-tent with the positions taken by other Anglican representatives in dialogue with the Orthodox, COCU, and the Lutherans, is a matter that can only be treated in a more detailed cross-analysis of all these dialogues.

The immediate and practical and pastoral impact of all this ARC dialogue in the life and work of both churches throughout the coun-try has already been indicated in discussing the procedures of local ecumenism above, and it has been remarked as a "notable feature" of ARC's work in the survey sponsored by the WCC. At the national level, this pastoral impact is further attested in the positive responses to the work of ARC and ARCIC given in the official resolutions of the U.S. Roman Catholic Bishops' Committee on Ecumenical and Interre-ligious Affairs and in those of the Episcopal Church's House of Bishops and General Convention. The BCEIA has hailed the ARCIC Windsor and Canterbury Statements as "unprecedented achieve-ments," and Presiding Bishops Hines and Allin have called these same documents "major milestones in the long journey toward reconcilia-tion between our two churches." In sum, it is no longer possible for either church to conceive of its future apart from the other, separated though they still are. In their "Common Declaration" of April 1977 Pope Paul VI and Archbishop Coggan of Canterbury stated that the time must shortly come when the conclusions of this dialogue between the two churches will need to be evaluated by the authorities of each, and this time—for moving from dialogue to decision—may well be near at hand. For the Episcopal Church in the U.S.A., it seems highly probable that such an evaluation and decision can be, will be, and should be, positive.

3. *The Consultation on Church Union*

Procedures

The Consultation on Church Union presently involves ten denominations, as follows:

The African Methodist Episcopal Church
The African Methodist Episcopal Zion Church
The Christian Church (Disciples of Christ)
The Christian Methodist Episcopal Church
The Episcopal Church
The National Council of Community Churches
The Presbyterian Church in the United States
The United Church of Christ
The United Methodist Church
The United Presbyterian Church in the U.S.A.

The work of the Consultation is done through five commissions and two task forces, on each of which all the participating denominations are represented. These are:

The Commission on Generating Communities
The Commission on Interim Eucharistic Fellowship
The Commission on Middle Judicatory Concerns
The Theology Commission
The Commission on Worship
The Task Force on Disabled Persons
The Task Force on Women's Concerns

Each of these commissions and task forces pursues its own business under the coordinating leadership of an Executive Committee and with the assistance of a staff headed by the Executive Secretary, with an office permanently located in Princeton, N.J. Periodic plenary sessions of the Consultation make recommendations to the member churches on the basis of the work of the commissions and task forces.

Dialogue on faith and order issues, carried on focally in the Theology Commission, is thus only one aspect of COCU, although it is unquestionably central to the aims of the Consultation. Characteristic of the procedures of COCU is the existence of what may be called proleptic embodiments of a united church in the shape of interim eucharistic fellowships and generating communities.

The diversification of COCU's work has been gradual. The Consultation began in 1961, when the Episcopal Church in General Convention accepted the invitation of the United Presbyterian Church to join with it in inviting the United Methodist Church and the United Church of Christ to explore the establishment of a united church. It was the achievement of the first years of COCU to agree upon *Principles of Church Union* (1966). This agreement was the basis of *A Plan of Union* (1970), which included a restatement of the theological premises on which the representatives of the several churches were agreed and also the outlines of a constitution for "The Church of Christ Uniting." Reaction to *A Plan of Union* resulted (1973) in the appointment of a Commission to Revise the Theological Basis. This Commission in its turn recorded three achievements:

a. An affirmation "Toward the Mutual Recognition of Members," adopted by the Episcopal Church and the other participating churches.
b. A revision of the theological portions of *A Plan of Union,* entitled *In Quest of a Church of Christ Uniting.* This was commended to the member churches as "a statement of an emerging theological consensus" by the plenary meeting at Bergamo, Ohio, in 1976. It is now under study.
c. The statement entitled "An Alert on the New Church-Dividing Potential of Some Persistent Issues," which takes up the problems of Racism, Sexism and Institutionalism as they bear on the problems of Church unity.

At present, in addition to the continuing work of the other commissions and task forces, the Theology Commission is at work on Chapter VII ("Ministry") of the report *In Quest of a Church of Christ Uniting*.

It is a significant factor in the continuing work of COCU that it is now 17 years old, and that the persons responsible for dialogue on questions of faith and order (as well as those involved in concrete projects of co-operation) belong to a second, and sometimes even a third, generation of participants.

In the course of these seventeen years, the character of the work of the Consultation has changed. In the opening years of COCU, scholarly papers were produced which dealt with theologically central issues for church union—Scripture and Tradition, for example, or sacramental theology, or the character and meaning of "apostolic succession." The agreements achieved through such work laid the foundation for *The Principles of Church Union,* which in turn enabled 1970's *A Plan of Union.* Theological discussion since that time has been concerned with concrete issues created by the apparent necessity for revising *A Plan of Union,* it being presupposed that the fundamental agreements originally achieved are still valid. The character of discussion has further been changed, however, by two significant developments. The inclusion in COCU of the principal black denominations and the "arrival" of the question of the place of women in the Church (and in society generally) have compelled COCU to take cognizance of the problems of racism and sexism in a more than ceremonial way. This development has not only affected the discussion of constitutional issues (though it has certainly done that), but has also raised basic theological issues which have proved difficult to deal with inside the framework of a revision of texts.

Goals

There can be little question what the goal of the Consultation is. It is church union which includes institutional and organizational unification as well as mutual recognition of members and ministries. This fact is indicated by the very terms of *A Plan of Union,* which prescribes constitutional as well as theological bases for "The Church of Christ Uniting." The Church envisaged is one which will be, to use the traditional COCU phrase, "truly catholic, truly evangelical, and truly reformed," and will for that reason represent "a more inclusive expression of the oneness of the Church of Christ than any of the participating churches can suppose itself to be" (*Principles,* p. 12). This church will be a *uniting* as well as a *united* church: that is, it will continue after its formation to admit its own "incomplete and provisional character" (*ibid.,* p. 17) and to press toward even wider unity.

While this has been the formal goal of the Consultation, and indeed remains so, its *parousia* seems to have been postponed. *A Plan of Union* summons the member churches to "covenant together in the Plan of Union for The Church of Christ Uniting" (p. 9). The failure of the churches to take this step meant not only delay but acknowledgement and acceptance of delay. The document *In Quest of a Church of Christ Uniting* asserts: ". . . these seven chapters describe a starting point for a common inquiry and search with a specific goal, namely mutual recognition of members and ministers as a stage on the way toward a Church of Christ Uniting" (p. 6). This statement clearly marks a change of outlook. COCU is no "dialogue." Its ultimate aim is the union of a particular group of churches. Its proximate goal, however, is now "mutual recognition of members and ministers."

Achievements

The achievements of the Consultation on Church Union have been significant, and they have not been confined to the area of statements of theological accord. The involvement of black churches in the Consultation has meant that of all ecumenical undertakings in which the Episcopal Church is officially engaged, COCU alone involves dialogue with churches which represent both black culture and black religion. This is not to say that the issue of such encounter has always been a creative or even a useful one. One of the principal grounds for criticism of *A Plan of Union* was, after all, the constitutional provisions made to safeguard the rights of black membership and black leadership in the united church. COCU stumbled, at least in part, because of its attempt to be committed to practical racial justice and equality. Nevertheless it remains the sole arena where the "mainline," predominantly white, denominations can engage in serious dialogue with black churches.

In the second place, one must note the practical achievements which are represented by mutual recognition of members, interim eucharistic fellowships, and generating communities. The first of these represents a significant breakthrough whose implications, when considered and worked out, may prove surprising.

Finally, as a matter of fact, COCU has achieved a remarkable consensus in the realm of faith and order. Prior to the round of bilateral discussions which have occurred in the wake of the Second Vatican Council, COCU anticipated many of the conclusions to which present-day dialogues are beginning to come. On the authority of Scriptures and creeds, on the nature of the Church as Body of Christ, on the matter of worship, and even in the matter of theology of sacraments, COCU led the way in the United States towards what may now be an "emerging consensus" which embraces many more church bodies than those belonging to the Consultation. From an Anglican point of view, it is especially important to note that COCU has achieved essential agreement on all items of the Lambeth Quadrilateral. These accords have been achieved, moreover, in such a way that these guarantees of catholic order are at the same time seen as instruments of the reformed and evangelical character of the church.

Evaluation

Once these achievements have been noticed, it is no disloyalty to say that COCU today has problems.

In the first place, its goal of creating a Church of Christ Uniting has not, after 17 years, been achieved—though it would be unfair to say that the churches involved in COCU have not come closer to one another through its work. What is more, most people would agree that these are no longer times when that goal is likely to capture the imagination of many. COCU was born in an era when "the institutional church" was at a height of its success in the United States. Today, the same institutional church shows all the symptoms of decline. It clutches, therefore, in all its manifestations, at tested securities while it wonders what its future may be. It talks continually of "mission" and "evangelism," even as it pulls in horns and antennae and tries to believe that to do the expected is to confront the world with the scandal of the Gospel. In such a setting, COCU appears as a risky enterprise—as a luxury and a dangerous one. COCU, therefore, has a public-relations problem.

In Episcopalian circles, moreover, and no doubt in others as well, the formal goal of COCU has appeared more as a threat than as a matter for hopeful anticipation. A union of nine, or, as it is now, ten denominations would, it is thought, produce little more than another, vaster denomination whose only achievement would be a body within which no one would feel at home. Such a denomination would, it is suspected, produce a huge, centralized ecclesiastical bureaucracy of the sort no one wants; and what is more the resultant body would be one in which distinctively Anglican or "catholic" emphases would have little chance of fruitful survival, given the overwhelmingly "liberal Protestant" complexion of the Consultation. It is of course true that the denominational representatives to COCU have agreed on matters of creeds, sacraments, and the like, and that these agreements are in principle acceptable to Episcopalians. Do the several churches, however, including the Episcopal Church, actually practice what the COCU texts guarantee? Not often. It is, after all, a long way from the theological conference-table to the life of the church.

In addition to these problems, which concern the fashion in which ordinary people see COCU's aims and the possible results of success in achieving these aims, there is also an internal problem. The theological agreements on which COCU has based its hope of church union are, no doubt, both far-reaching and, in their fashion, sound. Nevertheless, new issues have arisen. New theological currents are moving, and the old agreements sometimes look as though they must be reconsidered in such a way as to incorporate the fruits of more recent reflection. One might, of course, argue just the contrary. The point is, however, that this is a problem which COCU must face and deal with.

Facing it, furthermore, may involve a reconsideration of COCU's very aims. If new circumstances and new theological developments have overtaken the Consultation on Church Union, shall it, by way of adjustment, turn itself into a continuing "dialogue," or admit that the way to church union is likely to be a long, slogging one? Shall it, in short, adjust its sights to a more distant consummation? If so, though, what is its use? Ecumenical conversations are not, after all, the best situations for serious theological reflection. They aim not at theological but at institutional results. Yet institutional results—at least in the very near future—may be just what cannot be had.

On the other hand, the churches involved in COCU belong together because they share a field of mission and because even now they do not understand one another well enough. There is safety in international confessional dialogue (and use as well, no doubt). It is arguable, however, that the hardest, and therefore the most important, people to talk to are the ones who operate just next door. The Episcopal Church must decide whether the COCU churches are its neighbors, and if so, how to let this truth shape its life.

4. *Lutheran-Episcopal Dialogue*

This report needs to be read in the context of the 1978 Lambeth Conference Resolution on relations with Lutheran Churches:

> The Conference encourages Anglican churches together with Lutheran churches in their own area:
> 1) To study the report entitled "Anglican-Lutheran International Conversations" [The Pullach Report, 1972], Resolution 2 of the second meeting [Dublin, 1973], and Resolution 5 of the third meeting [Trinidad, 1976] of the Anglican Consultative Council;
> 2) To give special attention to our ecclesial recognition of the Lutheran Church on the basis of these reports and resolutions; and
> 3) To seek ways of extending hospitality and of engaging in joint mission.

The International Anglican-Lutheran conversations met in four sessions between September 1970 and April 1972. From the beginning, these conversations sought to determine the conditions necessary for "mutual recognition and fellowship between the two churches" in the context of the mission of the Church to the world. Such convergence and present agreement was found to exist in matters theological, liturgical, creedal, in sacramental life and practice, as well as the place and role of the ordained ministry, that the conversations recommended a mutual recognition by Anglican and Lutheran churches seeing each other as "a true communion of Christ's body possessing a truly apostolic ministry." It is important to note that the Anglican participants could not foresee "full integration of ministries apart from the historic episcopate." It was suggested that this present agreement and convergence was sufficient to justify increasing inter-communion and eucharistic sharing as the context for further grow-ing together in the mission of the Church and theological discussions.

The 1973 Anglican Consultative Council meeting in Dublin re-ceived with satisfaction the report of the Anglican-Lutheran Interna-tional Conversations, commended it to the member churches for rec-ognition, approved the setting up of the Anglican-Lutheran Joint Working Group to receive and examine the comments from the churches and to take account of other international conversations in which Anglicans and Lutherans were involved. The 1976 Anglican Consultative Council meeting in Trinidad received the Joint Working Group's report which noted that while there is wide agreement be-tween the two traditions, several areas call for further discussion, espe-cially concepts of justification, eucharistic presence, apostolicity and episcopacy, with attention being given to the role and place of the bishop—and not only the more functional idea of *episcope*. This exhor-tation from Lambeth and these reflections of the international discus-sion and the Joint Working Group do reflect both the continuing urgency and also some of the most important historical influences which help shape the continuing Lutheran-Episcopal Dialogue in the U.S.A.

Procedures
Participants for the First Series of the Lutheran-Episcopal Dialogue were appointed by the Joint Commission (now Standing Commission) on Ecumenical Relations of the Episcopal Church and by the Division of Theological Studies of the Lutheran Council in the U.S.A. (which was at that time the cooperative agency for the American Lutheran Church, the Lutheran Church in America, and the Lutheran Church–Missouri Synod). Six meetings were held between October 1969 and June 1972. A series of papers on key issues was presented and discussed as follows:

1. Detroit, Michigan, October 14–15, 1969: "The Meaning and Au-thority of Scripture in the Life of the Church Today"
2. Milwaukee, Wisconsin, April 7–9, 1970: "The Relationship of the Church's Worship and Sacramental Life to the Unity of the Church"
3. New York, New York, November 17–19, 1970: "Our Baptismal Unity and Its Ecumenical Significance"

4. St. Paul, Minnesota, April 14–16, 1971: "The Apostolicity of the Church"
5. New York, New York, November 10–12, 1971: "What Would Be Needed for Full *Communio in Sacris* between Our Two Churches?"
6. New York, New York, May 31–June 1, 1972: Completion of Final Report

The Final Report submitted to the two sponsoring agencies is divided into four parts: Preamble, Summary, Statements Deriving from the First Four Dialogues, Recommendations, and Enabling Legislation. In the report the participants sought to make possible the practical implementation of mutual recognition by the Episcopal and Lutheran churches and local eucharistic intercommunion as soon as possible. Following the pattern of the international discussions whose work and conclusions influenced the first-round discussions, and without whose report the local discussions would seem less than fully documented, this report also has a statement addressed to each of the communions written by a participant to show how such a consensus and such far-reaching implications could rightly have come about. The reception of this report by the Joint Commission on Ecumenical Relations over the next few years indicated:

1. That the report was received and recommended to the Episcopal Church for study.
2. It was noted that this approach of interim eucharistic fellowship was at odds with the approaches followed in our dialogues with Rome and in the Consultation on Church Union, and it was suggested that all three dialogues should be consistent with each other.
3. Others on the Commission wondered whether we did not need more historical and theological documentation, as well as a fuller explanation of our concept of apostolicity.
4. Others asked whether this ecclesial recognition which seemed appropriate to the Lutheran Communion was to be extended to a general recognition of all mainline Protestant churches.
5. The JCER recommended a second series of discussions to be approved by the General Convention to continue the Lutheran-Episcopal Dialogue.

Participants for Series Two were appointed by the SCER and the presidents of the four Lutheran churches participating in the Lutheran Council in the U.S.A. (the fourth, beyond the three in Series

One, being the Association of Evangelical Lutheran Churches). Five of possibly seven sessions have taken place:

1. Alexandria, Virginia, January 18–31, 1976: "What Is the Gospel?" (A statement was shaped by this session but was not officially signed or submitted to either church. Also, certain historical quotations taken from *Anglicanism,* compiled and edited by Paul E. More and Frank Leslie Cross (Milwaukee: Morehouse Publishing Company, 1935), pp. 397–403, which dealt with classical Anglican writers and attitudes to non-Episcopal orders, were appended to this statement. The writings of Richard Hooker, John Cosin, and John Bramhall were felt to indicate that the first-round conclusions could well be substantiated within classic Anglican tradition and perspective. The reason this material was not issued was due to the fact that the second series of discussions was at this point not entirely clear as to its task and method.)
2. St. Louis, Missouri, January 26–28, 1977: "The Office of Bishop in Anglicanism and Lutheranism"
3. Sewanee, Tennessee, September 21–27, 1977: "Historic Profiles, and Apostolic Succession in the New Testament"
4. Columbus, Ohio, March 29–April 1, 1978: "Justification by Faith"
5. Nashotah, Wisconsin, September 20–23, 1978: "Apostle in the New Testament, Apostolic Succession and the Historic Episcopate" (This session authorized the release of an agreed statement on "Justification.")

Subsequent sessions will need to deal with Christ's presence in the eucharist, the authority of Holy Scripture, similarities and differences in Lutheran and Anglican approaches to doing theology and to proclamation of the Gospel.

Goals
The general mandate of the Lutheran-Episcopal Dialogue was to consider the feasibility of longer unity discussions. It is clear that both the international discussions and the Lutheran-Episcopal Dialogue in the United States felt impelled from the very beginning, due to the similarities of both communions, to go beyond a mere discussion about feasibility and to enter into a process leading to rather strong recommendations. The goals of Series One became

1. The exploration of the possibility of a recommendation of ecclesial recognition, and

2. The possibility of the recommendation of *Communio in Sacris* or Altar and Pulpit Fellowship.

The goals of Series Two were determined after a period of hesitancy during the first and second meetings of the series. They are threefold:

1. the theological exploration of the themes suggested to us by the Anglican-Lutheran joint working group and the Standing Commission on Ecumenical Relations.
2. the furthering of mutual understanding of each other on a parish level (to this end the Lutherans have brought in a church publications man and we have had frequent discussions concerning how our work might be more directly helpful on the parish level).
3. the possible reiteration of the recommendations of Series One.

Findings
The following is an attempt to sketch very briefly what seem to be the findings of major significance.

Series One
1. Apostolic Succession: A Many-Splendored Thing
Anglicans, in the opinion of the participants of this dialogue, have tended to think of apostolic succession in too narrow a fashion and have thought of continuity with the apostles almost entirely as mediated through the historic episcopate. Actually, the early church may be said to have expressed its continuity with the Apostles' fellowship, prayers, and the breaking of bread in a fourfold strand. This fourfold strand is conveniently expressed in the content of the Chicago-Lambeth Quadrilateral. The succession of the church in the apostles' fellowship involves faithfulness to apostolic teaching, hence, the canon of Scripture; instruction of the faithful in the rule of faith, ultimately given shape in the creeds; eucharistic, baptismal life and practice, hence, the Gospel sacraments and liturgies; and ordained leadership, hence, the historic episcopate, the presbyterate, and the diaconate. It is important to note that, unique to Anglicans and Lutherans as communions at the time of the Reformation, is what has been called the "conservative principle of reform." This is an attitude which delights in continuity with the pre-Reformation Church wherever such continuity could be had in agreement with Scripture and in accord with the treasured and positive experience of the Church. All that was found helpful and good and customary insofar as it was in agreement

with or was compatible with the witness and teaching of the Apostles found in Holy Scripture and insofar as it furthered the apostolic life and mission of the Church was to be retained. This principle or attitude sets Anglicans and Lutherans apart from all other churches which underwent the Reformation.

Hence, Anglicans and Lutherans look into one another's faces and see a very striking family likeness—a common eucharistic tradition, a common use of the church year, etc. It is further worthy of note that Anglicans have discovered in other settings that even where the historic episcopate is intact, true and full apostolic succession is not thereby guaranteed. The historic episcopate participates as an expression of, a channel of, and a living sign of a far wider succession in the fellowship of the apostles. Lutherans, for their part, have seen in our Prayer Book and its implicit teaching sufficient continuity in doctrine to recognize in us those who teach and confess the apostolic faith even though we do not have quite the same relation to the Reformation confessional writings which they have. This too needs to be recognized, that succession in right doctrine is not only preserved through elaborate confessional writings.

2. Episcope *and the Episcopate*

The Anglican participants in Series One learned, and believe it is important for other Anglicans to understand, that the Lutherans do take the ordained office of Word and Sacrament and pastoral care to be an office in the church *jure divino* (of divine appointment). Further, that the Lutherans have carefully sought to preserve "oversight" (*episcope*) in the Church through a variety of institutions and by those who occupy the office of Word and Sacrament. Also, they see succession in office to be good for the right order of the Church. In some parts of the Lutheran Communion, they have retained the historic episcopate. Lutherans, in principle, are willing to listen to Anglicans explain why the development of the historic episcopate within the church is the most appropriate and truest expression of *episcope* in the body of Christ.

3. *Ecclesial Recognition and Recognition of Ministries*

Anglicans in this dialogue became convinced that both the general Anglican attitude evidenced in historic Anglican practice, and the statements of the Lambeth Conferences, indicate that in the mutually schismatic body of Christ Episcopalians can recognize in other communions true churches, even where the fullness of historic order is not present. In a case where apostolic succession in the widest sense is so fully represented as it is in the Lutheran Communion, it seems surely appropriate for Episcopalians to look upon their sister communion and say to her, "We recognize in you a member church in the body of Christ in the apostolic succession." And if Anglicans see in them a true celebration of the Lord's Supper and a true teaching of the apostles' doctrine, must we not also see in their ministry one which stands in some real continuity in the fellowship of the apostles?

4. Interim Eucharistic Fellowship as the Context for Further Cooperation in Life and Mission and Theological Discussion

It is clear that the Lutheran-Episcopal Dialogue has taken a different approach from some of our other dialogues. The question is whether or not such an approach is consistent with other approaches, and whether it is in itself justifiable. This dialogue has concluded that where such common agreement and likeness in apostolic succession is to be found and recognized, as this discussion believes it has found in each other, it is imperative that we recognize sharing in the Lord's Supper or eucharistic fellowship to be appropriate when local conditions make it possible. It would seem to be in the context of sacramental unity that we would find the proper setting for closer sharing in the apostolic work and witness of the church and for continuing theological discussions and discussions about the kind of unity, outward and visible, and about the integration of ministry to which the Lord would be calling us. One can make a case that within the life of any given Christian congregation the Lord's Supper is both the expression of an existing unity, i.e. the sacramental celebration and expression of that unity, as well as a call to deepen that unity and to live it out. The eucharist is never simply the end of the road, but it is always also a means of grace and a context for a pilgrimage. Should it not also be so between Episcopalians and Lutherans? Such is the question posed by this dialogue.

5. Other Elements of Agreement

There are many other elements of agreement in ethos noted in both of the reports. One could simply say that when both Lutherans and Episcopalians (or Anglicans) are faithful to their own deepest and richest traditions, their likenesses become more and more evident. The ethos in each communion is remarkably one. It is impossible to give a true impression of this by simply detailing discrete elements. Ultimately, it is the living unity of all of them together, a *Gestalt,* in which one discovers two churches remarkably alike amid their diversities.

Series Two

1. Ignorance of Each Other and Two Historical Sketches

It has become clear that Episcopalians do not know Lutherans very well and Lutherans do not know Episcopalians very well. Lutherans have been much preoccupied with intra-Lutheran fragmentation and the search for Lutheran unity, and Anglicans have been preoccupied with our discussions with Rome of late and interdependence in the Anglican Communion. Two historical sketches presenting the Anglican and Lutheran experience in America were written and shared. It is strongly to be recommended that these two sketches be published and made available for adult education in the two communions.

2. *"Agreed Statement on Justification"*

The Second Series has now issued an "Agreed Statement on Justification," and the participants hope that this will be studied widely.

3. *Confessional Statements of Lutheranism and Their Positive Attitude towards the Historic Episcopate*

Picking up once again the theme of apostolic succession, *episcope,* the historic episcopate, and the office of the bishop, this particular round discovered anew the positive statement and attitude in the Lutheran confessional documents concerning the historic episcopate. Its rediscovery came with fresh impact. Anglican participants, indeed, began to wonder whether the Lutheran Church must no longer ask "Why the historic episcopate?" but, given the early and universal development of the historic episcopate, and given the positive attitude in the confessional writings, and given the conservative principle of Reformation: "Why *not* the historic episcopate?"

Several of the Lutheran bodies in this country have voted to use the title of "Bishop" for their presiding regional officers. This is, of course, not yet the full recovery of the historic episcopate from an Anglican viewpoint, but in a conservative tradition the use of biblical and historic terms brings with it a certain sensitivity to the realities of which those speak. There seems a growing openness among Lutherans, even on a popular level, to the historic episcopate. The Second Series will continue to talk about this subject and may well come to a fresh statement about it at some point.

Evaluation

1. *Significance*

The call and significance of these discussions needs to be taken very seriously. As the Anglican-Lutheran Joint Working Group points out, the United States of America is one of two places in the world where Anglicans and Lutherans live side by side in large numbers, and hence these discussions have a particular significance. Other geographical settings do not pose the issue with the same sharpness and clarity. This is said, being fully cognizant of the fact that the timing of this discussion alongside the ARC and ARCIC discussions has taken something of the sense of drama away from the Anglican-Lutheran discussions. The size of Rome, her lateness in coming into the ecumenical discussions, the attraction which Rome has held for many Anglicans, have so to speak "upstaged" the boldness and the breakthrough which many find in these international and national discussions with the Lutherans.

2. Anglican and Lutheran Difficulties in Discussing Church Order

The conservative principle of reform should show the way forward to both Anglicans and Lutherans in their historic difficulties in speaking about the historic episcopate. The Anglican difficulty can be expressed in the question, "How can Anglicans hold that the historic episcopate is a legitimate development in the life and mission of the Church, without at the same time requiring of partners in ecumenical discussion a doctrine of the historic episcopate which approaches an *esse* position, which position has never been held dominantly within Anglicanism?" Anglicans, thus, have been content to have the fact of the historic episcopate without insisting upon any one required doctrine about it, although this Anglican insistence upon "the fact" is often suspected by our ecumenical partners in dialogue to be a defense of some one particular doctrine of the historic episcopate.

The Lutheran difficulty, with their doctrine of *adiaphora* (that is, that in matters of church order the historic episcopate is neither expressly commanded by nor excluded by the Apostolic teaching in Scripture), has been that her doctrine so easily slips over to an attitude of indifference or even hostility to the historic episcopate. Either attitude, indifference or hostility, is a clear shift away from the conservative attitude which characterizes her principle of Reformation and towards a more radical attitude to reform of churchly tradition. Surely the "freedom" of the Gospel does not imply that there is nothing in between the absolutely essential and necessary and the purely pragmatic considerations of effective communication of the Gospel. Historic development, symbolic appropriateness—these are the things which Lutherans have long treasured and which in their confessional writings are treasured highly. One need only appreciate again the irenic and catholic nature of the Augsburg Confession to believe that the way forward in discussions about the historic episcopate between these two bodies is through a renewed appreciation of the conservative principle of reform common to Lutherans and Episcopalians.

3. Mutual Recognition of Churches and Ministries

For Anglicans to recognize formally the Lutheran churches and ministries would not be to say that the proper form of that ministry in its fullness has been preserved, but that *episcope* has continued, that faithfulness to eucharistic celebration, baptismal celebration, apostolic proclamation, and apostolic mission has continued, and that the office has been preserved in succession, though its form and integration into the historic episcopate was broken at the time of the Reformation in most places in Lutheranism. Anglicans also need to state clearly to Lutherans that we do not believe that the proper sign of the unity of the Church in time and space can be given its truest and fullest expression in the realm of church order except in the episcopate in historic succession. On the other hand, it would seem to many equally right for us to say that, where the historic succession has been retained but has failed to be faithful to that of which it itself is an expression, i.e. a sign of continuity in apostolic mission, apostolic teaching, and apostolic fellowship in sacramental life, such succession in order falls under judgment and is understandably abandoned for the sake of a more acceptable concept of apostolic succession until such time as it may be regained in faithfulness to the Gospel. Can we not, therefore, putting aside past misunderstandings, recognize the apostolic character and quality of the Lutheran Church in its ministry, even while asking the question: "Why not now, the historic episcopate?"

4. The Local Impact of the Discussions

The local impact of the international and national discussions between Lutherans and Episcopalians has not been as dramatic as that of the Anglican–Roman Catholic discussions. On the other hand, it has been more widely felt than many have realized. There have been meetings of diocesan clergy of both communions discussing the First Series reports and international reports. There have been so-called LARC gatherings in which parishes and congregations of the Lutheran, Anglican, and Roman Catholic communions have gathered together for common worship and prayer and have sought to understand each other better and to ask how they could in their local region more effectively carry out the mission of the Church together. There are congregations which have partially become one under one ordained leadership. Most dramatic is the agreement between the Dioceses of Michigan and Western Michigan and the Michigan Synod LCA, the Michigan District ALC, and the English Synod AELC, which have in effect acted affirmatively in that local area on the recommendation of Series One of the discussions. Their agreement and the theological documentation for so acting has been made available in a document entitled "Lutherans and Episcopalians: Free to Share," in which both Lutherans and Episcopalians offer their own documentation as to why they have acted positively on these recommendations.

5. Lutherans, Roman Catholics, and Episcopalians in "Trilogue"?
The question arises, in the light of the measure of agreement found
in the official dialogues between the Lutherans and Roman Catholics
and between the Lutherans and Episcopalians, as to whether these
three dialogue partners ought not from time to time sit down in common discussion, perhaps once a year, addressing together some common theme. It would be at least advisable to ask each of the dialogues
whether they believe that would be a helpful procedure.

5. *General Theological Evaluation*

As the preceding reports show, the Episcopal Church during the past
some years has engaged in a significant series of ecumenical conversations with other Christian groups. The conversations have ranged
from situations of dialogue in order to increase mutual understanding to a serious commitment to explore some form of visible and
organic unity. It is only appropriate that an analysis of each of those
conversations (a term used generically to cover all of the various ecumenical involvements) should be made in order to determine more
clearly the directions which they have taken in the past and to pose
some questions about the directions which they might take in the
future. As is evident from the separate reports, each conversation has
had its own set of goals. In some cases the goals are reasonably clear,
even though it may not yet be clear when those goals will be accomplished. That is true, for example, of COCU, where some form of
visible and organic unity is clearly envisioned, but how and when that
will be accomplished is not yet clear. In other cases the goals are less
clear, as in our long-standing conversations with the Orthodox
Churches. In the conversations with the Lutheran Churches, on the
other hand, certain immediate goals became clear during the course
of the conversations, even though they have yet to be implemented.
The conversations with the Roman Catholic Church have been particularly significant on both a national and international level and have
led to the hope that certain proximate goals can soon be
accomplished.

Behind each of these conversations lies a serious commitment on
the part of the Episcopal Church to some form of visible unity, but the
form or nature of the unity to which we are committed needs careful
examination lest we fall into one or another of two dangerous places.
On the one hand, our present ecumenical conversations, simply because of their diversity, could enable us to use ecumenical dialogue as
an excuse for doing nothing at all; there can be much pleasure and
self-satisfaction in simply talking. On the other hand, we might well

run the risk of moving too precipitously into a form of unity which would of itself be the occasion for new divisions. The history of the Christian Church in the United States amply demonstrates the dangers involved when denominational mergers are undertaken without serious theological and experiential foundations.

In the analysis that follows, certain questions will be asked that seem fundamental for determining the future course or courses which the conversations might follow:

1. Is there a discernible movement towards visible unity in a form acceptable to all groups involved?
2. Is there any sign from the several conversations about the possible model or shape which such visible unity might take?
3. On the basis of the present conversations, can a particular or unique role be discerned for the Episcopal Church, and do the conversations suggest how the Episcopal Church must change in its self-understanding in order to fulfill its role?
4. Are there any concrete actions which might be taken or ought to be taken now as a result of the conversations?

1. Is there a discernible movement towards visible unity in a form acceptable to all groups involved?

The term visible unity is not itself altogether clear, in part because of the complexity of the issues which divide us from other churches and in part because of the diversity of different forms of unity which have developed in the history of the Church. That latter problem will be considered in the next section. Here we are concerned to analyze more clearly what visible unity might mean in terms of a theological and experiential consensus among the several churches. It does seem true to say that the Episcopal Church (and the Anglican Communion as a whole) is in a rather unique position to talk about what kind of theological and experiential consensus is necessary for visible unity because of our history of "communion in diversity." Unlike many of the churches with whom we are involved, we have neither a clear confessional statement of our position on many doctrinal matters nor have we some form of Magisterium to which we can appeal as the source of our unity. From time to time Episcopalians have been wont to ask what it is, in fact, which does enable us to maintain visible unity with one another.

Based upon the preceding reports and the conversations which they reflect and upon various official and quasi-official statements of the

Episcopal Church, it would seem that a necessary consensus for visible unity (prescinding from the question of the form that unity might take) should—from an Anglican viewpoint—mean the following:

1. A mutual recognition that the Holy Scriptures of the Old and New Testament are the Word of God as they witness to God's action in Jesus Christ and the continuing presence of His Spirit in the Church. They are the authoritative norm for catholic faith in Jesus Christ and for the doctrinal tradition of the Gospel. Therefore we can declare that they contain all things necessary for salvation.

2. A mutual recognition that the Ancient Creeds are the form through which the Christian Church, early in its history in the world, under the guidance of the Holy Spirit, understood, interpreted, and expressed its faith in the Triune God. The continuing doctrinal tradition is the form through which the Church seeks to understand, interpret, and express its faith in continuity with the Ancient Creeds and in its awareness of the world to which the Word of God must be preached.

3. A mutual recognition that the Church is the sacrament of God's presence to the world and the sign of the Kingdom for which we hope. That presence and hope are made active and real in the Church and in Christian men and women through the preaching of the Word of God, through the Gospel sacraments of Baptism and Eucharist, and through our apostolate to the world in order that it may become the Kingdom of our God and of his Christ.

4. A mutual recognition that apostolicity is evidenced in continuity with the teaching, the ministry, and the mission of the apostles. Apostolic *teaching* must be founded upon the Holy Scriptures and the ancient fathers and creeds, drawing its proclamation of Jesus Christ and His Gospel for each new age from these sources, not merely reproducing them in a transmission of verbal identity. Apostolic *ministry* exists to promote, safeguard, and serve apostolic teaching. All Christians are called into this ministry by their Baptism. In order to serve, lead, and enable this ministry, some are set apart and ordained in the historic orders of Bishop, Presbyter, and Deacon. We understand the historic episcopate as central to this apostolic ministry and to the reunion of Christendom. Apostolic *mission* is itself a succession of apostolic teaching and ministry inherited from the past and carried into the present and future. Bishops in apostolic succession are, therefore, the focus and personal symbols of this inheritance and mission as they preach and teach the Gospel and summon the people of God to their mission of worship and service.

On the basis of these four points, how are we to evaluate the conversations in which we have been involved?

Our conversations with the Orthodox Churches are the most difficult to evaluate. They have gone on for many years and at times have seemed to make considerable progress. As the report makes clear, much progress had been made towards mutual understanding, and there was a sense, even though not clearly defined, that there existed between us a "special relationship." Recently, however, the profound cultural and theological differences between us— differences that had not always been faced in the early conversations—came to the surface over two issues: the continued inclusion of the *Filioque* clause in the Creed and the ordination of women. These two issues have shown the profound theological differences between us because they epitomize the fundamentally different ways in which the Orthodox and the Anglicans regard the authority of Scripture and tradition and the authority of secular movements upon the Church's life. Until these more fundamental questions are dealt with it would seem unlikely that there can be any formal agreement on the part of either Church in the four areas of mutual recognition. As the report makes clear, our conversations have only reached that first stage of "deepening mutual knowledge and understanding."

Perhaps the most dramatic advance in ecumenical conversations has been achieved with the Roman Catholics. The various documents cited in the report and the report itself imply that a substantial degree of unanimity in the four areas already exists between our two communions, to such a degree that they can be referred to as "sister churches." However, the report points to the several areas of concern which yet remain between us. As we continue our conversations with the Roman Catholic Church the following questions need to be dealt with.

1. The principal area of difficulty between us, in spite of the Venice Statement, is still the question of authority in the Church. Episcopalians must ask themselves if even the moderate statement of papal authority and the way in which that authority is exercised in the Church's life, is, on the one hand, agreeable with our experience of authority in our ecclesial life, and, on the other hand, comfortable with the consensus which we have already developed with non-Roman Catholic churches.

2. Certain traditional sources of doctrinal disagreement between us seem to have been bypassed in our conversations. Is this really the case? Can they be bypassed? Other than the papal office the most obvious source of difficulty would seem to be the development of Marian doctrines and the manner in which these doctrines have

been promulgated by an infallible Magisterium. Has the context changed so drastically that these issues can legitimately be left behind? Or do they reflect, as some Episcopalians might suspect, a deeper disagreement which has not yet been honestly faced?

3. The report mentions that the theological foundation for social ethics is yet to be explored by ARC. What fundamental differences about the authority of Scripture and Tradition may emerge as that question is investigated in greater depth?

4. The Roman Church's condemnation of Anglican Orders continues to be an offense to many Episcopalians. At the present time our Orders are not recognized officially by the Roman Church and the bull by which they were condemned is still an official document of the Magisterium. That can only mean that while we may be agreed on the theological principles concerning the ordained ministry, in practice the Roman Catholic Church can not yet establish with us a mutual recognition of this ordained ministry nor eucharistic fellowship. It is not sufficient to say that the condemnation of Anglican Orders can simply be forgotten. How can the Roman Catholic Church change its position in this matter without compromising other principles?

5. We believe that it is important for us to continue our conversations with COCU and with the Lutheran Churches, and Rome believes it important to begin more serious conversations with the Orthodox. Is there a potentiality for conflict as a result? Will we be required to make concessions towards the Protestant Churches (for example, in our understanding of the episcopate and apostolicity) which might compromise our conversations with Rome? Will Rome be required to make concessions towards the Orthodox (for example, on the ordination of women) which might compromise their conversations with us?

6. Certainly there has been a tremendous growth of trust between our two Churches, but have Episcopalians (and the Anglican Communion at large) reached the point where they can trust the seemingly authoritarian way of making decisions in the Roman Curia and among some of the Roman hierarchy?

If our conversations with Rome show the most dramatic advance, our involvement with COCU is in many ways the most problematic. As the report makes clear our relationship to COCU is of a different order than our conversations with other churches. In COCU we have committed ourselves to explore a form of church union "which includes institutional and organizational unification as well as mutual recognition of members and ministries" (p. 91). In none of the other conversations has such a commitment been made. At the same time, as the report admits, our relationship with COCU has serious problems. It is without doubt that COCU has made tremendous, even radical, advances in all of the areas of doctrine, ministry, sacraments, and mission. There has developed a theological consensus in all those areas which scarcely seemed possible some years ago. In addition, COCU has been and is essential to the ecumenical life of the Episcopal Church because it has required of us that we deal seriously with our neighbors, accept and deal with the reality of pluralism in American Christianity, and confront the social issues of the United States. In our conversations with other churches some or all of those areas could be avoided, but in COCU we are confronted with them concretely as part of the reality of our own ecclesial life. However, while recognizing the profound achievement of COCU, as the report makes clear, certain very serious problems remain, and they are problems which give rise to serious questions.

1. In spite of the considerable consensus which has been reached among the participating churches on doctrinal matters (p. 92), we must ask ourselves seriously if that consensus accurately reflects the life of the churches involved. That is, it is one thing for theologians and ecumenists to write theological documents, but it is another thing altogether for those documents to be accepted in the ordinary life and thinking of an ecclesial community. The diversity of churches in COCU is at one and the same time a strength and a weakness. The theological consensus may be acceptable to many in the Episcopal Church because to a large degree it reflects our heritage, but will it be equally acceptable to those who come from a more congregational and less sacramental experience? For example, we in the Episcopal Church have had a long history of living with the episcopate as an office which is pastoral, administrative, and sacramental; for many of the COCU churches, however, such a conception of bishops would essentially be imposed upon their history and experience. In a similar way, Espicopalians, in spite of their diversity, have a spirituality which has been nurtured for many centuries by the structured and formal worship of the Book of Common Prayer. This has not been the case for many of the COCU churches. Will the movement towards such a sacramental and structured spirituality be another imposition upon some COCU churches and therefore unacceptable to them?

2. Will the kind of institutionalism which COCU has developed be acceptable to us, given our particular history and experience? In spite of a significant theological consensus on the doctrine of the

Church, the hope which COCU holds out still reflects its origin as the coming together of a group of denominations. Is the proximate goal of COCU—"mutual recognition of members and ministers" (p. 91)—an acceptance, at least for the foreseeable future, of denominationalism? Would the Episcopal Church be comfortable, either theologically or practically, with such a vision of the Church?

3. Finally, does our serious involvement with churches representing a strong protestant and evangelical tradition comprise our conversations with other churches such as the Lutheran and Roman Catholic? That is, of course, a tension which has always existed in the Episcopal Church itself between our "catholic" and "protestant" heritage. Can we as an institution survive the deepening of that tension if we move simultaneously towards the protestant and evangelical churches and towards those of a more catholic structure and life?

Even when all of these questions have been raised, however, it is important to repeat the conclusion of the report: "The Episcopal Church must decide whether the COCU churches are its neighbors, and if so, how to let this truth shape its life" (p. 94).

The Lutheran-Episcopal Dialogue, has, without question, made the most significant advances, to the point that some form of communion between the two churches has become a serious possibility and, indeed, to a limited degree has already been established in Michigan. The advances made are deeply encouraging not only for the churches involved but for the ecumenical movement itself. The report on the Dialogue gives an extensive and thorough examination of the agreement reached on the essential points of mutual recognition, and it is not necessary to repeat those here, except to emphasize the one area which seems to be the most significant, namely, that while both churches represent the Reformation in the sixteenth century, both also represented a conservative stance in that they sought to maintain continuity with the past history of the Church through some form of apostolic succession. The report points out that the Anglican theological tradition can see in the Lutheran form of apostolic succession a legitimate expression of the apostolic nature of the Church. Our problem is to overcome some of the unfortunate emphases on historical succession in the episcopal office which we developed in the nineteenth century in order to resolve some of our own difficulties. It may be very difficult for some Episcopalians to abandon or modify that fairly recent development in our own theological tradition, especially if they are not convinced by the evidence that this Dialogue has provided.

The problem posed by the Lutheran-Episcopal Dialogue and by the conclusions reached during the first series is not what ought to happen between our two churches. In the view of the participants in this dialogue, there would seem to be no serious theological objection to the establishment of Eucharist and pulpit fellowship between us. The problem is rather how that would affect our other ecumenical conversations. Were such a relationship established between us, some of the churches involved in COCU might legitimately ask us why we felt it necessary to insist upon the notion of the historic episcopate in our agreements with them. We might well find ourselves hard pressed to define the differences on a serious theological level between a conservative principle of reform and something else. From another direction, such a move might well add to our current differences with the Roman Catholic Church on the nature of the apostolic ministry. Some might think it helpful to us if conversations between the Lutheran Churches and the Roman Catholic Church resolved some of the difficulties before the Episcopal Church moved in any official manner. On the other hand, the establishment of communion between our two churches would be an encouraging sign to many and could provide the beginning, at least, of a model for visible unity.

2. *Is there any sign from the several conversations about the possible model or shape which such visible unity might take?*

On the basis of the preceding, rather lengthy analysis of the movement towards some kind of visible unity, the second question can be answered more succinctly. It would appear that as yet no significant model for church unity has emerged from our various conversations. The reason for this is twofold.

On the one hand, the reason why no clear model of unity has yet emerged is that certain fundamental problems remain unsolved. In spite of the mutual recognition achieved between us and the Roman Catholic Church in many areas of theological controversy, the central question still remains: What does unity with the Holy See involve? What changes would be required of us in order that we might accept the institution of the papacy, and what changes would be required of the papacy in order that it might be acceptable to us? The Lutheran Churches pose to us an equally serious question: Is the Episcopal Church prepared to recognize a non-episcopal form of government and pastoral leadership even though it can recognize, theologically, the apostolicity of the Lutheran Churches? How fundamental is episcopacy for us? The COCU conversations require us to face the question of denominationalism. Can denominationalism be overcome when unity is seen in terms of the merger of institutional structures? In such a united and uniting Church would unity mean a loss of our own identity and heritage? It is especially sad that our conversations with the Orthodox have floundered because they, perhaps more than any other communion, do offer a model of union for churches sharing a common tradition. But our experience with the Orthodox Churches would seem to suggest that we are far away from a time when such a model can be made visible in the life of the Church.

On the other hand, no church, with the possible exception of the Roman Catholic Church, has a clear picture of what the visible unity of the Church might involve. And the Roman Catholic Church is only a *possible* exception because the model which it has officially known, namely, submission to the Holy See, is radically unacceptable to most other ecclesial bodies of the East and West, and even that official view would appear to be in the process of transformation and development. To this point, the paper prepared by Fr. Ryan for this study bears witness. In addition, the question can seriously be asked, although certainly not answered here: Has the Christian Church ever had in its history a model of unity acceptable to all? Has there ever been a time when the One Church was not rent and divided by schisms of various kinds? As the various churches move towards unity it may become increasingly obvious to us that the unity we seek is an eschatological hope that must be given to us and of which we cannot now have a clear image. For that reason we might well ask: How can separated churches understand what unity might mean until they have experienced some form of unity? Is it possible that we need to establish eucharistic and pulpit fellowship now with other Christians, despite all of our problems, as a legitimate means towards unity? This method has been suggested by the Lutheran-Episcopal Dialogue, but has not yet been implemented by either church.

3. *On the basis of the present conversations can a particular or unique role be discerned for the Episcopal Church, and do the conversations suggest how the Episcopal Church must change in its self-understanding in order to fulfill its role?*

That the Episcopal Church does have a particular, and even a unique, role in ecumenical conversations is evident from the separate reports and from the very questions which are raised in this evaluation. We pose questions to other ecclesial bodies out of our particular historical development and present experience which they must consider. Here are those which seem most obvious from the preceding material.

1. In our history we have been required to learn to live with diversity in doctrine and liturgical practice while maintaining some form of

visible unity with one another. While the particular manner in which we have done that obviously cannot be transferred to other churches, it can enable us to bring to the diversity of ecumenical dialogue both a vision and some practical experience.

2. We have experienced the episcopate as a pastoral office and as a sign of unity. While the emphasis which we have placed upon apostolic succession in the episcopate, sometimes to the exclusion of other considerations, may need modification and correction, it has, nonetheless, meant for us a sense of continuity with the past and a notion of hierarchy as service rather than juridical power.

3. With all the variations we have known, the Episcopal Church does seem to have developed a discernible form of sacramental spirituality and liturgical worship. Obviously we have much to learn from other traditions in these matters, but we can also offer something out of our heritage of worship and sacramental practice.

4. The Episcopal Church, as part of the Anglican Communion, has had a unique history of understanding itself as deeply rooted in the American experience, while at the same time having ties and responsibilities to a very international and diverse communion of churches. As Anglicanism itself has ceased to be quite so identifiably English, so too has the Episcopal Church begun to experience a greater degree of identity with our national culture and with the diversity of cultures elsewhere. That experience may be the greatest gift we have to offer the ecumenical movement in the United States.

Our strengths, however, have their converse weaknesses. It is not simply an ecumenical platitude to say that we have much to learn from the history and experience of the churches with whom we are in conversation. Self-criticism is difficult, and those other churches can certainly see our weaknesses more clearly than we can. However, certain very clear areas of need have been shown to us through our ecumenical conversations.

1. Our conversations with the COCU churches have demonstrated to us more clearly than anything else that we must overcome our sense of exclusiveness and privilege. At one time the Episcopal Church may have been justified in thinking of itself as the Established Church, but that day has long since gone, even though the mental attitudes it produced have not. COCU is requiring us to learn how to deal with our neighbors as equal partners.

2. Our conversations with the Roman Catholic Church may well show us that the somewhat nebulous and un-reflected notion of authority which we have developed is no longer appropriate in a world which requires radical moral and spiritual decisions if the Church is to fulfill its mission. Responsible pastoral care to the world may require us to take the authority of the Gospel and of the Church's tradition more seriously than has been our wont.

3. In the past we have relied upon the historic episcopate and our liturgical forms to provide us with a sense of unity. Our conversations with the Lutheran Churches would seem to be suggesting to us that we need to develop a greater awareness of the meaning of Apostolicity in the Gospel and, therefore, a greater flexibility in the interpretation of the *episcope* in the Church.

4. The Orthodox Churches, out of their present pain at what has happened between us, may well be our most helpful and severe critics as we continue in conversation with them. They offer not only to the Episcopal Church but also to western Christendom a vision of spirituality, theological reflection, and faithfulness to the past which all of the churches of the west need to recapture even if not to imitate slavishly.

4. Are there any concrete actions which might be taken or ought to be taken now as a result of the conversations?

Since this area is one of the chief concerns of the entire Triennial Ecumenical Study, it cannot be discussed at any length here. It is certainly true to say, however, that just as there is no conversation which ought to be abandoned so also there is no conversation which could not be strengthened. What the preceding sections have shown is that we have many serious questions before us as a church if we are to be honest with ourselves and with others in our future conversations. The danger for the Episcopal Church will always be that of speaking out of both sides of our mouth simply because we have that tension among ourselves.

NOTES

1. Partial listings are to be found in L. B. Guillot, *Ministry in Ecumenical Perspective* (Rome, 1969), pp. 114–124; N. Ehrenström and G. Gassmann, *Confessions in Dialogue*, 3rd edition (Geneva, 1975), pp. 69–70; and *A Workbook of Bibliographies for the Study of Interchurch Dialogues*, ed. J. F. Puglisi (Rome, 1978), pp. 33–34. For extensive bibliography of both ARC and ARCIC, including official documentation, see the last-mentioned work.

2. *Pro and Con on Ordination of Women* (New York: Seabury Professional Services, 1976).

3. Ehrenström and Gassmann, *op. cit.*, p. 71.

Appendix A:
List of Current Participants

Anglican-Orthodox

Anglicans: Bishop Donald J. Parsons (chairman), Bishop Robert E. Terwilliger, John Andrew, John Backus, Mother Mary Basil, Winston F. Crum, William B. Green, James E. Griffiss, Jr., William A. Norgren, Richard A. Norris, Jr., Lloyd G. Patterson, Jr., David A. Scott.

Orthodox: George S. Bebis, Demetrios Constantelos, John Erickson, Florian M. Galdau, Robert Haddad, Radovan Milkovich, Paul Schneirla, Stephen Sedor, Nomikos Michael Vaporis, Serge Verkovskoy.

Anglican–Roman Catholic

Anglicans: Bishop Arthur A. Vogel (chairman), Bishop David Reed, Bishop William Weinhauer, V. Nelle Bellamy, Peter Day, Eleanor McLaughlin, Charles P. Price, Henry B. Veatch, J. Robert Wright.

Roman Catholic: Bishop Raymond W. Lessard (chairman), Bishop Daniel E. Pilarczyk, Frederick M. Jelly, O.P., Allan Laubenthal, John R. Portman, Herbert J. Ryan, S.J., J. Peter Sheehan, Georges Tavard, Sara Butler.

Consultation on Church Union Theology Commission

Anglican: Richard A. Norris, Jr.
African Methodist Episcopal: Handley A. Hickey
African Methodist Episcopal Zion: George B. Thomas
Christian Church (Disciples of Christ): Paul A. Crow, Jr.
Christian Methodist Episcopal: Thomas Hoyt, Jr.
Presbyterian Church in the U.S.: Jorge Lara-Braud
United Church of Christ: Walter A. Brueggemann
United Methodist: John Deschner
United Presbyterian Church: Lewis Mudge
At Large: Margrethe B. J. Brown, J. Robert Nelson, Susan Savell, Otto Sommer
Observer Consultants: William G. Rusch (Lutheran Council), Avery Dulles, S.J. (Roman Catholic Church)
Secretariat: Gerald F. Moede, John Brandon

Lutheran-Episcopal

Anglican: Bishop William G. Weinhauer (chairman), Peter Day, Reginald H. Fuller, J. Ogden Hoffman, Jr., William Petersen, J. Howard Rhys, John H. Rodgers, Jr., Louis Weil.

Lutheran: Robert L. Wietelmann (chairman), Carl L. Bornmann, Stephen Bremer, Robert J. Goeser, Frank W. Klos, Jerald C. Joersz, Paul D. Opsahl, Ralph Quere, Frank C. Senn, Richard L. Trost, Cyril Wismar.

Appendix B:
Selected Bibliography

Anglican-Orthodox

Handbook of American Orthodoxy (Cincinnati: Forward Movement Publications, 1972): "Guidelines on Anglican-Orthodox Relations," pp. 11–14.

"A Reaction to the Proposed Ordination of Women," Diocesan Press Service of the Episcopal Church, June 25, 1973.

Ecumenical Bulletin no. 8, 1974: "Anglican Orthodox Consultation: Common Statement of Purpose," pp. 17–18. Also *Diakonia* X, 2, 1975, p. 188f.

Ecumenical Bulletin no. 16, 1976: "Statement on the Ordination of Women," pp. 26–28.

International:

Ecumenical Bulletin no. 19, 1976: "Anglican-Orthodox Joint Doctrinal Discussions: Communique," pp. 16–17.

Anglican-Orthodox Dialogue: The Moscow Statement (London: SPCK, 1977).

Anglican–Roman Catholic

ARC-DOC I and II (United States Catholic Conference, 1977; reprinted from I [1972] and II [1973]): "ARC IV Statement on the Eucharist," p. 3f.; "ARC VII Statement on the Eucharist," pp. 9–22; "Doctrinal Agreement and Christian Unity: Methodological Considerations," pp. 101–5; "Comment on the 'Agreed Statement on Eucharistic Doctrine' of the Anglican–Roman Catholic International Commission," pp. 106–8.

ARC-DOC III (United States Catholic Conference, 1976): "Anglican/ Roman Catholic Commission in the U.S.A. Agreed Statement on the Purpose of the Church," pp. 1–11; "ARC Response to ARCIC Canterbury Statement," pp. 82–84.

Pro and Con on Ordination of Women (New York: Seabury Professional Services, 1976).

Ecumenical Bulletin no. 22, 1977: "Initial Response to the Venice Statement on Authority in the Church."

Ecumenical Bulletin no. 28, 1978: "Second Response to the Venice Statement."

Ecumenical Bulletin, no. 27, 1978: "Where We Are: A Challenge for the Future, a 12-year Report."

International:

ARC-DOC I and II: "Agreed Statement on Eucharistic Doctrine," pp. 45–50.

ARC-DOC III: "Ministry and Ordination: Statement on the Doctrine of the Ministry," pp. 74–81.

Final Report: Commission on the Theology of Marriage and Its Application to Mixed Marriages (United States Catholic Conference, 1976).

Agreed Statement on Authority in the Church (United States Catholic Conference, 1977).

Ecumenical Study Guides on the Eucharist, Ministry and Authority (Garrison, N.Y.: Graymoor Ecumenical Institute).

Consultation on Church Union

Ecumenical Bulletin no. 10, 1975: "Toward the Mutual Recognition of Members: An Affirmation," p. 21f. Supplementary material in *Ecumenical Bulletin* no. 17, 1976, p. 40; and *Ecumenical Bulletin* no. 20, 1976, p. 21.

Ecumenical Bulletin no. 18, 1976: "Consultation on Church Union: Insights from Women in Sacramental Ministry," pp. 29–33.

In Quest of a Church of Christ Uniting (Princeton, N.J.: Consultation on Church Union, 1976).

Principles of Church Union (Cincinnati: Forward Movement, 1966).

Lutheran-Episcopal Dialogue

Lutheran-Episcopal Dialogue: A Progress Report (Cincinnati: Forward Movement, 1972), pp. 11–46.

International:

Lutheran-Episcopal Dialogue: A Progress Report, pp. 139–75.

Selected Other

A Workbook of Bibliographies for the Study of Interchurch Dialogues, James
    F. Puglisi (1978) (Available: Centro pro Unione, Via S. Maria
    dell'Anima, 30, 00186 Rome, Italy.)

Confessions in Dialogue, Nils Ehrenström and Gunther Gassmann. Faith
    and Order Paper no. 74; 3d rev. and enlarged ed. (Geneva: World
    Council of Churches, 1975).

Lutherans in Ecumenical Dialogue: An Interpretive Guide, Report of a Task
    Force Convened by the Division of Theological Studies, Lutheran
    Council in the U.S.A., and the Office of Studies, USA National
    Committee of the Lutheran World Federation, 1977.

Search for Understanding, Warren A. Quanbeck (Minneapolis: Augs-
    burg, 1972). (For Lutheran dialogue only.)

"The Bilateral Consultations between the Roman Catholic Church in
    the United States and Other Christian Communions—A Theologi-
    cal Review and Critique by the Study Committee Commissioned by
    the Board of Directors of the Catholic Theological Society of Amer-
    ica, Report of July 1972," in *The Catholic Theological Society of
    America—Proceedings of the 27th Annual Convention* vol. 27 (1973).

The Eucharist in Ecumenical Dialogue, Leonard Swidler, ed. (New York
    and Paramus, N.J.: Paulist Press, 1976).

One Baptism, One Eucharist and a Mutually Recognized Ministry (New
    York: World Council of Churches, 1975).

For further information on any the dialogues and their agreed statements, please contact The Ecumenical Office of the Episcopal Church,
815 Second Ave., New York, N.Y. 10017.

Appendix C:
Brief Topical Guide to
Agreed Statements

Authority
    (Christ, Scripture, Tradition, Creed, Primacy, Conciliarity)
Anglican-Orthodox: Anglican-Orthodox Dialogue: The Moscow Statement,
    pp. 82–88
*Anglican–Roman Catholic: Agreed Statement on Authority in the Church
    Ecumenical Study Guide on Authority in the Church*
COCU: In Quest of a Church of Christ Uniting, pp. 24–28
Lutheran-Episcopal: Lutheran-Episcopal Dialogue, pp. 14–16, 145–154

Baptism
COCU: *In Quest of a Church of Christ Uniting,* pp. 31–32
Lutheran-Episcopal: *Lutheran-Episcopal Dialogue,* pp. 18–19, 155–156
World Council: *One Baptism, One Eucharist and a Mutually Recognized Ministry,* pp. 9–17

Eucharist
Anglican-Orthodox: *Anglican-Orthodox Dialogue: The Moscow Statement,* pp. 88–91
ARC-DOC I, II, *Agreed Statement on the Eucharist,* pp. 64–68 (old ed. pp. 45–50)
Ecumenical Study Guide on the Eucharist
COCU: *In Quest of a Church of Christ Uniting,* pp. 32–33
Lutheran-Episcopal: *Lutheran-Episcopal Dialogue,* pp. 16–17, pp. 156–157
World Council: *One Baptism, One Eucharist and a Mutually Recognized Ministry,* pp. 18–28

Marriage
Anglican–Roman Catholic: *Final Report, Commission on the Theology of Marriage and Its Application to Mixed Marriages*

Ministry
Anglican–Roman Catholic: ARC-DOC III, *Agreed Statement on Ministry and Ordination,* pp. 74–81
Ecumenical Study Guide on Ministry and Ordination
COCU: *In Quest of a Church of Christ Uniting,* pp. 34–44
Lutheran-Episcopal: *Lutheran-Episcopal Dialogue,* pp. 20–22, pp. 158–163
World Council: *One Baptism, One Eucharist and a Mutually Recognized Ministry,* pp. 29–56

Mission
Anglican–Roman Catholic: ARC-DOC III, *Agreed Statement on the Purpose of the Church,* pp. 1–11
COCU: *In Quest of a Church of Christ Uniting,* pp. 13–23, 29–30

The Roman Catholic Vision of Visible Unity

Herbert J. Ryan, S.J.

What vision of visible unity is held by the Roman Catholic Church? Fifty years ago Pope Pius XI issued the encyclical *Mortalium animos*.[1] If a Roman Catholic theologian were to have answered the present question in 1928, the theologian would merely have pointed to *Mortalium animos*. Pius XI's vision of the visible unity of the whole Christian Church was clear: the whole Christian Church should be the Roman Catholic Church. The unexpressed assumption underlying Pius XI's viewpoint was the Roman Catholic Church's understanding of itself to be coextensive with the true church. Since the Roman Catholic Church as it existed in 1928 was the one, true Church of Christ, simple logic demanded that the canonical and visible structure of the Roman Catholic Church provided the vision of visible unity which the Roman Catholic Church held.

Mortalium animos does not detail this vision of visible unity. Had the encyclical done so, the picture that would have emerged would roughly have been something like the following. The Bishop of Rome exercises by divine right a primacy of ordinary, immediate, and universal jurisdiction over the whole Christian Church. Each local ordinary (bishop) of a diocese is appointed by the Bishop of Rome and reports to the Bishop of Rome. As each bishop owes a profound allegiance to the Bishop of Rome as the Vicar of Christ on earth, so each baptized Christian owes the same type of allegiance to his local bishop and to the Pope, the Bishop of Rome. By reason of each Christian's baptism, every Christian is in a relation of "objective subjection" to the Vicar of Christ whose possession of ordinary, immediate, and universal jurisdiction is the cornerstone on which is built the visible structure of the church.[2]

If fifty years ago a group of Christians not in communion with the Bishop of Rome had sought as a group to enter into communion with the Pope, what would the Roman Catholic Church's operative model have been to negotiate the group's coming into union with the Pope? The Roman Catholic Church would have offered the group status in the Roman Catholic Church comparable to a diocese of the Latin rite of the Roman Catholic Church. Concretely this would have meant that the Pope would have to have been given some measure of authority consistent with his possession of ordinary, immediate, and universal jurisdiction over the whole church in the appointment of the group's bishop or bishops. The bishop or bishops so appointed would belong to the one college of bishops of which the Bishop of Rome was the head. The canon law of the group would have had eventually to be codified and brought into line with that of the Roman Catholic Church. The codification of the group's canon law would have tolerated divergence from the Latin rite in the group's liturgical and ascetical practices, if the divergence had been shown to be theologically consonant with the Roman Catholic Church's dogmatic teaching.[3]

Commencing fifty years ago with this canonical model of the Roman Catholic Church as the exclusive model for the visible unity of the whole Christian Church, three European Roman Catholic theologians, Emile Mersch,[4] Max Pribilla,[5] and Karl Adam,[6] began in the late 1920s the Roman Catholic scholarly reflection on the problem of achieving unity among Christians. Their research stimulated interest in Christian unity among other Roman Catholic ecumenical pioneers. The gifted historian Joseph Lortz[7] initiated the Roman Catholic reassessment of Martin Luther and the sixteenth-century church. The German Jesuit whom Hitler beheaded in 1944, Max Metzger,[8] saw visible Christian unity as an imperative precondition for world peace. To achieve world peace through the cooperative effort of all Christians, Metzger founded the International Fellowship of Reconciliation and the Una Sancta Brotherhood, activities that eventually cost him his life in Hitler's Germany. In 1932 Paul Couturier[9] adapted to France a popular movement, the Church Unity Octave, which was begun in the United States by Fr. Paul Wattson of Graymoor.[10] Out of Couturier's movement under the aegis of Pierre Michalon, the Roman Catholic Church over the course of the next thirty years evolved its theology of "spiritual ecumenism" by which Roman Catholics actively shared with others the riches of the interior life of prayer. "Spiritual ecumenism" proved to be the most effective pastoral catalyst for the Roman Catholic Church to engage in "grass-roots" ecumenical activity.

Even though Couturier changed the yearly Church Unity Octave into a week of prayerful petition for the "realization of unity such as it is willed and demanded by Our Lord Jesus Christ," neither Couturier nor the other Roman Catholic ecumenical pioneers developed a vision of visible Christian unity that differed from that which underlay Pius

XI's encyclical *Mortalium animos*. The first steps beyond the juridical vision of visible ecclesial unity were proposed in 1937 by a young French Dominican of the Paris Province, Marie-Joseph Congar, O.P.

Congar's *Chrétiens désunis: principes d'un oecuménisme catholique* is a landmark in Roman Catholic theology.[11] No other single book has had such a profound influence on any church's ecumenical position. Congar's book had three purposes: (1) to explain the Catholic Church's unity and catholicity; (2) to analyze the non-Roman Catholic churches; (3) to develop a basis and strategy for uniting those churches with the Roman Catholic Church. For Congar the unity of the church refers primarily to what the church is given by God. The catholicity of the church is to be understood in terms of what the church receives from human beings. Congar conceived the ecumenical task in terms not of unity but of catholicity.

The catholicity of the church is the capacity of its "principles of unity" (sacraments, dogma, hierarchical authority) to assimilate, fill, exalt, win to God, and join together in God every human person and all human persons, as well as every value of humanity. For Congar all of humanity's religious experiences must be assimilated into the church for their divinely intended fulfillment. Thus the Catholic Church must respect the legitimate diversity of non-Roman Catholic religious expressions and ought not to reduce them to a common denominator as they are assimilated into the Roman Catholic Church. Congar sees the Roman Catholic Church as a vast "sacrament" in which everything is a sign and a means of an inward unity of grace.

Congar's vision of the church, though stressing its interior or mystical aspects, did not obscure the importance of its visible structure. If the church were a "sacrament" it must be a *visible* sign. The visible elements of the church would be its sacramental rites, dogmas, priestly hierarchy, and canon law. Moreover, the church would have a visible head and "regulator" of its "social" life, the Bishop of St. Peter's see at Rome.

How does Congar's vision of visible ecclesial union differ from that which underlay Pius XI's in his encyclical *Mortalium animos?* For Congar, one discerns or finds the unity that God has given and is giving to the church through the action of the Holy Spirit. Unity is discovered; it is not created by the establishment of juridical relationships between human individuals or groups. A church is truly catholic if it is a church within that human realm in which the gifts of the Holy Spirit have been operative since Pentecost and manifesting catholic elements (sacraments, dogma, hierarchic priesthood) that mediate the Trinitarian life to humankind. Congar sees all these catholic elements in the

Roman Catholic Church. Nowhere, however, does Congar state that the Roman Catholic Church has developed all the elements fully. Another Christian church may possess some of the catholic elements and may have developed these elements more fully than has the Roman Catholic Church.

Congar's vision of visible ecclesial unity is profoundly theological and multi-dimensional. When treating the canonical and jurisdictional dimension of the church, Congar upholds Pius XI's teaching in *Mortalium animos*. Yet Congar's vision touches other and deeper dimensions of the church, and for that reason it opened the Roman Catholic Church to the possibility of making a positive assessment of other Christian churches. By admitting that other Christian churches, especially the ancient Christian churches of the East, possess Catholic elements in rich development Congar laid the groundwork for the Second Vatican Council's assertion that the Church *subsists* in the Roman Catholic Church. The Council did not claim that the Roman Catholic Church is totally coextensive with the Catholic Church since there are churches not in communion with the Roman Catholic Church that possess in a richly developed manner genuinely catholic elements. Thus Congar's work, while keeping in step with Pius XI's canonical understanding of the Roman Catholic Church, successfully replaced the unexpressed assumption upon which Pius XI's comprehension of the church was founded. Congar showed how the Roman Catholic Church could still be the true Church of Christ without excluding other Christian churches from the Church of Christ. In Congar's view the ecumenical task for the Roman Catholic Church was to discover and to appreciate the catholicity of other Christian churches that canonically were independent of the Roman Church.

Though almost twenty-five years were to elapse between the publication of Congar's *Chrétiens désunis* and Pope John XXIII's calling of the Second Vatican Council, no other Roman Catholic theologian expanded the vision of the Roman Catholic Church in the matter of visible ecclesial unity to the extent and with the depth that Congar's work did. It is not an exaggeration to say that the strengths and weaknesses of the current position of the Roman Catholic Church's understanding of visible ecclesial unity are the strengths and weaknesses of Congar's theology. Why is this so?

Rarely in the history of the Roman Catholic Church has a decree of an ecumenical council of that church owed so much to one man and to one book. It is fair to say that the Decree on Ecumenism (*Unitatis Redintegratio*) of Vatican Council II borrowed heavily from Congar. The great Dominican theologian was present throughout the sessions of the Council and exercised considerable influence on the Council's various drafting commissions. The Decree on Ecumenism incorporates Congar's theology and commends Michalon's approach to "spiritual ecumenism." The decree does not advance the vision of visible unity beyond Congar's position as he elaborated that vision in 1937.

The vision of visible unity as expounded by Congar was accepted by the Roman Catholic Church at the Second Vatican Council. The Constitution on the Church (*Lumen Gentium*) expresses his doctrine that the Church of Christ *subsists* in the Roman Catholic Church.[12] The Pastoral Constitution on the Church in the Modern World (*Gaudium et Spes*) accepts his vision of human aspirations and re-echoes Metzger's insights into the necessity of Christian unity for the achievement of world peace.[13] The Decree on Ecumenism (*Unitatis Redintegratio*) sets the ecumenical task of the Roman Catholic Church in terms of discovering the catholic elements in churches not in communion with the Roman See.[14] The strength of Congar's vision was that it opened the Roman Catholic Church to participate in the worldwide ecumenical movement and to engage appreciatively in ecumenical dialogue not only with other Christian churches but with non-Christian religions as well.

But there were weaknesses inherent in Congar's vision. That vision provided no procedure for the Roman Catholic Church to enter into communion with a church which, after extensive theological dialogue, the Roman Church saw had all the catholic elements except one—visible, full, ecclesiastical communion with the See of Peter. Moreover, Congar never treated the question of how the Bishop of Peter's See as "regulator" of the church's "social" life should relate to those churches which were found to possess all the catholic elements except they were not in union with Rome. If these churches had by the action of the Holy Spirit richly developed some of the catholic elements such as *magisterium* (teaching office) or sacramental ordained *episcope* in the apostolic succession (ordained ministry) in a manner different from that of the Roman Catholic Church, why would these elements have to relate to the "regulator" of the church's "social" life in the same way that these elements were related to the Pope in the Roman Catholic Church? Suppose the Anglican Communion were seen to possess all the Catholic elements except ecclesiastical communion with the See of Peter. Ought the Pope be the "regulator" of the Anglican Communion's "social" life in the same way that he is the "regulator" of the "social" life of the Roman Catholic Church? The logic of Congar's position would suggest that the Pope could not be the "regulator" of the Anglican Communion in the same way that he fulfills that role for the Roman Catholic Church. Yet Congar's vision of ecclesial union gives not a clue as to how the Pope is to be the "regulator" of the Anglican Communion once the Roman See is in full, visible, ecclesiastical communion with the 23 autonomous churches of the Anglican Communion.

Adopting Congar's ecumenical theology with its strengths and its weaknesses, the Roman Catholic Church after the Second Vatican Council began official, ecumenical theological dialogues with the Anglican Communion, the world confessional families (Lutheran, Methodist, Reformed or Calvinist traditions), the World Council of Churches, and the ancient Christian churches of the East. Official dialogue between the Anglican Communion and the Roman Catholic Church proceeded simultaneously on both the international and national levels. The Anglican/Roman Catholic International Commission (ARCIC) was the dialogue group beween the whole Anglican Communion and the Roman Catholic Church. The Anglican/Roman Catholic Consultation in the USA (ARC) was the official dialogue group between the Episcopal Church and the National Conference of Catholic Bishops in the United States. The Roman Catholic participants in both ARCIC and ARC closely followed the documents of the Second Vatican Council. Thus their ecumenical theology owed much to Congar's approach. In both dialogues the Roman Catholic members were eager to find and explore the Catholic elements in the churches of the Anglican Communion.[15]

In the course of articulating substantial agreement on the doctrines of the eucharist and the ordained ministry many of the Roman Catholic members of both dialogue groups became increasingly aware that the Episcopal Church and the other churches of the Anglican Communion might possess *all* the catholic elements except full, visible, canonical ecclesiastical communion with the See of Peter. The Roman Catholics were also aware of the weaknesses in Congar's vision of visible unity. If ARC and ARCIC were to make further progress and take up the topic of authority in the church, it would be necessary for the Roman Catholics to have some general guidelines on what visible unity would entail from the Roman Catholic point of view if the churches of the Anglican Communion were to enter into full, visible, canonical, ecclesiastical communion with the Roman See.

These guidelines were given by Jan Cardinal Willebrands of the Vatican Secretariat for Promoting Christian Unity on January 18, 1970, in an address at Great St. Mary's, Cambridge, England.[16] Cardinal Willebrands proposed as a model of visible unity the concept of *typos* or "sister church" and elaborated that model with certain ideas that had been suggested in dialogue with the World Council of Churches by Dom Emmanuel Lanne, O.S.B.[17] Willebrands' adaptation of Lanne's model envisioned the whole Christian Church as a communion of *typoi* (sister churches), each maintaining its own traditions of theology, liturgy, spirituality, and canonical discipline. Each of the "sister churches" *subsists* in the Church of Christ. The Roman Catholic Church is one *typos*. Once, through ecumenical dialogue, the Roman Catholic Church and its partner in dialogue are seen to be one in the faith, they should recognize themselves as "sister churches" or *typoi*. Neither *typos* would have to undergo major change in entering into full, visible, canonical, ecclesiastical communion with the other. This vision of visible unity was explicitly endorsed by Pope Paul VI on the occasion of the canonization of the Forty English Martyrs.[18] It was reiterated by Cardinal Willebrands during his lecture at the Great Hall of Lambeth Palace on October 4, 1972.

When ARCIC set about to draft its Agreed Statement on Authority in the Church (Venice Statement), ARCIC tried to express the faith of both the Anglican Communion and the Roman Catholic Church. The church which the Venice Statement describes is the whole Catholic Church in which both the Anglican Communion and the Roman Catholic Church subsist as "sister churches" or *typoi*. The Venice Statement does not describe either of the "sister churches" exclusively, but the whole Catholic Church.[19]

The current agenda of ARCIC, as the group tries to complete the Venice Statement, arises from the Roman Catholic Church's having articulated an understanding concerning the whole church that initially, at least, seems alien to the Anglican Communion's understanding of the whole church. The Roman Catholic Church believes that because the Holy Spirit abides in the church the whole Catholic Church is infallible. Moreover, the Roman Catholic Church believes that the Bishop of Rome when he teaches the whole church on matters of faith and morals is endowed with (*pollere*) that infallibility with which the whole church is endowed.[20]

If ARCIC succeeds in reaching agreement on the difficult problem of infallibility, what effect will this have on the Roman Catholic Church's model of visible unity? Suppose the Anglican Communion and the Roman Catholic Church were in full, visible, canonical, ecclesiastical communion. Suppose also that the Pope believed that he ought to exercise the infallibility which the whole church possesses by teaching the whole church on some vital matter of faith or morals. As the two reputed instances (1854 and 1950, with the dogmas of the Immaculate Conception and the Assumption of the Blessed Virgin

Mary) of the exercise of infallibility by the Bishop of Rome involved prior worldwide consultation of the *magisterium* of the Roman Catholic Church, some consultative process in keeping with the *typos* of the Anglican Communion would also be required. But a problem still remains. Is such an exercise of the church's infallibility compatible with the Anglican *typos*?

What vision of unity is held by the Roman Catholic Church? Many Roman Catholics, even today, would answer that question in the terms of Pius XI's *Mortalium animos* of fifty years ago. Roman Catholics who are more informed would be aware of the ecumenical advance of their church, which was so much the work of Marie-Joseph Congar, O.P. The Roman Catholic Church officially, especially in regard to the churches of the Anglican Communion, would agree with the vision expressed by Cardinal Willebrands: a vision of "sister churches" or *typoi* subsisting in the Catholic Church. However, even this official vision of unity espoused by the Roman Catholic Church is more akin to Congar's description of the ecumenical task of discovering the catholicity of the church through Michalon's "spiritual ecumenism" and theological ecumenical dialogue than to preparing clear organizational models for visible church union. Moreover, within the official Roman Catholic vision of unity—which presupposes substantial agreement in the faith—there remains an unresolved problem. What is the role of the Bishop of Rome, whose prerogatives are matters of faith for Roman Catholics, in the life of those churches which enter into visible, full, canonical, ecclesiastical union with the Roman See?

The role of the Bishop of Rome is a vital issue for any Church that would enter into union with the Roman See. Yet the question of that role is too neuralgic and too universal to be investigated only by Roman Catholic theologians. Their current research indicates that the primacy of the Roman See and of its Bishop is a service of love for other Christian communities which is provided by the local church at Rome. The Bishop of Rome because he is bishop of that local church which is sanctified by the martyrdom in that community of Peter and Paul inherits the global evangelical and missionary task of these apostles. This is the reason why the Bishop of Rome is called the servant of the servants of God, *servus servorum Dei*.

But how are the servants of God to be served by the local church at Rome and its bishop? Surely Christian communities that have been visibly estranged for centuries from the Roman center of pastoral care must be asked what service they seek Rome to provide for them by entering into visible communion with the Roman See. No Roman Catholic theologian can properly essay this task. However, once the separated community has articulated for itself what it seeks from Rome, then a joint theological effort will be required to determine the manner in which the Roman See and its Bishop is to provide the desired service. The manner in which Rome is to serve the once separated Christian community may have more far-reaching consequences than the service itself. Broadening how Rome's service of love is exercised will enable the whole Church to be truly united.

Anglican theology is richly equipped for this required theological reflection and mutual collaboration with the Roman Catholic tradition. No Christian theological tradition surpasses the depth with which the *Ecclesia Anglicana* has analyzed the task of the Church and the role of its members, has been more creative in polity or more sensitive to the imperatives of Christian conscience. The Anglican ethos sees that organizational authority in the Church varies directly with the role which the communicant member is prepared to undertake to advance the tasks of the Church. From vestry to Lambeth Conference the forms of organizational authority in the Anglican Communion are perceived ideally to be functions of evangelization. In this area the Roman Catholic Church will gratefully and gladly learn from her "beloved sister Church" whose missionary efforts have brought the Gospel to tens of millions who in turn have created a polity suited to evangelize each differing culture in which the Anglican communion thrives.

NOTES

1. *Acta Apostolicae Sedis,* XX (1928) 5–16.
2. This understanding of *Mortalium animos* was expressed by the Lambeth Conference of 1930. Cf. *Lambeth Conference: 1930* (London, 1930), p. 131.
3. A very clear essay on this type of ecclesiology is E. F. Hanahoe, *"Vestigia Ecclesiae:* Their Meaning and Value," in E. Hanahoe and T. Cranny, editors, *One Fold* (Graymoor, 1959), pp. 272–83. Cf. Also C. Korolevsky, *L'Uniatisme* (Gembloux, 1927).
4. Cf. J. Levie, "Mersch, Emile," *New Catholic Encyclopedia,* vol. IX, 693–94.
5. Max Pribilla, *Um Kirchliche Einheit—Stockholm, Lausanne, Rom* (Feiburg, 1929). L. Swidler, *The Ecumenical Vanguard: The History of the Una Sancta Movement* (Pittsburgh, 1966) is a rich source on the ecumenical pioneers of the Roman Catholic Church.
6. Cf. P. Misner, "Adam, Karl," *New Catholic Encylopedia,* vol. XVI, 4–5.
7. J. Lortz, *The Reformation in Germany* (New York, 1968). This is a translation of the third German edition (1949) of Lortz's two-volume study (vol. I was first published in 1939 and vol. II in 1940).
8. Cf. L. Stevenson, *Max Josef Metzger, Priest and Martyr: 1887–1944* (London, 1952). Also M. Mohring, *Täter des Wortes, Max Josef Metzger* (Freising, 1966).

9. M. Villain, *L'Abbé Paul Couturier* (Tournai, 1957). Also G. Curtis, *Paul Couturier and Unity in Christ* (London, 1964).

10. C. Angell and C. La Fontaine, *Prophet of Reunion: The Life of Paul of Graymoor* (New York, 1975).

11. Y. M. J. Congar, O.P., *Divided Christendom: A Catholic Study of the Problem of Reunion* (London, 1939). Congar's ideas on catholicity derive from the theology of another French Dominican, Ambroise de Poulpiquet, O.P. Cf. G. Thils, *Les notes de l'église dans l'apologétique catholique depuis la Réforme* (Paris, 1937), pp. 250–53.

12. J. Alberigo *et al.*, editors, *Conciliorum Oecumenicorum Decreta* (Bologna, 1973), p. 854. Hereinafter *COD*. (*Lumen Gentium*, 8.)

13. *COD*, pp. 1125–29 (*Gaudium et Spes*, 77-82).

14. *COD*, pp. 909–10 (*Unitatis Redintegratio*, 3).

15. H. J. Ryan, S.J., "La dichiarazione di Windsor intorno alla dottrina sull' Eucaristia," *La Civiltà Cattolica* 2983 (5 October 1974), pp. 26–35; and Arthur A. Vogel, "In the United States," the epilogue in B. and M. Pawley, *Rome and Canterbury through Four Centuries* (New York, 1975), pp. 364–87.

16. *Documents on Anglican–Roman Catholic Relations* (Washington, D.C., 1972), pp. 32–41.

17. E. Lanne, O.S.B., "Pluralism and Unity: The Possibility of a Variety of Typologies within the Same Ecclesial Allegiance," *One-in-Christ* VI-3 (1970), pp. 430–51.

18. *Documents on Anglican–Roman Catholic Relations*, pp. 42–43. For the shift of Anglican opinion regarding the papacy, cf. J. Robert Wright, "Anglicans and the Papacy" in P. J. McCord, editor, *A Pope for All Christians* (New York, 1976), pp. 176–209.

19. E. J. Yarnold, S. J., and H. Chadwick, *Truth and Authority: A Commentary on the Agreed Statement of the Anglican–Roman Catholic International Commission: Venice, 1976* (London, 1977).

20. *COD*, p. 816. The best contemporary statement of the position of Vatican Council I (1870) on this point is P. Chirico, S.S., *Infallibility: The Crossroads of Doctrine* (Kansas City, 1977), pp. 222–44.

The Vision of Unity Held in the Lutheran Churches

William G. Rusch

Preface

As I understand my assignment, it is to sketch out how Lutherans today view the question of church unity and then to describe how this view could affect future Lutheran-Anglican relations. At first glance, such an endeavor does not appear unmanageable. Nevertheless, the task is not as simple as it might seem, and for several reasons. First of all, both Lutheranism and Anglicanism are not homogeneous. Both communions have within themselves differing emphases. Lutherans, or for that matter of fact, Episcopalians, find it perplexing to state what is essential for their own identity.

In addition, another problem must be considered. Quite apart from the internal variations within each tradition, there is the matter of the differing character of Lutheranism and Anglicanism. This has often been overlooked because of the obvious commonality of the two communities: both traditions have origins in the sixteenth century and in a separation from the western church headed by the Bishop of Rome. But in spite of both these factors, there is a fundamental incongruity which the following two citations set in bold relief. H. R. McAdoo in *The Spirit of Anglicanism* declares, "Anglicanism is not a theological system, and there is no writer whose work is an essential part of it, either in respect of content or with regard to the form of its self-expression."[1] On the other hand, Eric W. Gritsch and Robert W. Jenson in *Lutheranism* state, "Lutheranism is a confessional movement within the church catholic that continues to offer to the whole church that proposal of dogma which received definitive documentary form in the Augsburg Confession and the other writings collected in the Book of Concord. . . . The Lutheran proposal of dogma has one great theme: justification by faith alone, apart from works of law."[2]

The relationship of Lutheranism and Anglicanism, especially since the seventeenth century, could be compared to how Karl Barth viewed his rapport with Rudolf Bultmann. Barth once wrote to Bultmann, "It is clear to you where you and I are. To me it is as if a whale and an elephant had met in utter bewilderment on some oceanic shore. In vain the one sends spouts of water high up into the air. In vain the other beckons now amicably, then threatening with his trunk. They lack a common key to what both, each from his proper element and in his own language, obviously and so anxiously want to say to the other."[3] This is largely true of Lutheranism and Anglicanism. They have much in common, but their lives have been lived in different worlds. Their relationship has not been polemical, but rather, until recently, largely non-existent. Now from their different worlds, eager to communicate and share, Lutherans and Episcopalians are finding that they have a Christian responsibility to express their oneness in Christ and that the task is not always simple.[4]

Therefore, this essay will delineate a Lutheran understanding of church unity and of church union as a model for unity. Then some differences and similarities between the Lutheran and Episcopal communions will be pointed out. Next, some of the accomplishments of the international and national Anglican-Lutheran dialogues will be noted. Finally, there will be a concluding word.

I

In order to understand how Lutherans approach the question of the unity of the church, it is necessary to turn to the Lutheran Reformation of the sixteenth century. This may seem to be an ironic statement in view of the fact that it was this cataclysmic event that ripped the fabric of unity of, at least, the western church. But this comment discloses a contradiction between what the Lutheran churches have become in the vicissitudes of history and what was the fundamental intention of the Lutheran Reformation.

Luther and his fellow reformers always insisted that they were not establishing a new church. Whenever the suspicion arose that they were doing this, they reacted with strong feelings, declaring they were part of the one universal church. This sentiment can be found repeatedly in Luther's writings. The first Lutheran was not a sectarian but an ecumenist![5]

The Lutheran reformers also maintained that the church of Jesus Christ had continued to exist under even the papacy. It was not necessary, therefore, to develop a link with the true church at some earlier point in the history of the church. The Augsburg Confession, one of the principal confessions of every Lutheran church, states in article 7, "It is also taught among us that one holy Christian church will be and remain forever."[6] The Lutheran Reformation thus had one main focus: the *continuity* of the *one* church. Its followers were convinced that the issue between them and the Roman church was nothing less than the essential of the Christian faith: the Gospel of unmerited grace given by God in Christ, and that this issue could never be a concern of a separate church but contained a dimension that affected all Christendom. The Gospel had not been lost in the medieval Roman church, but the followers of Luther believed it had been obscured and must be uncovered and purified to shine forth once more. The reformers had an ecumenical emphasis in their stress on the continuity of the church and in their desire to present the true Gospel.

As the events of the sixteenth century disclose, the Lutheran reformers operated with this ecumenical stress and, only after forced by a series of circumstances, became reconciled to be separate churches with their own confession, structure and life.[7] In spite of this necessity of history, or perhaps even more so because of it, the Reformation's confession of the continuity and unity of the church, with an acknowledgement of a responsibility to all Christendom, should make it incumbent upon any Lutheran church in any age to seek dialogue and fellowship with other churches.

Bishop Andreas Aarflot in an address to the Sixth Assembly of the Lutheran World Federation in Tanzania this past summer spoke of these ecumenical intentions of the Lutheran Reformation.[8] He identified four ecumenical dimensions: (1) The principle of going back to the Holy Scriptures. The Lutheran Fathers were willing to discuss any doctrinal questions with anyone who was willing to submit to the authority of Scripture. (2) The principle of going back to the ancient church. Luther, Melanchthon and others wanted to express their deep conviction in consistency with the writers of the early church. Note the inclusion of the three ancient creeds and patristic quotations in the Book of Concord. (3) The principle of willingness to enter into discussion and dialogue. The spirit is reflected in the entire Augsburg Confession. In the sixteenth century, Lutherans sought dialogue with Catholics and the Reformed. (4) The principle of discriminating between fundamental and non-fundamental articles of faith. For Lutherans the key question was: Is there the same understanding of the Gospel as expressed in justification by faith? This was the only fundamental; polity, liturgy were non-fundamental.

This ecumenical openness and commitment of the Lutheran Reformation are seen specifically in article 7 of the Augsburg Confession. This document was written by Philip Melanchthon and presented to the Diet of Augsburg in 1530. Representing the theological consensus of those who accepted the Lutheran Reformation, it became a

confession of faith of the Lutheran churches. Its influence and significance for subsequent Lutheran theology cannot be overestimated, for
it stands second to the Scriptures themselves as authoritative for
Lutherans. Article 7, entitled "The Church," like article 19 of the
Thirty-Nine Articles, deals with the unity of the church. Article 7 is
fundamental for any Lutheran view of church unity. Succinct and
simple, it reads: "It is also taught among us that one holy Christian
church will be and remain forever. This is the assembly of all believers
among whom the Gospel is preached in its purity and the holy sacraments are administered according to the Gospel. For it is sufficient for
the true unity of the Christian church that the Gospel be preached in
conformity with a pure understanding of it and that the sacraments be
administered in accordance with the divine Word. It is not necessary
for the true unity of the Christian church that ceremonies instituted
by men should be observed uniformly in all places. It is as Paul says in
Ephesians 4:4–5, 'There is one body and one Spirit, just as you were
called to the one hope that belongs to your call, one Lord, one faith,
one baptism.'"[9]

The teaching of the article is: What is equally essential for both the
existence and unity of the church is that the Gospel is preached in its
pure form and that the sacraments are administered in accord with it.
Where both of these things happen, there is the church. Where Christians and churches concur on this, there is the unity of the church, and
all that is needed for church fellowship has been met. The article
anchors the existence and unity of the church in true proclamation of
the Gospel in Word and sacrament. It clearly states that uniformity in
rites and ceremonies of men is not required. Article 7 draws a sharp
distinction between what is absolutely necessary and an area of responsible freedom. Thus the article indicates clear ecumenical guidance without merely giving a general confession on church unity.

The history of Lutheran ecumenical efforts could be traced in the
light of this article. Lutherans have generally been concerned with the
understanding of the Gospel, and the proclamation of the Word and
administration of sacraments. When common agreement is found
here, Lutherans have acknowledged the existence of church fellowship. They have also affirmed that differences of church structure,
liturgies and polity are of secondary importance and can be retained
within fellowship—a notion which probably strikes many Episcopalians as strange.

Although Lutherans assert a highly significant role for article 7 in
an understanding of church unity, they have come to recognize certain limits inherent in the article. These strictures are caused in part

by the fact that the context of the article in the sixteenth century no longer exists today. The practice of fellowship and visible unity, while in extreme danger in 1530, had not yet been lost. The task of the church in our century is not to maintain visible unity but to attempt to regain it. Naturally, article 7 of the Augsburg Confession does not directly address our situation. But even with this acknowledgement, Lutherans have continued to identify with the ecumenical commitment of this article. However, they recognize that the framework of familiarity and practical fellowship, taken for granted by article 7, is not now present. Therefore, some Lutherans today admit that unity cannot be limited to the quest for theological agreement only, but must also be sought in the midst of familiarity and fellowship, and that this context must be developed alongside efforts aimed at theological concord. This means that different forms of worship and church order, which were not obstacles until the sixteenth century, but have been burdens in the centuries of division, must be part of the ecumenical endeavor today. Such items include the Anglican tradition's stress on episcopal succession from the apostles and on communion with the archbishop of Canterbury.

This approach, giving attention to theological and non-theological factors, can be seen in two documents of the Lutheran World Federation. "More Than Church Unity" and "Guidelines for Ecumenical Encounter" reflect a theological understanding resulting from involvement by Lutherans in the ecumenical movement.[10] Both documents are worthy of careful study. They do not surrender as a goal the attempt to formulate a theological consensus, but they recognize multiple expressions of doctrine, life and action as valid. Dr. Harding Meyer of the Strasbourg Institute for Ecumenical Research has spoken of this new theological understanding, expressed in these documents as follows: "Today it is possible to say that the traditional principle 'doctrinal conversation and doctrinal agreement first, and only then church fellowship' has, even on the Lutheran side, been recognized as too rigidly one-sided and has therefore been considerably modified. . . . On the Lutheran side considerable emphasis is still placed on the importance of a common formulation and expression of theological consensus of confession. There is no doubt that today this is still a characteristic and important facet of the Lutheran understanding of the church, of ecumenical endeavor and of church unity. But, at the same time, it is recognized that there is a clear interrelation, a sort of 'circle,' between the fact of living and experiencing fellowship on the one hand, and explicit agreement on faith and doctrine on the other."[11] Meyer reflects the most recent position of many Lutheran theologians, who would argue today that for Lutherans the most satisfactory concept of church unity is one of a fellowship in which confessional particularities and differences are not blended but reconciled as legitimate pluralism. Such a view rejects an overall, uniform Christian identity as a non-entity in history and favors a confessionability open for, and exposed to, change.[12]

Bishop Aarflot in his address referred to above declared that Lutheran ecumenical commitment calls for a *critical* conciliarity or a *purified* as well as a reconciled diversity. He stated that true teaching and proclamation of the gospel and the administration of baptism and Holy Communion are the necessary prerequisites for every kind of unity of the church. And this has to be maintained against any tendency of relativism or pluralization. Factors, however, such as church structures, forms of ministry, etc., cannot jeopardize the real unity of the church.

In regard to "reconciled diversity," Aarflot sees the term of some help as long as it is a purified and critically examined diversity which describes a way to unity which does not automatically entail the surrender of confessional traditions and confessional identities. "This way to unity is a way of living encounter, spiritual experience together, theological dialogue and mutual correction, a way on which the distinctiveness of each partner is not lost sight of but rings out, is transformed and renewed, and in this way becomes visible and palpable to the other partners. There is no glossing over the differences. Nor are the differences simply preserved and maintained unaltered. But they lose their divisive character as they are reconciled to each other."[13]

Much of the language of Bishop Aarflot's address was picked up in a report from the recent assembly of the Lutheran World Federation, "Lutheran Churches in the Ecumenical Movement."[14] This report gives high priority to the continuation and extension of bilateral dialogues. In the "models of unity" section of the report, the understanding of unity which allows room for the diversity of confessional traditions and the existence of fellowships to cherish these traditions is encouraged. The assembly believed reconciled diversity comes close to the concept of "conciliar fellowship" as recently developed in the World Council of Churches except that the latter term does not seem to take seriously enough confessional differences and the need to preserve them. The assembly stated that the concept of "reconciled diversity" in itself does not provide a detailed and final description of the goal of our striving for the unity of the church. The Lutheran World

Federation did not officially adopt this concept of unity but saw it as well suited to provide help at the present moment of the ecumenical struggle.

· In light of the nature and origin of Lutheranism, such a position is not difficult to understand. It reflects the Lutheran proclivity for theological agreement and reaffirms the Lutheran fondness for bilateral discussion as an approach to the problem of church unity. Yet it acknowledges that the difficulty is more than common theological formulae.

This position hints at the cause of Lutheran apprehensions of movements for church union between Lutherans and non-Lutherans, viz., concern over compromises in the area of doctrine. Thus in the year 1960 Lutherans in the United States did not take part in the Consultation on Church Union. This decision was reached in large measure because of historic Lutheran mistrust of church-union negotiations which resulted from efforts in the nineteenth century to achieve a Reformed-Lutheran union in Germany. On the international scene, developments were also taking place. Here incentive began before the 1963 Assembly of the Lutheran World Federation when the South Indian and East African Lutheran churches involved in union discussions asked for guidance. The history of this concern may be traced in a series of articles which appeared in *Lutheran World*.[15] The result was, in 1970 at its assembly in Evian, the Lutheran World Federation adopted a "Statement Concerning the Attitude of the Lutheran World Federation to Churches in Union Negotiations." The document is worthy of quotation.[16]

Statement Concerning the Attitude of the LWF to Churches in Union Negotiations

When a member church of the LWF decides to enter union discussions with one or more non-Lutheran churches it may request advice and counsel from the LWF, which shall use the following guidelines in making a response:

a) Consistent with respect for both the fellowship and autonomy of member churches, the LWF will not attempt to prevent them from participating in union discussions but will rather assist them upon request.

b) A union of churches must be seen as a proper expression of the unity of the church when uniting churches have agreed upon a confessional statement of faith that witnesses to a right understanding of the gospel to serve as a guide for preaching and the administration of the sacraments. Becoming a part of a united church by a member church should not lead to a break in relationships with the LWF if the united church's confessional statement is in substantial agreement with the doctrinal basis of the LWF. Since united churches differ in nature, however, the LWF must find its appropriate relationships to such churches on an individual basis.

c) United churches which have or have had Lutheran constituencies, but which do not become members of the LWF, may be invited to send official visitors to LWF assemblies. Representatives of these churches may also take part in commissions, national committees, and other meetings under LWF sponsorship as consultants, or under certain circumstances as full members of commission (Executive Committee minutes, 1965, p. 2).

d) Since a united church will discover its full integrity only after union is complete, all concerned parties should recognize that the church might well prefer not to maintain relationship with any organization representing a confessional family of faith. At the same time it should be recognized that a united church may desire a relationship with more than one confessional family. The LWF is willing to appoint representatives to discuss interchurch relationships with representatives from uniting churches and from the organizations of their families of faith.

e) The LWF has the conviction and desire that when member churches which have received aid from sister churches in the past unite with churches not of the Lutheran family, the donor churches should continue such financial support as will benefit the receiving church. The LWF will act in the same way.

This statement does not imply that Lutherans endorse all forms of church union. But it does indicate that a new attitude has arisen which still does not reject the Lutheran concept of unity. Probably most Lutherans still believe that church union is not the most adequate model for unity. Nevertheless, the Lutheran World Federation and some respected Lutheran theologians now recognize church union as a viable option in some circumstances.

From this depiction of Lutheran views of unity, two key characteristics emerge with some clarity. First, Lutheranism possesses a strong dogmatic theology. It has been, and is, at home with doctrinal decisions and formularies. Second, Lutheranism has throughout its history downplayed the importance of church polity in and of itself. It must be acknowledged that both this Lutheran stress on theology and de-emphasis of church structure probably strike Episcopalians as alien to their own understanding of the church. Of course, Lutherans conversely tend to react in a like manner to what they perceive as Episcopal emphasis on polity and disinterest in theology. While such generalities preserve a certain measure of truth, they are oversimplifications, especially when the conclusion is drawn that Lutherans are indifferent to polity, Episcopalians to theology. Admittedly, the generalizations accurately disclose that Lutherans and Episcopalians tend to put their emphases in different places. However, this is not to say that such differences are incompatible. In fact, they could be complementary and mutually enriching. It is precisely this determination that Episcopalians and Lutherans must make jointly. Indeed they have been involved in this task, and the preliminary judgment is one of Lutheran and Episcopal complementarity rather than of incompatibility. But before these efforts are described in some detail, attention should be given to the nature and limits of Lutheran-Episcopal commonality upon which this initial assessment, has been made. This may be done most conveniently by briefly exploring several topics. The following is not intended to be exhaustive.[17]

First, there is the matter of the origin of both churches. Lutheranism and Anglicanism have their beginnings in the Reformation of the sixteenth century. Both claimed a rediscovery of the primitive message of Christianity. In their formative documents the statement is put forth that both traditions are substantially older than the Reformation and indeed have their roots in primitive Christianity. Admittedly, this common experience aids each tradition in understanding the other. Nevertheless, even within this similarity there are differences to be noted. For Anglicans the separation from the papacy had a stronger and sharper political accent than for Lutherans. Henry VIII to a large extent cut the bonds with Rome. Luther and his followers were excommunicated. Also, there is no parallel in Anglicanism to the role of Luther. The Reformation in Germany could be largely seen as the personal achievement and biographical sequence of the events in Luther's life, but Ridley, Latimer and Cranmer did not fill such a role in the development of Anglicanism. Another difference to be observed is that Luther and his followers separated themselves from humanism. This was not true of early Anglicans. This difference of approach to humanism may be traced in the subsequent history of both communities.

Second, attention should be given to the place of Scripture. Once again a common feature is noticeable. Lutheranism and Anglicanism are marked by an energetic urging to return to the Bible and by preaching the Biblical message in the language of the people. But there are also dissimilarities. Anglicanism has not been characterized by the intensive hermeneutical work on texts that has been true for Lutheranism. The Lutheran distinction between Law and Gospel is not a feature of Anglicanism. Unlike Lutheranism, there is the impression that the Anglican community accepts the Bible as something given rather than as a task for appropriation, filled with problems. Thus for Anglicans the Bible is often used as an ethical imperative and a guide for life in a way which Lutherans find strange.

Third, there is the question of justification. Justification through grace by faith alone is the article by which the church stands and falls for Lutherans. The quotation of Gritsch and Jenson describing Lutheranism reveals the centrality of this doctrine. This teaching of justification is certainly affirmed within the Episcopal church. (See article 11 of the Thirty-Nine Articles.) But it does not have the same kind of pivotal significance and function as it does for Lutheran churches.

Fourth, mention could be made of the teaching about the incarnation. Both Lutherans and Episcopalians reject the ancient heresies of docetism and ebionitism. Both are concerned with asserting the full humanity of Jesus to guarantee the work of salvation. Lutherans and Episcopalians have given preference to the Greek concept of one nature of God-man become flesh, as taught by Cyril of Alexandria, to Tertullian's doctrine of two natures, which is basically a rational construction. Both accept Chalcedon. Still, differences remain. Anglicanism employed Platonism for the construction of a world view and theory of reality. Platonism had no such effect on Lutheranism. Thus, although Lutheranism and Anglicanism agreed on the fundamentals of the incarnation, different stresses occurred. Richard Hooker provides an example.[18]

Fifth, there is the nature of ministry and the closely related topic of apostolicity. Here, too, there is a common point of view. Lutheranism and Anglicanism recognize an "aristocratic" character of ministry, i.e., in the sense that it does not derive from a democratic election by the community. Rather, the church acknowledges a particular endowment (charisma) that has become visible and audible. The picture of the church with its various functions, as seen in 1 Corinthians and Ephesians, is of binding significance. The origin of ministry is a commission from God who in the Old Testament called prophets and who in the New Testament in his Son called and sent disciples who thus became apostles. The legitimation of ministry is by the Lord of the church himself. This divine character remains the decisive fact of ministry. Thus far there is Lutheran and Episcopal agreement. Lutherans see these views of ministry in accord with article 14 of the Augsburg Confession. Lutherans stop at this point; Anglicans continue. They claim the canonical, primitive Christian and essentially divine character of the episcopate as the leading organ of the church. For Anglicans, apostolic succession belongs to the ministry as an essential element, a determinative qualification. On the Lutheran side the apostolic succession of bishops is viewed in regard to its purpose of maintaining and handing on the original Christian message and the doctrine belonging to it. Anglicans accord apostolic succession a value and weight of its own. It supports the significance of ministry. For Anglicanism the weight possessed by apostolic succession bears witness to the sanctification of history. The uninterrupted succession of legitimate office-bearers testifies to the Lord of history who acts continually and not occasionally.

All five of the above points disclose that there is much which unites Episcopalians and Lutherans. Yet, in every issue where a commonality can be found, dissimilarities can also be observed. These differences may be no more than a difference of emphasis within the legitimate pluralism of Christian expression. But it is the answer to this question that is needed before fuller unity between these two communities can be affirmed. By lack of theological precision, has the Anglican community run the risk of losing the Gospel? This is the Lutheran question. By an apparent indifference to polity, have the Lutherans run the risk of losing an essential of the Christian faith? This no doubt is the Episcopal question. Episcopalians and Lutherans in dialogue have attempted to answer these questions, for they form the prerequisites for further unity. It is a description of these attempts as found in bilateral conversation which is given in the next section.

II

Although contacts between Lutherans and Episcopalians can be discovered from the sixteenth century onward, it is only within the last twenty years that serious theological discussion on the highest official levels has occurred.[19] Lutherans and Episcopalians had probably supposed that there were differing stresses within each community on the doctrine and form of ministry, or on the place of theology and confession, but no major theological differences. Yet it is exactly the presupposition which required substantiation when at various places around the world Episcopal and Lutheran churches met in negotiations leading to church union. These negotiations must be regarded as one of the main causes of Lutheran-Anglican conversations in recent times. This is especially true on the world level.[20]

Thus in 1963 the Lutheran World Federation through one of its commissions took action looking toward a conversation on the world level between Anglicans and Lutherans. Contacts with the Archbishop of Canterbury led to the formation of an ad hoc planning committee which met in 1967. This committee proposed to both the Lambeth Conference and the Executive Committee of the Lutheran World

Federation that Anglican-Lutheran conversations be held. This proposal was accepted in 1968. Between the years 1970 and 1972, an international Anglican-Lutheran dialogue met four times. At this last meeting, April 4–8, 1972, it drew together its final report, the so-called Pullach Report, named for the meeting site in West Germany near Munich.[21] There were nine Lutherans and ten Anglican participants, coming from Europe, North America, Asia and Africa. Attempts were made to see that both groups had representation of the different theological thinking and views of church life within each.

From the very beginning the dialogue turned to examine the conditions for mutual recognition and fellowship between the two churches. In order to secure a theological basis, five specific areas were examined: sources of authority, the church, the word and the sacraments, apostolic ministry and worship. Provisional statements were drawn up and then revised and integrated into the final report. Included in the Pullach Report are personal statements by the two co-chairmen, Bishop Williams of Leicester, England, and Archbishop Hultgren of Uppsala, Sweden. These statements explain the key points in language familiar to each of the two traditions.

The common statement in the report discloses considerable agreement in all five areas, although certain qualifications are mentioned in regard to the historic episcopate. With this exception, the existing differences are judged to reflect differing historical developments and thus are not ultimately divisive. The one controversial issue between the two confessions is the historic episcopate. Nevertheless, the gulf between the differing positions has been reduced by a common agreement that apostolic mission and episcopacy are more basic realities than apostolic succession in the shape of the historic episcopate. Both communions assert that they are exercising the essential function of oversight but in differing ways. The report states that while beliefs of each tradition are in part incompatible, they do not prevent mutual recognition. This conclusion is supported by the findings in the other areas.

There is a short section of the Lord's Supper. The participants agreed that in the Supper the church receives the body and blood of Christ, the forgiveness of sins and all other benefits of his passion. The real presence of Christ, without describing the "how," is affirmed. Agreements were reached that Christ's sacrifice was offered once and for all, and yet the eucharist in some sense involves sacrifice. Whether the church's offering of itself is caught up into Christ's self-offering is not answered.

The Pullach Report does not deal explicitly with justification, presumably because this doctrine was not regarded as controversial. The personal statement of the Lutheran co-chairman reports that in further dialogue, especially if concerned with the establishment of church fellowship, the Lutherans will insist that more attention be given to this topic so that future conversations say more clearly and fully that the gospel proclaims the unmerited grace whereby God declares men righteous through faith in Jesus Christ.

In spite of its somewhat modest scope, the Pullach Report recommends a mutual recognition among Anglican and Lutheran churches as a true communion of Christ's body possessing a truly apostolic ministry. The Anglican participants could not foresee full communion with the integration of ministries apart from the historic episcopate. But this position did not in their opinion preclude increasing intercommunion. The Lutheran participants declared that while their churches are free to accept the historic episcopate it should not become a necessary condition for interchurch relations or union. In reaching these conclusions the international dialogue adopted a point of view quite close to that of the Lutheran-Episcopal dialogue conducted in the United States.

Between October 1969 and June 1972, six meetings were held of the Lutheran-Episcopal dialogue in the U.S.A. Participants were chosen by the joint Commission on Ecumenical Relations of the Episcopal Church and by the Division of Theological Studies of the Lutheran Council in the U.S.A. Lutherans who took part came from The American Lutheran Church, the Lutheran Church in America and The Lutheran Church–Missouri Synod.

A report was submitted to the sponsoring agencies which included: preamble, summary statements, recommendations, enabling legislation and a separate document addressed to each tradition. The structure discloses that the participants wished a means of practical implementation. The separate statement to each confession seeks to explain and justify how the consensus came about.[22]

The mandate given to the dialogue was "to define the possibilities and problems for a more extended dialogue having more specific fellowship or unity or union goals."[23] Early in the series the focus shifted to altar and pulpit fellowship, *communio in sacris*. Here the participants were going beyond their mandate. Nevertheless, in spite of their enthusiasm to manifest oneness, political realities in both groups had their influence. The final recommendations fall short of any claim for union or organic unity now. The suggestion was for a limited, almost experimental *communio in sacris* as a matrix out of which further unity might develop.[24]

The group stated that they were able mutually to affirm the presence of the gospel and apostolicity in their respective communions and to agree that remaining problems between Anglicans and Lutherans could better continue to be explored in communion with one another than out of communion. Agreement of a significant degree was noted on Holy Scriptures, worship, centrality of preaching and eucharist, and baptism and confirmation. There was a mutual affirmation of each other's ordained ministry, although the agreement on apostolicity was limited. In fact, apostolicity became a central concern of the dialogue.

It was because of agreement on some of these fundamental aspects of church life and doctrine that the participants recommended that, subject to the consent of the appropriate local authorities, communicants of each communion should be commended to services of word and sacrament of the other. This was to include intercommunion between parishes and congregations which might find it appropriate to do so. The intention was for selective and local implementation.

There was also the call for a structure that would continue theological study of pertinent issues to accompany the suggested limited intercommunion. To be discussed would be the nature of the gospel, common forms of ordained ministry, *episcope* and further reform and renewal of the church.

The differences and difficulties appear more clearly in the separate statements to each communion than they do in the common report. The Lutheran statement, reflecting the consensus of all the Lutheran participants, declares in effect that where the situation described in article 7 of the Augsburg Confession is found to exist by those responsible for making the assessment, consequences should follow which express and strengthen that situation.[25] The Episcopal statement, authored by one participant, admits that the question of episcopacy remains a serious problem. The statement seeks to broaden the concept of apostolicity and points to historical precedents where intercommunion had been practiced and non-episcopal ministries recognized. Yet it maintains that all four points of the Lambeth Quadrilateral must be met before full communion or structural reunion can occur.[26] The document looks forward to the restoration of the episcopate in historical succession among Lutherans.[27]

While the dialogue itself indicates there is much still to be done, several things were accomplished. Lutherans and Episcopalians disclosed that they were willing to listen to each other. They also affirmed that they had no desire to abridge the doctrine of the gospel. This is true of Lutherans speaking of justification and of Episcopalians in their commitment to continuity with the apostles. Episcopalians and Lutherans came to some agreements on *episcope*. Episcopalians were willing to recognize that *episcope* was being exercised by the ministry of the Lutheran churches. Lutherans acknowledged that where the church is there is *episcope* and that they do not see a three-tiered ministry as the only way in which this *episcope* could be exercised. Any Lutheran willingness to move their ministry into three tiers would not be out of necessity but of a desire to serve the unity of the church. One weakness of the dialogue is that it left unanswered key questions about the nature of ministry and the meaning of ordination.

A strength of the dialogue report is its concern for establishing a positive climate at the local level. This may ultimately be more significant than national pronouncements. The recognition that the eucharist may not only be the goal of unity but a means to attain unity is significant and in keeping with contemporary views of article 7 of the Augsburg Confession.[28] This is also true of the suggestion of the dialogue that limited intercommunion be initiated now as the appropriate context for further exploration of unity. The suggestions of this dialogue could have considerable procedural implications for further conversations and relationship between these two confessions and other bilaterals. At this time neither the Episcopal Church nor any Lutheran church has taken official action on these suggestions. Nevertheless, the dialogue has had some impact at both the parish level and among church body executives, especially in regard to intercommunion. Within the framework of a "reconciled diversity," this dialogue does offer a way to an ecumenical convergence.

There is in progress in the United States a second series of Episcopal-Lutheran dialogue, sponsored by the Standing Commission on Ecumenical Relations of the Episcopal Church and by the Division of Theological Studies of the Lutheran Council in the U.S.A., and begun in 1976, but it has not yet completed its work. Therefore it is too early to see what contribution it may make to future Episcopal-Lutheran relations.

A Concluding Word

From the above account, what can be concluded about future Episcopal-Lutheran relations from a Lutheran point of view? Hopefully, it has become apparent that Lutherans can, and do, affirm the visible unity of the church. As an option, but not an essential, Lutherans are able to accept an episcopal structure of church polity. No doubt, this position is perplexing for Episcopalians. The only conditions which Lutherans should need to declare their unity with other Christians are to be found in article 7 of the Augsburg Confession. Yet, history has shown that this requirement even among Lutherans has been deceptively simple. Nevertheless, in the light of all that the Anglican and Lutheran traditions share and of the conclusions of their first dialogues, these are optimistic signs which seem to indicate that closer relationships and more intimate expressions of unity will be possible between Lutherans and Episcopalians in the future. When this long overdue development occurs, thankfulness will be the only appropriate reaction.

NOTES

1. H. R. McAdoo, *The Spirit of Anglicanism* (New York: Scribner's, 1965), p. v.
2. Eric W. Gritsch and Robert W. Jenson, *Lutheranism: The Theological Movement and Its Confessional Writings* (Philadelphia: Fortress, 1976), pp. 5–6.
3. Eberhard Busch, *Karl Barth: His Life from Letters and Autobiographical Texts*, trans. John Bowden (Philadelphia: Fortress, 1976), quoted by Martin E. Marty in *Context* (Chicago: Claretian, Oct. 1, 1977), p. 3.
4. For a comparison and description of Anglican-Lutheran relations, see Martin Schmidt, "Anglicanism and Lutheranism—Similarities and Contrasts," in *Lutheran World*, 12, 1 (1965), pp. 209–224. This entire issue is useful for documenting Anglican-Lutheran relations before bilateral discussion.
5. Martin Luther, *Sincere Admonition to All Christians* in *Luther's Works*, vol. 45, edited by Walther I. Brandt (Philadelphia: Muhlenberg Press, 1962), pp. 70–71.
6. The confessions of the Lutheran churches may be found in the original German or Latin in *Die Bekenntnisschriften der evangelisch-lutherischen Kirche* (Göttingen: Vanderhoeck & Ruprecht, 1959). The best English edition is *The Book of Concord*, translated and edited by Theodore G. Tappert (Philadelphia: Fortress, 1959). The quotation is from the Tappert edition, p. 32.
7. See, for example, Hans J. Hellerbrand, *Christendom Divided: The Protestant Reformation* (New York: Corpus, 1971), esp. pp. 139–140.
8. Andreas Aarflot, "The Lutheran Church and the Unity of the Church," in the *Proceedings of the Sixth Assembly of the Lutheran World Federation*, June 13–26, 1977, Tanzania, edited by Arne Sovik (Geneva: The Lutheran World Federation, 1977), pp. 35–47.
9. *Book of Concord*, p. 32.
10. "More Than Church Unity" and "Guidelines for Ecumenical Encounter" in *Lutheran World*, 17, 1 (1970), pp. 43–58.
11. Harding Meyer, "The LWF and Its Role in the Ecumenical Movement," *Lutheran World*, 20, 1 (1973), pp. 19–31, especially p. 20. This view is also seen in the Strasbourg document on Eucharistic Hospitality in *Lutheran World*, 20, 4 (1973), pp. 353–360, and a new statement on communion practices developed by The American Lutheran Church and the Lutheran Church in America, *Communion Practices, A Study of the Proposed Statement*, commentary S. D. Schneider, edited M. Roloff and R. Tiemeyer (Philadelphia: Fortress, 1977).
12. See also Harding Meyer, "Confessional Identity and Christian Unity," *Consensus: A Canadian Lutheran Journal of Theology*, 2, 4 (1976), pp. 3–12.
13. Aarflot, *op. cit.*
14. "Lutheran Churches in the Ecumenical Movement." See the *Proceedings of the Sixth Assembly of the Lutheran World Federation*, June 13–26, 1977, Tan-

zania, edited by Arne Sovik (Geneva: The Lutheran World Federation, 1977), pp. 173–175 and p. 200.

15. On the question of the relationship of Lutheran churches to church union in South India see H. W. Gensichen, "The Church of South India," *Lutheran World*, 1, 4 (1954), pp. 297–308; H. W. Gensichen, "Conversation between the CSI and the Federation of the Evangelical Lutheran Churches of India," *Lutheran World*, 2, 1 (1955–56), pp. 74–78; H. W. Gensichen, "New Conversations between CSI and the Lutheran Churches of South India," *Lutheran World*, 3, 2 (1956–57), pp. 178–181; Vilmos Vajta, "The Problem of Church Union in South India," *Lutheran World*, 3, 2 (1956–57), pp. 110–132; H. W. Gensichen, "The Lutheran Churches in South India and the Church of South India: New Developments Since 1956," *Lutheran World*, 5, 1 (1958–59), pp. 84–88. On the question of Lutheran churches and church union in Africa, see H. Meyer, "The Ecumenical Significance of Maranger," *Lutheran World*, 2, 4 (1955–56), pp. 380–382; A. Sovik, "Confessions and Churches—An Afro-Asian Symposium," *Lutheran World* 3, 4 (1958–59), pp. 363–374; Paul E. Hoffman, "Antsirabe, 1960," *Lutheran World* 7, 2 (1960–61), pp. 183–185.

16. *Sent into the World: The Proceedings of the Fifth Assembly of the Lutheran World Federation,* Evian, France, 1970, edited by La Vern K. Grose (Minneapolis: Augsburg, 1971), pp. 142–143.

17. A still valuable resource for exploring this topic is the article by Martin Schmidt cited in footnote 4. The presentation given here is indebted to Professor Schmidt's work, but cannot in limited space give full justice to it.

18. See Martin Schmidt, *op. cit.*, p. 219.

19. See for example Neelak I. Tjernagel, *Henry VIII and the Lutherans* (St. Louis: Concordia, 1965) and D. S. Armentrout, "Lutheran-Episcopal Conversations in the Nineteenth Century," *Historical Magazine of the Protestant Episcopal Church*, 44, 2 (1975), pp. 167–187.

20. See Nils Ehrenström and Günther Gassmann, *Confessions in Dialogue,* Faith and Order Paper No. 74; 3rd, revised, and enlarged edition (Geneva: World Council of Churches, 1975), pp. 14–18.

21. *Anglican-Lutheran International Conversations,* the report of the conversations 1970–1972 authorized by the Lambeth Conference and the Lutheran World Federation (London: S.P.C.K., 1973), also in *Lutheran World*, 19, 4 (1972), pp. 387–399.

22. All this material with some selected papers was published in *Lutheran-Episcopal Dialogue: A Progress Report* (Cincinnati: Forward Movement Publications, 1973). Besides the official dialogue report, two valuable resources are: *Lutherans in Ecumenical Dialogue: An Interpretive Guide* in *Studies* (New York: Lutheran Council in the U.S.A., 1977) and Warren A. Quanbeck, *Search for Understanding* (Minneapolis: Augsburg, 1972).

23. *Progress Report,* p. 13.

24. *Ibid.,* pp. 23–24.

25. *Ibid.,* pp. 31, 33.

26. *Ibid.,* p. 41.

27. *Ibid.,* p. 43.

28. See notes 11 and 12, above.

All in Each Place One
The Consultation on Church Union
Gerald F. Moede

Introduction

The assignment given to the writer of this paper was to describe the vision of visible unity which animates the Consultation on Church Union, to remind the Episcopal Church, as it studies its ecumenical commitments, why church union is important, what its intention is, and therefore why in my opinion this church should continue its participation in COCU's effort to achieve a united church in the United States at this time.

In the pages that follow I shall attempt to do the former by addressing myself directly to the latter. This attempt will involve describing some of the building blocks or basic ingredients with which union works, blocks which, I believe, have to do with the very existence of the Church itself.

A final introductory remark is this: I appreciate greatly the fact that the Episcopal Church is undertaking the study of its ecumenical relationships and commitments. All too often particular churches are still indifferent to the ecumenical dimension of their discipleship. Or, if they take it seriously and get involved on various fronts, often their "right hand does not know what their left hand is doing." For years the Faith and Order Commission of the World Council of Churches has been urging the churches to study their own efforts, the better to co-ordinate them, that each facet may supplement and complement the others, not contradicting or duplicating them, as has sometimes been the case. A thoroughgoing review such as this gives each dimension opportunity to be understood and appreciated for what it is, and to find its proper place in the whole. The various strands in the fabric of unity all have a place. The challenge of our day is to find the design and to weave this fabric in a way that is compatible with the nature of the Church of Christ.

I. *Church Union as a Form of Ecumenical Endeavor*

A. The Intention

Church union takes many different forms, and manifests itself in different ways. But inherent in each union is the desire that there be one visible manifestation of the catholic Church where previously there were several. All unions spring from the conviction that the unity among Christians for which Christ prayed was intended to be a unity in faith, worship and witness; that it should be, in fact, a unity which is not merely spiritually experienced by believers (important though that may be), but a manifest reality, apprehensible even by those who are not Christians at all.

Basic to the understanding of the elements of unity on which union builds is the famous "New Delhi paragraph" agreed to by the member churches of the WCC at the New Delhi Assembly in 1961. This statement clearly stimulated efforts to bring churches together "in each place." Between the New Delhi and Uppsala Assemblies no fewer than 22 unions were consummated. Most of these were built around the very elements of unity included in that description. That paragraph is reproduced here as a reminder to the reader:

> We believe that the unity which is both God's will and His gift to His Church is being made visible as all in each place who are baptized into Jesus Christ and confess Him as Lord and Saviour are brought by the Holy Spirit into one fully committed fellowship, holding the one apostolic faith, preaching the one Gospel, breaking the one bread, joining in common prayer, and having a corporate life reaching out in witness and service to all and who at the same time are united with the whole Christian fellowship in all places and all ages in such wise that ministry and members are accepted by all, and that all can act and speak together as occasion requires for the tasks to which God calls His people.[1]

The bones of the skeleton can be identified in this paragraph of Pauline proportions. This skeleton had emerged from years of Faith and Order discussion; it represented an important milestone of agreement.

Between 1925 and 1975, 63 major church unions were concluded, incorporating the above-mentioned elements. There are at present 34 negotiations toward union underway in the world, involving more than 120 churches, of which more than a third are already united churches.

B. A Change in Atmosphere?

We must consider the question: Are such unions obsolete? Do they bring about a type of unity no longer desirable? Are the present negotiations pursuing a will o' the wisp?

To be sure, it is true that some unions, especially in the West, have striven to attain too uniform a structure, and have thereby resembled corporate mergers (take-overs?) in business, more than a body with many members. This type of objection against union has long been voiced. (It was one of the clearest questions raised by the half-million people who studied the 1970 *Plan* of the Consultation on Church Union. COCU is therefore committed to maintain diversity, but is not yet sure how this may be done. Thus it is working first to attain the mutual recognition of members and ministers.) But new objections are being raised as well. The Anglican Consultative Council (ACC), in its 1976 Trinidad meeting, listed several factors behind such objections: (1) consciousness of membership in a world-wide body; (2) sociological and non-theological factors; (3) the appearance of the Roman Catholic Church as a serious participant in ecumenical discussion; (4) church leaders most immediately involved in union negotiations have not always been sensitive to the voice of the constituency they serve; (5) the office of bishop has continued to be a source of difficulty; (6) practical ecumenism has become more popular.[2] Since the ACC represents, in a certain way, the Anglican communion, we must take its observations seriously.

The ACC also observed that "since the last meeting of the Council we have seen the collapse of a significant number of negotiations towards Church union in which Anglicans have been involved . . . we must try to hear what 'the Spirit says to the Churches' through these failures."[3]

The six factors identified above are doubtlessly related to a changing set of circumstances which confront union negotiators as they go about their work. But such negotiations have usually required a full generation of time to come to fruition; they have usually had to adapt to changes in the *kairos*. In all candor, it must be said that the word "collapse" which the ACC utilized is, as was Mark Twain's obituary, somewhat premature! At least it would surprise negotiators who are still at work to achieve union in Ghana, New Zealand, and Sri Lanka, to learn that their negotiations had "collapsed." It is true that each of these negotiations has experienced recent delays. And Anglican participation in the work in Canada has, as a matter of fact, ceased. But such delays have been par for the course in other negotiations; why are they suddenly written off now as "failures"? It must also be said that in each of these four negotiations, it was members of the Anglican communion who have raised the public concerns causing the delay.

The Trinidad meeting of the ACC did concede:

> . . . with the encouragement of successive Lambeth Conferences, united churches have come into being with a strong conviction that they have entered into an organic union according to the mind of Christ, and in order to promote the mission and witness of the Church in their lands. These united Churches are learning to grow together in common life with courage and perseverance. They are also developing further negotiations towards visible unity with other churches in their own land.[4]

But the Council pointedly refrains from commending union to those still negotiating, or encouraging those confronting difficulties.

At this point I shall quote sentences regarding organic union from the *preceding* meetings of the ACC in Limuru, Kenya, and Dublin, Ireland.

> The degree of commitment to unity among Christian Churches can be plotted on a kind of scale. At the top of the scale are the Churches which are organically one, sharing a common faith, a common name, a common discipline, and a common structure. Other Churches are in full communion with each other, or in a less complete relationship for which the term intercommunion is used.[5] The Council (ACC) will follow with interest and will pray for the progress of these union discussions and encourages those participating to go forward in hope. It further suggests that the structure ought to be such that the bishops will have maximum opportunity for that pastoral ministry which we believe is of the very essence of their function in the Church.[6]

> The Council looks forward to the inauguration of the united Church of Lanka . . .[7]

Or consider a statement from the 1973 meeting of the Council in Dublin:

> It is necessary that the goal of actual church union should emerge again as a powerful motive. The co-operation of Christians is now in a phase which cries out for intercommunion; but local intercommunion may lead to confusion and even sectarianism unless there are more than local approaches to the unifying of ministries and Churches. There must be no shrinking from the conviction that, to use the New Delhi phrase, 'all in each place' should be one in ordered fellowship as well as in faith and sacrament. While avoiding any quest for uniformity or for centralization, we

reaffirm the conviction that organic union in the sense of united Churches is a goal for which intercommunion alone or federation alone is no substitute.[8]

The quotations cited above do reveal "a shrinking from the conviction," or at least a growing criticism regarding organic union in the Anglican Consultative Council. It probably is not possible to know the basic reasons behind this turn. But one given great attention, seems to be the assumption that *conciliarity* indicates a departure from, and even a repudiation of, the organic union of churches. Conciliarity is looked upon very favorably. In section III of this paper I shall investigate this question in greater depth, and indicate why I think this position represents a misunderstanding of the conciliarity debate. But before doing this, I shall describe some of the ecclesiological questions which union addresses directly, which, I contend, make it an authentic attempt to overcome division within Christ's Church.

II. *Ecclesiological Questions Which Union Addresses*

A. Faithfulness in Mission

It is important to note that the New Delhi Assembly joined witness and service inseparably together, *within* the same phrase in which it mentioned the "corporate life." This is simply to say that it is the body which reaches out in mission; its very existence is tied up with the mission of God in the world. The *means* by which the good news is preached must be congruous with the nature of the salvation preached—a "making whole," a healing of all things in Christ Jesus. How can divided churches which are not whole themselves, be authentic instruments of this "making whole"? This is only to say that the division of the churches contradicts the very nature of the Gospel.

It can be accurately stated that many of the insights of "union theology" have grown out of renewed mission consciousness among Western Christians. Burgeoning "missions" in the "third world" countries in the 18th and 19th centuries produced several kinds of fruit. One of the varieties was the awareness that the task of evangelism was too large for any one association or Church to carry out alone—the results were comity arrangements by which areas for mission responsibility were divided by mutual agreement.

By about 1900, however, another fruit was ripening, ready to be harvested (and to plant new seeds) at the Edinburgh Missionary Conference in 1910: the realization that even comity was not an adequate response to the imperative of unity for the sake of mission. It became steadily more clear, especially among third world Christians, that divided Churches were contradictions in terms, luxuries left from a Christendom situation they could not afford.

To conclude this point, it should be said that, to be a credible sign of its Lord (drawing all people to the Cross, John 12), the Church needs to bring into its fellowship people of every race and culture. For this to happen, these various people need to be *present,* in face-to-face encounter and reconciliation, around the preached Word and the supper on the Lord's Table. This is one reason the task of union goes so slowly. The Consultation on Church Union, for example, has committed itself to tackle humanity-dividing issues of the present, as well as the theological questions that have divided the churches in the past. But how else can the church be a first-fruit, a foretaste of the unity of humankind?

The growing awareness of the interdependence of obedient mission and unity has been reflected in an ever-growing number of church unions and negotiations. It is at this point, *in the context of mission and witness,* that the questions of sacramental life and *episcope,* should, and do emerge.

B. Sacramental Life

As long as churches live apart (even if they belong to the same Council of Churches or are in full communion with one another), sacramental sharing continues to be the exception rather than the rule; the mutual forgiveness and renewed fellowship that stem from the week-by-week gathering of the people around the Word and Sacrament simply do not occur.

Cooperation at all levels among churches is a very positive development, but in so far as it leaves untouched the basic realities by which the Church lives its life (faith, worship, sacraments, congregational fellowship) it can neither solve the basic problems existing between the churches nor fulfill their potential.

Common worship at the local level is central to the whole enterprise of union, for it incorporates the dimension of the reconciliation of persons (and not only institutions) to one another, persons who may have lived across the street from one another, but whose worship lives had always been separated from each other. A "fully committed fellowship" without at least the *possibility* of regular sacramental sharing is difficult to envisage by New Testament witness. For fellowship to live and develop, some kind of form and structure becomes necessary. The mutual recognition of members and ministers that is accomplished in all union plans plays a crucial role here. The critical point is that the recognition is not only formal or theoretical, but effective and practically at work. Eucharistic sharing and mutual recognition are possible because a theological framework has been worked out, usually after years of labor. The experience of about fifteen "Interim Eucharistic Fellowships" of the Consultation on Church Union already bears out the priceless nature of shared eucharistic worship among previously divided Christians.

The "all in each place" ideal of worship is especially important at this point. Union usually involves a conscious attempt to obey the biblical injunction to be one at the place where such unity will be visible—at the congregational level, the gathering together of Christians in a certain place.

> The stress on local unity has theological significance. The Church is always a concrete fellowship. It exists wherever the Gospel is proclaimed and men have felt themselves called, wherever they celebrate the eucharist, and are sanctified as a fellowship and as individuals. It always exists in particular places.[9]

The union finds its primary effect in the eucharistic fellowship and mission of the local congregation and parish. It is there that the tests of reconciliation, new life in Christ, and involvement in mission are passed—or failed. If the presence of Christ, breaking down social, economic, and racial barriers, reconciling, liberating, cannot be detected in the local gathering, any more universal forms of fellowship (important in their own right) are seriously called into question.

The united Church of South India has made this point very clearly. By its explicit decision to bring together into single congregations the various economic, racial, intellectual, and even caste strata, it made vividly clear that redemption in Christ is, by itself, enough to reconcile into a fruitful fellowship people previously divided at all levels. Union such as this recognizes the validity of the fact that there are theological and social questions which are decisively shaped by, and can only be settled in, the context in which churches live and encounter one another locally. Such "each place" eucharistic reconciliation and fellowship is one of the stated goals of COCU as well.

C. Corporate Life

The element of church union that seems to provide the most ground for controversy and objection is that enigmatic term in the New Delhi paragraph "having a corporate life reaching out in witness and service." Why a corporate life of its own? Why a loss of previous corporate identities? What kind of super-bureaucracy will result?

It is true: by its attempt to create a new united manifestation of corporate life, church union makes clear that it assumes unity in *gov-*

ernment is an important aspect of Christian unity, and it is at this point that it differs primarily from federations of churches on the one hand, or a "communion of communions" on the other. Church union, in its insistence that oversight (as well as authority) is involved in the unity of the Church, manifests that there is an organic relation between apostolic witness, sacramental leadership, and oversight.

1. *Episcope*

Most theologians will now agree that at least one part of the role of a true bishop is the sacramentalizing of the unity between a given eucharistic celebration and the Eucharist of the entire Church. (The Trinidad ACC calls him the "sign and focus of unity.") The advocate of union carries this sacramentalizing one step further. He asks: If the bishop is the sacramental person standing at the point of intersection between the local eucharistic celebration and that of the universal Church, can ecumenical endeavor be satisfied with several bishops (or corporate episcopacies), organized under separate, autonomous, and even competing jurisdictions, claiming and exercising oversight of separated parts of the Christian fellowship in a particular place? This person answers "No." The inter-relationship of the persons who exercise oversight is also a vital part of being "one in each place." Indeed, it can thus be said that such a taking seriously of the oversight of the church is a mark of the union approach. To paraphrase the words of Colossians 2:19, the joints and ligaments, which knit the body together, need to be part of the same body!

Those who advocate recognition of members-ministers, or even "full communion" as an adequate goal of unity efforts need to be reminded that such recognition existed among many "free churches" in North America and Europe for generations without making discernible differences in their day-to-day life in isolation from one another. (Have Anglicans had similar experiences with churches with whom they are in full communion?) Encounter and relationships between members of different traditions really develop only when the governing agencies of their church are implicated (threatened?) and make possible (necessary?) that relationship. This observation is one of the most clear of the gleanings being gathered from COCU's Generating Communities.

I have been suggesting that there is a need to take united governance seriously, even though there is a danger of developing bureaucracy. To deplore bureaucratic operational style, however, is not to invalidate a united church *government*. One has only to examine the "structure" of the Church of South India to understand that union does not necessitate bureaucracy; one can not equate union with a proliferation of functionaries. The heart of organic union is not a highly centralized administrative type of organization, but rather a fully shared experience of inter-connected life. True organic unity is present when a single stream of life flows through all parts of a church and no part of it is shut off from any aspect of the common experience. The various types of united churches have shown that different types of *episcope* can provide for such life. But the disaffection with current administration should remind us of the great importance, and difficulty, of working through a kind of corporate life that takes its form from the life and ministry of Jesus, at least in this era, in this country.

Our question boils down, in the last analysis, to the difference between an organization and an organism. The Consultation is attempting to employ the former in behalf of the latter. Perhaps what I am attempting to describe may be included within a full definition of "communion" as it was articulated in the Second Vatican Council. In a passage dealing with "perfect incorporation," the Constitution on the Church uses "communion" as a comprehensive term to include the "joining effected by the bonds of professed faith, of the sacraments, of ecclesiastical government."[10] Organic union attempts to bring about this kind of communion.

2. National Church

Concern is also voiced, often in the world confessional families, that many united churches have aimed at, and accomplished union, within their national boundaries, sometimes even within the context of nation-building. This is somewhat ironic, since most of the members of world families are "nation-churches," that is, churches whose boundaries (except for their "mission fields") are co-terminous with their nation's.

There are, of course, dangers to be recognized. Historical influences played a role in this evolution; it was assisted by the *cuius regio eius religio* principle, bringing about a certain uniformity within a particular region. And the evolution of the nation state influenced this ideal as well, coinciding with the formation of "denominations" in the United States, until in our time most Protestant churches, even those who come out of "local autonomy" traditions, utilize a national context for their "regional" organization.

But it must be said that most union negotiations recognize these dangers. The Consultation on Church Union puts it this way:

> Because a uniting church is only a step toward the reunion of Christ's church, its commitment is toward a wider unity both

within this nation and outside its borders. There is danger in a church organized solely within one nation, since nationalistic attitudes may pervert or silence the judgment of God's Word on the cultural, social, and political shape of national life. Nevertheless, a church is sent to the society within which it is called; and apart from this society, it cannot bear true and responsible witness in its world (Gal. 2:7–10).[11]

Union does not, by *definition,* seek national boundaries. Several examples may suffice. The most famous united church, the Church of South India, is regional in character, comprising seventeen dioceses in southern India. Its new partner, the Church of North India, is likewise regional in makeup.

Furthermore, one of the dioceses of the CSI (Jaffna) is located in India's neighbor, Sri Lanka (international).

Again, for almost forty years negotiators who prepared the plan of union for the CNI and the Church of Pakistan worked together. With the evolution of separate governments (and the need to obey local laws), the two churches emerged separately, but in full communion with one another. In almost all respects these two plans are identical.

These three illustrations are cited only to remind the reader that union *per se* is not automatically tied to national expressions of the church.

But, *national* union negotiations also have *positive* value. There is a good, as well as a potentially bad, reason for a church to tie its existence to a national expression of a peoples' life, and not *primarily* to a world-wide family fellowship. That reason has to do with its being truly the church *for its place.* What does it mean to be "one in each place"? Lesslie Newbigin states the ideal well:

> The "place" is not just the latitude and longitude of the spot where this church happens to be . . . but its place in the fabric of human society. The Church cannot be described unless it is described as the Church *for that place,* and the meaning of the preposition "for" is determined christologically; that is to say, it is determined by what Jesus Christ has done, is doing, and will do with and for the world as its author, redeemer, and consummator. The Church in each place is the Church for that place . . . and in this sentence the word "place" must mean the whole secular reality of the place including its physical, social, cultural, and political aspects.[12]

The truth of this statement validates the national organism of the Church.

It should also be remembered that each of the COCU member churches has evolved a type of "national" government, at least in its legislative branch. These national bodies do have limitations, but there is no principle within them which would, as such, prevent these churches from relating themselves to some common personal symbol of Christian unity at the world level. Even churches which have traditionally formed provincial or super-national relationships through "communion," such as the Episcopal Church, have found it desirable in the American context to develop a type of national government. Thus, the Episcopal Church has a minimal "national staff" bureaucracy, but it is governed by a General Convention, a representative assembly comprising bishops, clergy, and laity. In fact, it is a kind of union of regional dioceses in a national setting.

Even Lutherans, who have traditionally used the "altar and pulpit fellowship" principle to describe their communion, have been gradually bringing together their various ethnic strands into larger united Lutheran churches—American churches. It appears that when sufficient doctrinal agreement can be reached, the implication of united government is also compatible with Lutheran ecclesiology.

The foregoing probably illustrates that American Christians have been influenced by their political culture more than they would admit. It can be observed that it is primarily the Western Protestant churches which have evolved (with their mission offspring) a representative national style of government in which the laity have indispensable place and voice, and that this evolution was profoundly influenced by secular political ideals since the time of John Locke. But such a development *can* be interpreted as motivated by the Holy Spirit as well, working in history to give (finally) the entire People of God genuine authority as well as theological respectability! In fact, the voice and authority of the laity in the Episcopal Church may well represent one of the more basic problems to be faced as it attempts to reach agreement on the question of authority with the Roman Catholic Church. As Professor M. Shepherd has pointed out, "It is most unlikely . . . that the Anglican churches would abandon the participation of their laity at all levels of decision-making processes, or the non-veto of a primate over collegial decisions of the episcopate."[13]

We have been trying to remind the reader that a variety of churches have formed themselves along national lines, and therefore that newly united churches should not be faulted for seeking unity within national borders, especially if they are aware of the need to enlarge their fellowship beyond those boundaries.

D. The Question of Identity

This point leads to a final consideration, which we can only mention in conclusion. What of my denominational identity, my heritage, the *ethos* in which I have lived my Christian life? Must it be sacrificed, given up, lost sight of forever?

It is clear that Christians treasure their various identities, histories, idiosyncracies, their *ethos* as such. These treasures have their positive sides, and the more inclusive unions have usually attempted to make possible some remembrance of these heritages in the new church, through a variety of worship styles, for example. There is a value in, and a need for, diversity in an inclusive church. No one is advocating uniformity, or "monolithic" institutions.

But to the extent that these identities remain exclusive enclaves, hugging their life to themselves to the detriment of mission, or compete with one another, giving contradictory testimonies to Christ in their settings, they bear witness that, to them, Christ is *not* a sufficient center of unity to enable them to live with the others in one household. The advocate of union feels that to the extent they allow their founders' viewpoints to continue to dictate separated lives, they are, in the words of the Apostle Paul, carnal.[14]

The union of churches does, in the end, involve some change in the identities of constituent bodies. This change constitutes both the pain and the potential of union. Reformation and reconciliation are the goals of such change, but pain is an inevitable concomitant; repentance cannot be avoided by *any* of the constituent bodies. To this extent union calls into question types of reconciliation which settle for minor adjustments rather than radical change, for "co-habitation without commitment."

Representatives of many united churches which are members of the WCC, meeting in June, 1975, put it this way:

> As members of united churches and church union committees, we emphasize the call to organic union. . . . We believe God is calling us to overcome the sinfulness and pain of our present divisions, leaving behind personal and group security, to serve the needs not only of individuals but also of divided communities and nations. . . . It is as we have entered upon a costly unity of the Church which is a death to the selfhood we cherish but new life at command of the Risen Lord that we have been set free to face the conflicts and tensions of our present situations in the world . . .[15]

World Council of Churches studies, too, have recognized that at the end of the road of unity discussions, each church's separate identity (at least in its present state) is called into question. This is a hard truth to accept, but it is made clear in most WCC statements (although these paragraphs do not usually gain wide publication, or at least popularity!).

For example, the famous New Delhi statement on unity was followed by these two sentences:

> The achievement of unity will involve nothing less than a death and rebirth of many forms of church life as we have known them. We believe that nothing less costly can finally suffice.[16]

Church of England Bishop Patrick Rodger has cogently commented:

> I am not sure what weight we should give to that little word "finally," but it is certain that the way of the Cross and Resurrection, the way of Christ Himself, is one which we see quite clearly and one from which our human weakness shrinks again and again. Frantic appeals are still heard to some inviolable national or confessional tradition; wearisome denunciations are directed against some imagined threat of "uniformity"; and the unspoken prayer of many is "O Lord, make us one, but not yet." For this adversary there is surely no remedy even in the very best kind of theological argument. "This sort goes out but by prayer and fasting."[17]

The Nairobi Assembly of the WCC continued to recognize the need for shared identity when it stated:

> Organic union of separate denominations to form one body does mean a kind of death which threatens the denominational identity of its members, but it is dying in order to receive a fuller life. That is literally the "crux of the matter."[18]

Indeed, when we bring these identities to the Cross, what is implied in terms of a new body? That is the question.

The goal and style of church union owes much to thinking and initiative from the World Council of Churches in the past thirty years. At this point, it is important to illustrate that union is still implicitly, and even explicitly, a central element in the continuing discussion in the international Faith and Order movement. To that subject we now turn.

III. *A Conciliar Fellowship of Local Churches, Themselves Truly United*

Since at least the 1968 Uppsala Assembly of the World Council of Churches, a term not heard recently has found its way into the ecumenical discussion again: "conciliar fellowship" and "conciliarity." Has a new goal been discovered, a new way forward? How does church union fit into "conciliar fellowship," if indeed at all? Since Professor J. Robert Nelson has recently written a substantial paper on the subject of conciliarity for the Faith and Order Commission of the National Council of Churches as well as for this Triennial Ecumenical Study of the Episcopal Church, I shall not go into it exhaustively. However, we do need to examine what relationship it may have to the subject of church union.

A. A New Way?

Indeed, the Trinidad meeting of the ACC felt that this concept represents a "new approach to visible unity," a "pillar of light." To quote several passages from the text of that meeting:

> The facts as we hear them reported from many parts of the Anglican Communion seem to question the older model of organically united national churches, and to make us look for new thinking, new approaches and new models of visible unity at local, national and international levels. We know only too well how easy it is to stick to the well-trodden ways in ecumenism as in any other activity . . .
> WCC discussions in recent years have led to new concepts:
> a) In 1961, New Delhi emphasised that *visible unity means local* . . .
> b) In 1968, Uppsala added that *visible unity means diversified unity* . . .
> c) In 1975, Nairobi added a further dimension which gathered together some of these insights—*the Church is conciliar fellowship.*[19]

The ACC expressed a preference now for the term "visible unity" over the term "organic unity." It then moved to a discussion of the idea "conciliarity," which, it feels, is intended to gather together "these notions." It said:

> We believe conciliarity would be attained when (through covenanting or otherwise) the churches in a country or region had reached the stage of:
> —the confession of a common faith
> —mutual recognition of membership
> —interchangeability of ministries
> —complete eucharistic fellowship
> —sharing of resources
> —streamlining of structures
> —maintenance and development of such diversity as enriches the whole Church.[20]

One can only welcome such a comprehensive statement of intention, even though this outline omits the crucial "corporate life" provision of the New Delhi goal. Of course each of these points is being striven for (and slowly attained) in the Consultation on Church Union, in a national setting.

But it is difficult to understand why this goal is counter-posed against organic unity, inasmuch as organic unity in the traditional sense would include all of the above. Perhaps the critical difference in goals is constituted by the two points which union includes which we mentioned in our second section: common *episcope* and governance.

Further evidence of the attraction of this line of thought among some Episcopalians is revealed in the "Twelve-Year Report" released by the Anglican–Roman Catholic Consultation on December 28, 1977, in which the ACC report on ecumenism is described: "Such new terms as 'visible unity' and 'conciliarity' seem to be opening a way to a different idea of Christian unity from the older concept of one monolithic church in each city, province, and nation."[21] One is astonished (and dismayed) that the misleading word "monolithic" is still used in an attempt to discredit union, when most united churches exhibit as much (or more) diversity as the Episcopal Church.

At this point I should like to turn to an attempt to relate church union to the concept of conciliarity or conciliar fellowship. It is my contention that there is no contradiction between organic union and conciliarity, that indeed, as presently understood, the latter presupposes the former.

B. Conciliar Fellowship

Dr. J. Robert Nelson, former chairman of the Working Committee of the Faith and Order Commission of the WCC, articulates well the danger:

> Conciliarity is by no means a household word, not even in the household of faith. As its use is promoted in ecumenical discussion, there is rising danger that it will be a piece of technical jargon. There is evidence that this is already happening. At worst, conciliarity is used as a substitute for, and a deliberate evasion of, the full, visible union of presently divided churches.[22]

The 1967 "Catholicity and Apostolicity" study group (composed of theologians appointed by the WCC and the Secretariat for Promoting Christian Unity of the Roman Catholic Church) reminded the Uppsala Assembly that "the Church in all times needs assemblies to represent it and has in fact felt this need." The necessity *that* they take place is due to conciliarity, which "is a constant structure of the Church, a dimension which belongs to its nature."[23] The principal intention here was "to preserve the fellowship of the Church in the Eucharist." This refers to councils, but it also speaks of the essential nature of the Christian Church as a somatic unity of faith, worship, and witness.[24]

At the 1968 Uppsala Assembly of the WCC a reference was made to a future genuinely universal Council as the possible ultimate goal of ecumenical effort.[25] Since that time the thread of "conciliar fellowship" has been continually woven into the Faith and Order fabric, usually understood as both process and relationship—the establishment of such relationships among the churches that a universal Council could again be conceived and convened.

Perhaps the crucial contribution to the development of this concept was made by the consultation on "Concepts of Unity and Models of Union," which assembled at Salamanca, Spain, in the autumn of 1973. The key paragraph emerging from that conference, which the ACC quotes with approval, was this:

> Jesus Christ founded one Church. Today we live in diverse churches divided from one another. Yet our vision of the future is that we shall once again live as brothers and sisters in one undivided Church. How can this goal be described? We offer the following description to the churches for their consideration: The one Church is to be envisioned as a conciliar fellowship of local churches which are themselves truly united. In this conciliar fellowship each local church possesses, in communion with the others, the fulness of catholicity, witnesses to the same apostolic faith and therefore recognizes the others as belonging to the same Church of Christ and guided by the same spirit. As the New Delhi Assembly pointed out, they are bound together because they have received the same baptism and share in the same eucharist; they recognize each other's members and ministries. They are one in their common commitment to confess the Gospel of Christ by proclamation and service to the world. To this end each church aims at maintaining sustained and sustaining relationships with her sister churches, expressed in conciliar gatherings whenever required for the fulfilment of their common calling.[26]

As becomes clear in the text and commentary following this paragraph, the word *conciliar* refers in this context to the mutual relationships of local churches within the *one* Church. It is derived from *concilium*, and does not refer to our present Councils of Churches. It can exist only if the churches recognize one another as holding and confessing the same truth, it is based on eucharistic fellowship, and it necessitates representative gatherings.[27]

The Salamanca Consultation wished to ascertain that its thinking not be interpreted as movement away from earlier Faith and Order statements regarding the appropriateness of union in achieving "oneness in each place." Thus it went on to say:

> The unity described in the preceding section requires union of the churches which are still separated today. There is no con-

tradition between the vision of a conciliar fellowship of local churches and the goal of organic union. Both terms point to the same calling. The conciliar fellowship will, therefore, become a reality only as the churches are prepared to face, at all levels, the implications and challenges of organic union.[28]

Thus, as Nelson points out, although there is some ambiguity in the use of words in the evolution of conciliar fellowship as a concept, there is no ambiguity in the insistence of Faith and Order that church union is presupposed in the evolution of conciliar fellowship.

Salamanca goes on:

> In particular, union negotiations at the national level need to be pursued. Since the local churches which form the universal conciliar fellowship must be truly united themselves, division at this level of the Church's life is particularly intolerable. But union negotiations at this level must recognize especially the necessity of finding appropriate ways to provide fully for emerging expressions of human diversities within the united church, as well as ways of expressing the worldwide dimension of the Christian community.
>
> God's great gift in Jesus Christ is the promise of a new community in which humanity's estrangements are overcome. The churches are called to seek to give visible institutional form to this new community—in a manner which will enable their members in each place to gather around the Word and sacraments and to work out their mission in the world together. Corporate union is such a form.[29]

The Nairobi Assembly of the WCC reaffirmed and built upon this understanding of conciliar fellowship. Section II of this Assembly, "What Unity Requires," put it thus:

> The term "conciliar fellowship" has been frequently misunderstood. It does *not* look toward a conception of unity different from that full organic unity sketched in the New Delhi statement, but is rather a further elaboration of it. The term is intended to describe an aspect of the life of the one undivided Church *at all levels.*[30]

The Assembly continues:

> True conciliar fellowship presupposes the unity of the Church . . . It is true that there is no community without structure, but structure must serve and facilitate good Church order, which is itself essentially and properly the expression of committed personal fellowship in Christ. Organic union of separate denominations to form one body does mean a kind of death which threatens the denominational identity of its members, but it is dying in order to receive a fuller life. That is literally the "crux of the matter."[31]

But it may be objected: "Perhaps the WCC discussion of conciliar fellowship does encourage union as a necessary step on the way; but wouldn't energy and involvement in union-oriented activities militate against Episcopalian rapprochement with the Roman Catholic Church? Don't Roman Catholic theologians prefer world-wide bilaterals, since they are not organized nationally themselves?"

Of course the Roman Catholic Church must converse and negotiate more as an international body than all of the other churches. Nevertheless, a group of Roman Catholic scholars, in assisting the WCC in its preparations for the Nairobi Assembly in the Joint Working Group, had this to say in a statement prepared and released jointly:

> We welcome the statement of the Salamanca Conference prepared as a basis for discussion at Nairobi. . . . This is a further development of the effort to state together the nature of the unity we seek. It presupposes and builds upon the earlier statements of New Delhi and Uppsala concerning the nature of the unity we seek . . .
>
> There has been in recent years a strong stress on conversations between confessions at the world level. This is partly the natural and proper result of the vigorous participation of the Roman Catholic Church, with its global perspectives, in the ecumenical movement. These discussions at the world level are necessary in order that the basic theological issues be not by-passed in the quest for unity at the local level. However, there is a danger that these may lead, and have in some cases led, to a weakening of the efforts among member churches of the WCC to seek organic union with their neighbors in the places where they live. We hope that all concerned, including the Roman Catholic Church, will agree that this ought not to happen. . . . We believe that all possible help and encouragement should be given to efforts for organic union at the national or regional level where the churches concerned believe that this is appropriate and possible, according to their understanding of the Church . . .
>
> We do not understand the word "conciliar" to imply any weakening of the fullness of organic union as envisioned in the New Delhi statement, but rather as describing something of the nature of that unity at all levels . . .[32]

I shall enter no further into the subtleties of the discussion on conciliar fellowship. Significant questions emerge from it, inasmuch as the discussion is not yet mature, but is only now evolving. Certain ambiguities, or at least ambivalences, are inherent in it, as one might expect at this state of its maturity.

This section of my paper has simply attempted to remind the reader that world ecumenical thinking since 1961 has not abandoned the ideal of union as a goal (or in the case of conciliar fellowship, as involved in reaching the goal). Rather, Faith and Order study of and concern for unity has continued on a steady course, building on the "all in each place" foundation laid in New Delhi, adding a ground-level wing regarding catholicity at Uppsala, and beginning to elaborate a super-structure at Salamanca and Nairobi.

Thus it is very important that churches do not misunderstand the "conciliar fellowship" concept as a departure from earlier approval of organic union, offering, as it were, a less expensive or demanding path toward unity.

Conclusion

The life of the Episcopal Church and its relation to the Anglican Communion are quite important in this discussion, inasmuch as in its own life the Episcopal Church holds together a comprehensive variety of viewpoints, theologies and ministries, but all within an episcopal communion of dioceses, with a modest national decision-making representative body. Thus it is itself a kind of model for the life of a united church.

Furthermore, the eucharistic, episcopal fellowship it enjoys with the other churches of the Anglican communion already anticipates some of the aspects of a conciliar fellowship, albeit in an intentional "Anglican" setting. That is to say, among the various churches of the Anglican communion there is mutual consultation of the bishops every decade, there is full eucharistic fellowship, interchangeability of members/priests, and now there are the beginnings of a consultative council. Some of the elements of the eventual wider fellowship are being developed and lived out within the Anglican communion.

This means that the experiences shared, and the insights won, the successes and failures, will be important in the development of a future universal fellowship of a more catholic makeup.

But it is the contention of the writer that the riches which the Episcopal Church and the Anglican communion have to bring will be enhanced and communicated to the fullest to the extent that they continue their commitment to, and support of, church union as one of the building blocks of conciliar fellowship. Indeed, a subcommittee of the bishops of the Anglican communion, when they last assembled at Lambeth in 1968, put the support of union as one of the "aims of Anglicanism":

> 1. To welcome, encourage, and be ready to give counsel in the merging of Anglican Churches in united national or regional Churches.
> 2. To enter into full communion with all such united Churches, even while certain anomalies remain . . .
> 4. To preserve and enrich our special insights, and to contribute them to the whole Christian Church and to the world.

> We believe that the Anglican witness and the Anglican role will
> continue; but the processes of church union will mean that the
> frontiers of Anglicanism become less defined.[33]

It is my hope that these aims of the bishops of the Lambeth subcommittee will continue to be the aims of the churches as well.

The family of Anglican churches has gifts to give, and others to
receive. In unions such as the Church of South India and the Church
of North India, in which Anglicans united with free-church traditions,
there is now widespread appreciation, among former free-church
members, of such treasures as episcopacy. And there is also a growing
appreciation in these churches, among "ex-Anglican" persons, for the
emphases the free churches brought into the new common life.

Robert McAfee Brown puts it well:

> If the fear is that denominational identity will be lost, the fear is
> well founded. But if the fear is that the distinctive gifts of the
> denomination will be destroyed, ecumenical experience leads to
> the opposite conclusion. The Church of South India is a case in
> point. . . . It brought together for the first time since the Refor-
> mation era churches from episcopal, presbyterian, and congrega-
> tional polities. In the intervening quarter of a century, no one of
> these has absorbed the others. On the contrary there has been
> mutual enrichment. Episcopacy has not destroyed the significance
> of the presbyter but has enhanced it. Powers given to the congre-
> gation have not smothered episcopacy but have helped all to see
> the relationship between bishop and congregation in new and
> more dynamic ways. The emerging pattern is that of enrichment,
> not diminishment of a denomination's contribution.[34]

Above all there is the conviction in these churches that preparation
for, and consummation of union brought about a necessary repentance and renewal of *each,* and that the newly united body is more a
faithful and obedient missionary witness to God's reconciliation of
persons to himself and to one another.

Thus it is my hope that the Episcopal Church, as it reviews its
ecumenical commitment, will continue to understand organic union as
one of the goals to be pursued and supported in the years immediately ahead, and that it will witness to the place of union in the development of a conciliar fellowship to the other churches of the Anglican
communion.

NOTES

1. W. Visser 't Hooft, ed., *The New Delhi Report* (London: SCM Press, 1962),
   p. 116.
2. *ACC-3, Anglican Consultative Council, Trinidad* (Coventry: Coventry Print-
   ers, 1976), pp. 9, 10.

3. *Ibid.*, p. 9.

4. *Ibid.*, p. 8.

5. *The Time Is Now, Anglican Consultative Council,* Limuru, Kenya (London: SPCK, 1971), p. 1.

6. *Ibid.*, p. 3.

7. *Ibid.*, p. 3.

8. *Partners in Mission, Anglican Consultative Council,* Dublin, Ireland (New York: Seabury, 1973), p. 2.

9. Lukas Vischer, "The Church—One People in Many Places," in *What Unity Implies,* R. Gorscurth, ed. (Geneva: WCC, 1969), p. 68.

10. *Lumen Gentium* 14.

11. *In Quest of a Church of Christ Uniting* (Princeton: 1977), p. 11.

12. Lesslie Newbigin, "What Is a 'Local Church, Truly United'?" *Ecumenical Review,* 29, 2 (April 1977), p. 118.

13. Massey Shepherd, "An Anglican Reply," in *The Plurality of Ministries* (New York: Herder, 1972), p. 95.

14. 1 Corinthians 1–3.

15. "Called to Witness to Christ's Cross and Glory," *Midstream,* 14, 4 (October 1975), pp. 542, 543.

16. Visser 't Hooft, *op. cit.,* p. 117.

17. Patrick Rodger, "Unity, a Wide Door and Many Adversaries," *Ecumenical Review,* 17, 2, p. 215.

18. *Breaking Barriers, Nairobi 1975,* ed. David M. Paton (Grand Rapids: Eerdmans, 1976), "What Unity Requires," p. 63.

19. *ACC, Trinidad,* p. 15.

20. *Ibid.*, p. 16.

21. Diocesan Press Service, "Where We Are: A Challenge for the Future," co-chairmen, The Most Rev. Raymond W. Lessard, The Rt. Rev. Arthur A. Vogel, document 77421, December 28, 1977, p. 10.

22. J. Robert Nelson, Conciliarity/Conciliar Fellowship, a study paper written at the Boston University School of Theology, 1977, p. 1; printed in *Midstream,* 17, 2 (April 1978), p. 97.

23. Cited in Nelson, *op. cit.,* p. 6 (*Midstream,* pp. 100–101); cf. *Councils and the Ecumenical Movement,* World Council Studies No. 5 (Geneva: WCC, 1968), p. 10.

24. Nelson, *op. cit.,* p. 6 (*Midstream,* p. 101).

25. *The Uppsala Report 1968* (Geneva: WCC, 1968), pp. 11–18.

26. *What Kind of Unity?* (Geneva: WCC, 1974), Faith and Order Paper No. 69, p. 121.

27. *Ibid.*, p. 122.

28. *Ibid.*, pp. 123–124.

29. *Ibid.*, p. 124.

30. David M. Paton, ed., *Breaking Barriers, Nairobi 1975* (Grand Rapids: Eerdmans, 1976), p. 60.

31. *Ibid.*, p. 60.

32. "What Unity Requires—A Comment," *What Unity Requires* (Geneva: WCC, 1976), Faith and Order Paper No. 77, pp. 14, 15.

33. "Renewal in Unity," *The Lambeth Conference 1968—Resolutions and Reports* (London: SPCK, 1968), p. 142.

34. Robert McAfee Brown, *Frontiers for the Church Today* (New York: Oxford University Press, 1973), p. 33.

The Orthodox Vision
of Visible Unity

Stanley S. Harakas

There is a special character to the Orthodox-Anglican relations which is substantively different from all other ecumenical relations which the Orthodox have maintained with other Christian bodies. In part, this can be attributed to some accidental and historically conditioned factors. On the other hand, this is clearly not an adequate explanation for the sense of communality which the Orthodox have felt over the centuries with their fellow Christians of the Anglican Communion. In this paper I wish to address this special relationship from the perspective of an Orthodox Christian who has not had the privilege of close involvement in the ongoing dialogue of many years standing between Episcopalians and Orthodox in this country. To choose such an author may prove to be a serious mistake on the part of those who have planned the Triennial Ecumenical Study, for most of the advances of the dialogue may well have taken place because of the increasingly intimate personal interchanges that come out of long-standing conversations in which I have not shared nor to which am I privy. Thus, it may also prove to be a serious mistake for me to undertake such a task, ignorant as I am of the nuances, the dynamics and the finer points of this dialogue. Yet, after due consideration, those who planned the Triennial Ecumenical Study have apparently decided to risk the dangers inherent in such a situation (that nothing significant or revealing may come from such an invitation), and I have been bold enough (in spite of contrary advice from sources of counsel which in the past have spoken wisdom consistently) to accept the invitation.

Thus, in truth, the following lines come from "outside" the dialogue. They do no more than represent the reflections and first conclusions of one who is at once committed to the integrity and truth of the Orthodox vision of the visible unity of the church as well as to the need to promote the unity of Christians through ecumenical endeavor.

I propose to address the issue by surveying, very briefly, the course of Orthodox-Anglican relations in the past. Then I hope briefly to sketch some of the ecclesiological principles which Orthodox hold central to the maintenance of the church's unity. Finally, with these two as background, I will venture an assessment of the present and future state of Anglican-Orthodox relations. I intend throughout this paper to use the terms "Episcopal" and "Anglican" interchangeably.

1. *The Orthodox-Episcopal Tradition of Relationships*

"The Contacts between the Orthodox and Anglicans cover the greater part of the history of Orthodox relations with the non-Orthodox."[1] These relations have been characterized by their variety, intensity, and consistency, as compared with Orthodox relations with all other churches since the time of the Reformation, including the Roman Catholic Church. They have been cultivated on many levels: personal, scholarly, diplomatic, academic, hierarchical, parochial, and even commercial. And they have not been without their darker moments in the past, such as during the decades preceding and following the turn of the century as a result of Anglican proselytizing activities and at present because of the ordination of women by the Anglicans.[2]

In the seventeenth century letters were exchanged between the archbishop of Canterbury and Orthodox hierarchs. The names of important figures from this period have a permanent place in church history. Cyril Loukaris, Archbishop Abbot, and Metrophanis Kritopoulos are among the more well known. The latter is connected with the Greek College at Oxford, an early ecumenical effort (1699–1705). English diplomatic presence in the Ottoman Empire and the increase of commercial and tourist travel served to increase contacts.

Personal and official contacts were facilitated by the establishment of Anglican dioceses in Jerusalem (1841) and Gibraltar (1842) and by official committees on the Orthodox in England and America from 1862. These became the background for increasingly frequent contacts and discussions. Thus, a decision of some practical significance was reached in 1869 when the patriarch of Constantinople and the archbishop of Canterbury agreed that Anglicans who died in predominantly Orthodox areas could be buried by Orthodox clergy with the use of a specially prepared Orthodox service. This was perceived by some as a first step to sacramental communion. Moscow also encouraged Anglican-Orthodox contacts, notably Metropolitan Philaret. In 1870 theological discussions took place in England with the visit of Alexander Lycourgos, Archbishop of Syros. The topics were characteristically divided into issues which required revision (i.e. the *filioque*), issues to be discussed (i.e. transubstantiation, the Seventh

Ecumenical Council), and issues regarding differences which could be maintained (i.e. the marriage of bishops).

Headway seemed to be made from the Orthodox point of view in the Bonn meetings of 1874–75 when a measure of agreement was reached on the issues of tradition, the *filioque,* and the Eucharist.

During the eighteenth century the contacts between the English Non-Jurors and Orthodox served to make bridges on two levels. The Non-Jurors themselves seemed to appreciate and approach the doctrinal positions of the East and even requested to be accepted into the Orthodox Church.[3] The Orthodox patriarchates responded with some caution, yet with willingness to pursue the issue since there appeared to be a possibility of doctrinal agreement between the two churches. However, when the archbishop of Canterbury revealed to the Eastern Orthodox the schismatic character of the Non-Jurors, the Orthodox broke off relations with them completely. In the first instance the importance of doctrine was emphasized in the quest for unity; in the second, the significance of canonical episcopal status was significant, both of which are important glimpses at the implications of Orthodox ecclesiology for church unity.[4]

An important step in Anglican-Orthodox relations took place in 1899 when Archbishop Frederick Temple officially wrote to the patriarch of Constantinople calling for a termination of proselytization on both sides, a proposal gladly and warmly accepted by the Orthodox. The implications of this agreement for future Anglican-Orthodox relations were great. It implied that unity would come about not by a bit-by-bit conversion of members, but by agreement and decision on the level of doctrine, church discipline and synodal decision. Further, it had the practical result of freeing the Orthodox to enter closer and friendlier contacts with Anglicans. Such contacts were encouraged by the interests expressed in the Oxford Movement with its obvious respect and interest and identification with the traditional catholic and orthodox faith and practices of the early church. The Orthodox were encouraged by this turn of emphasis. There was a tendency, it would appear, to interpret the Anglican Church as a whole from this image of it. What was completely lacking was an Orthodox comprehension or appreciation of "the well-known but ill-defined Anglican comprehensiveness." In a sense the balance of this history of Anglican-Orthodox relationships may be read as an Orthodox attempt to answer for themselves some of the questions placed by Anglicans to themselves, e.g. the question, in the "Anglican viewpoint *which* things *must* be believed, and which things *can* be *clearly* demonstrated from basic Christian sources . . ."[5] In practice, the Orthodox seemed to have worked on the assumption that the conservative, "high-church" approaches to these questions were normative for the Anglicans. The subsequent history of relations, however, tends to deny the normative character of this viewpoint and instead to display the Anglicans' own sense of their "doctrine of comprehensiveness." The nature of the contacts, their form, and their content seem to support this view.

Subsequently, in 1907, the Ecumenical Patriarch appointed an official representative to the archbishop of Canterbury. This was regarded by some as an indirect form of recognition of both Anglican Orders and the Anglican Church as well. The short but significant synod of the Russian Orthodox Church of 1917–18 passed a resolution encouraging relations and further study on Anglican-Orthodox relations.

A significant factor not often elaborated upon arose out of the increased emigration of Orthodox peoples from traditionally Orthodox lands to the West. Especially in America, this gave an opportunity for practical cooperation at the parochial level. Many small Orthodox congregations formed their first ecclesiastical homes in the basements of Episcopal Churches. This oft-repeated phenomenon is a witness to the fact that both Anglicans and Orthodox—even on the parochial level—sensed a shared (though not clearly defined) common heritage which caused Episcopal priests and vestries readily to welcome Orthodox into their buildings and which, conversely, was deemed an appropriate and acceptable course of action for the Orthodox. Though I cannot speak for Anglicans (would they have done the same for a Baptist congregation? Presbyterians? Methodists?), I can say with confidence that Orthodox people would never have accepted the same invitation into a Roman Catholic Church basement, and it never would have occurred to them to approach "the Protestants." A bond was perceived to have existed which was based more on ethos and feelings than on ecclesial decisions. Orthodox children, especially in areas of tiny Orthodox population, received instruction in Orthodoxy from Episcopal priests. Some even shared in Episcopal sacramental life.

Theological contacts were many and varied in this period. Official correspondence was exchanged once again under Patriarch Joachim III (1902–1904) and the issue of Anglican Orders became a subject of Orthodox theological debate. In America Archbishop Meletios Metaxakis, later of Athens and subsequently Patriarch of Alexandria, gave impetus to theological discussions.

The first expressions of the ecumenical movement further encouraged contacts. The Orthodox were represented for the first time officially at the Sixth Lambeth Conference in 1920. Seven meetings of theological discussions took place discussing issues of Baptism, Confirmation, the Seventh Ecumenical Council, the *Filioque*, the Thirty-Nine Articles, and the Eucharist. A year later the Church of England's Eastern Churches Committee published a document on terms of intercommunion in thirteen sections, all theological, a sign of a maturing dialogue. These became the basis of additional conversations, most notably those held on highest level at the Seventh Lambeth Conference in 1930. Significant were the questions placed by the Orthodox to the Anglicans; they betray a growing perplexity on the part of the Orthodox as to where to locate an authoritative voice with which to deal with the Anglicans. Questions with reference to who or what body "expresses the mind of the Anglican Church," "the supreme constitutional body in the Anglican Church," the status of Anglican individuals who utter "publicly opinions contrary to the faith of the church," and Holy Orders as "a link with the apostles" in "unbroken succession"[6] were raised by the Orthodox. These obviously were probing some assumptions which the Orthodox felt to be held by the Anglicans in common with them regarding traditional views of church unity, orthodoxy of faith, sacramental theology, and historical identity with the ancient undivided church.

The conclusion of these Seventh Lambeth discussions were cast in a form of statements of agreement and disagreement on doctrinal issues and a hesitancy, with some exceptions, to authorize general practical relations on the sacramental level.

That acceptable answers to the Orthodox, however, were ardently being pursued was evident in another set of meetings the next year.

In the meantime, Anglican Orders were recognized in 1922 by the Ecumenical Patriarchate, in 1930 by the Patriarchate of Alexandria, and in 1936 by the Church of Roumania; while in 1939, the Church of Greece refused to do so. Was this a sign of Greek conservatism, or a reflection of some questions which were beginning to arise in Orthodox minds? In 1948 a similar refusal was taken in Moscow, with the apparent approval of representatives of the Patriarchate of Alexandria and the Church of Roumania.

Since 1948 no positive steps to closer practical or ecclesial relations have taken place. Nor has inter-communion moved closer to reality. Formalities, such as the visit of Patriarch Athenagoras to Archbishop Michael Ramsey in London in November of 1967 and the visit of Nicholas VI, Patriarch of Alexandria, in May of 1970, continue to express the special relationships felt to exist between the Orthodox and the Anglicans.

But strains have appeared, as well. At present, the trend in the Anglican communion to approve the ordination of women seems to be causing a serious assessment of Orthodox attitudes toward this special relationship.

Overall, Vasilios Istavrides has well summarized this "special relationship":

> The two Churches feel themselves to be close to each other because of certain common characteristics, such as the Episcopal Office, a basically similar administrative system, similar attitudes toward Rome, their international character and the psychological factor.[7]

2. *Ecclesiological Dimensions of Visible Unity for the Orthodox Church*

Orthodox ecclesiology may be likened to a jewel which displays its wholeness through the multiplicity of its facets. Each facet is distinct and discrete, yet the light which shines through it is also filtered, colored, and refracted by the light transmitted through all of the other facets of the jewel. There is a constant tendency in all theology—Orthodox theology not exempted—to reductionism, i.e. to make one aspect of the whole Christian truth the dominant and almost exclusive determinant of all other aspects of Christian truth. Ecclesiology is no exception. The visible unity of the church is not determined exclusively by a single criterion, institution, practice, teaching, or factor, but by a complex configuration of many dimensions of the life of the church. It is vitally important to keep this in mind as these dimensions are separated out for discussion and study. In this paper we can do no more than to point to some of these dimensions and then show their interrelation as they affect the question of visible unity.

Basic to this discussion is the idea that unity is more than a wish or hope or desired future condition. From the Orthodox perspective unity is a fact—historical, empirical, and essential to the very nature of the church. "The Church is One," the title to Khamiakov's famous tract, states the essential truth from an Orthodox viewpoint. As a theological principle it is supported by the whole history of the church. It is not that the mystery of the unity of the church is fully comprehended or that it is possible to point to an absolute stage in history when there were not empirical challenges to it, but that in its self-understanding the church always perceived an inclusive and clear line between its own life and that which was outside of its life. This distinction, which marked off its life from that which was not of its life, was perceived on several levels and in several spheres. Thus, separation from the faith of the church was perceived as heresy which meant exclusion from the life of the church. So, also, was failure to be in communion with the hierarchy of the church, i.e. schism. Though differences in liturgy and practice may be tolerated and not cause division, so also identity in liturgical practice does not necessarily mean ecclesial unity. Division may be a consequence of ethical considerations, especially on the personal level. Less tangible, yet practically very significant, are the perceptions held by local churches of other local churches as to their Orthodoxy. The diptychs maintained by each of the patriarchs and heads of autocephalous churches are formal witnesses to that sense of Orthodox community by which a network of mutual recognition affirms membership of a local church in the One, Holy, Catholic, and Apostolic Church. Common to all is a sense of the shared tradition of basic identity in faith, worship, administration, sacramental unity, teaching, life, and practice.[8]

More specifically the visible unity of the church is delineated by several fundamental ecclesiological realities: Orthodoxy in faith, episcopal unity, unity of life, and the common tradition.

Orthodoxy in Faith is what was at the front line of discussion in most of the Anglican-Orthodox meetings. This is not an erroneous or false placing of the issue. Orthodoxy and heterodoxy have always been a major factor in the church's definition of the lines separating those who were "within," those who were "without," and those on the way in and out. The concern of St. Paul with the unique place of Christ in the salvation plan for mankind, and that it not be minimized or brought to nought, was essentially a call for Orthodoxy in faith.[9] False teachers were a concern to the early church.[10] God and his doctrine were not to be blasphemed,[11] sound doctrine was praised,[12] and heresies condemned.[13] The long patristic and conciliar history can be read as a struggle to define the faith and to condemn false teaching. Irenaeus' *Against Heresies* sought to exclude Gnostic heresies from the church. Athanasius' *Incarnation of the Word* was a defense against Arianism. The First Ecumenical Council and all councils subsequent to it made Orthodoxy of faith a criterion of membership in the One, Holy, Catholic, and Apostolic Church.

There is, of course, the need to clarify the parameters of Orthodoxy for the definition of the unity of the faith. Even in Orthodoxy there is a sort of "comprehensiveness." What is basic, essential and needed for salvation and what is open to free interpretation may be distinguished from one another. Often, however, it was not clear where the line was to be drawn: Thus, "loyalty to the fathers and their tradition implied that a distinction had to be drawn between an idea that had 'the confirmation of dogmatic formulation' and an idea that was merely 'a theory, albeit one that is set forth by a saint.'"[14] The first is doctrine, the second "theologoumenon." Difference in the first excludes from the unity of the church; difference in the second, not so. What determines the difference? The tradition, the *consensus patrum* as expressed in the ecumenical councils, the creed, and the common tradition, but, most concretely, the hierarchy.

Episcopal Unity is a multi-faceted guardian of the unity of the church. The episcopacy is the primary witness to the concreteness of the true faith, but it is much more than that. Thus Patriarch Sophronius of Jerusalem could in the sixth century write:

> An Apostolic and ancient tradition has prevailed in the holy Churches throughout the world, so that those who are inducted into the hierarchy sincerely refer everything they think and believe to those who have held the hierarchy before them . . .[15]

and anyone who contradicts those beliefs and teachings "even if he were an angel, was to be excommunicated and anathematized."[16] But the bishop as a focus of the unity of the church transcends even this important role as the one who defines and protects the faith. Just as there is a linear relationship with the episcopacy in apostolic succession through the ages, there is also a conciliar relationship with all Orthodox bishops. Communion with the episcopacy in general through canonical relations is an essential characteristic of the unity of the church. A man who held the true faith, who conducted worship in the accepted fashion, who claimed identity with the tradition, and yet who had not been ordained by canonical bishops or in a canonical fashion would not share in the unity of the church. Thus the bishop is the focus of church unity in terms of the Orthodoxy of the faith, and the bond with the apostolic foundations of the church. Equally, the bishop is the locus of the horizontal unity of the church, the signs of which are the diptychs, and the actual participation of the bishops in the synods of their national or patriarchal churches and their potential participation in an ecumenical council. Even more importantly, the bishop is the head of the Eucharistic synaxis which is, in the words of John Zizioulas, "the whole Church itself, the whole body of Christ."[17] Ecclesiastical fullness and catholicity of the church is located in each and every locale where a bishop presides canonically over the Eucharist. In the early church a bishop without a Eucharistic community, or a Eucharistic community without a bishop, was incomprehensible. "Only the Bishop was ordained to preside over the Eucharist and to offer it on behalf of the whole Church. The result was that separation from the Eucharist conducted by the Bishop for the whole people in one place meant separation from the Church."[18] The foundations for the unity of the church thus can be traced through a complex web of doctrinal faithfulness, episcopal guarantees of it through apostolic succession, the mutuality of episcopal action (synodal practice), and episcopal realization of sacramental (primarily Baptismal and Eucharistic) life. This latter constitutes one of the most important facets of ecclesial unity.

Sacramental Unity is in direct correlation to ecclesial unity. In a real sense they are indistinguishable from each other. When St. John Chrysostom commented on the passage in the passion narrative which described the blood and water that poured out of the Savior's side when it was pierced by the soldier's spear, he wrote:

> An indescribable mystery takes place; water and blood came forth. It was not by chance that these fountains came forth, for because it was from these two that the Church was constituted. Those who are initiated are equally reborn by water, and fed by blood and flesh.[19]

Baptism draws the dividing line between the "Old Man" and the "New Man."[20] The Eucharist constitutes and manifests the church in its fullness. The Eucharist is understood in Orthodoxy as the gathering "of all together at the same place"[21] which unites the whole church. It is the center of the mystery of the faith where the doctrines of Trinity, Incarnation, salvation, and eschatology are realized in the manifestation of the One, Holy, Catholic, and Apostolic Church. It is in the Eucharist, Orthodox believe, that the church is fully the church. Thus, in Father Meyendorff's words:

> Any local Church where the "divine liturgy" of the Eucharist is celebrated possesses the "marks" of the true Church of God: unity, holiness, catholicity, and apostolicity.[22]

To share in this sacramental action, which is presided over by the bishop (or his delegate, the presbyter), is to share in the unity of the church. To be excluded from it is to be excluded from the unity of the church. The Eucharist is the visible sign, the clear-cut determinant of membership in the church or exclusion from unity with it. But, as we have seen, it does not stand in isolation from the bishop. Without the connection with the bishop the Eucharist is not, indeed, an expression of the church; it is what the canons call a "parasynagogue," a gathering of persons in a conventicle, but not "the church."

Exclusion from the unity of the church, i.e., from the Eucharist, may be the result of a life-style, behavior, or defiance of the authority of the bishop.

Unity of Life, thus, is an additional facet of the unity of the church— as expressed in the ethical behavior of the faithful, the ethical expectations of the life of the church community, and in the common canonical tradition. The penitential tradition of the Orthodox Church expresses, in part, the ethical expectations of the church by prescribing most penances in terms of longer or shorter periods during which the penitent is "excommunicated," i.e., prohibited from receiving Holy Communion, but expected to live a life of remorse and repentance until he or she is restored to communion with the church. Thus, putting off "the old man with his deeds" is not only a liturgical consequence of Baptism, but an outgrowth and an imperative of oneness with the church.[23] Thus, the unity of the church is also related to its ethical and canonical discipline. Though not as precise and definitive as a "dogmatic horos" of an ecumenical council, the ethical and canonical tradition of the faith contributes to the unity of the church. The very authority of a church-wide council, so important to the Orthodox conciliar view of the church, could be and has been questioned on the basis of the canonical tradition. Thus, the critical facet of Orthodoxy in faith was itself subject to the "canons" which were at once an outgrowth of that faith and yet a judge of it as well. As Pelikan notes:

> . . . the authority of the councils, as indeed that of the doctors and even the Scriptures, was the authority of one changeless truth. When it was necessary, one could list reasons for declaring a particular council null and void, because it had not been "convened in accordance with the laws and canons of councils and with the rules of the church."[24]

This rather circular, interpenetrating view of the unity of the church is held together for the Orthodox by their dependence on the living *Tradition of the Church.* The tradition is never properly conceived as a static deposit which calls for a mere "theology of repetition." Father Florovsky has frequently noted that the proper understanding of the place of tradition in the Orthodox vision of the unity of the church is a dynamic loyalty to the tradition which is faithful to the patristic spirit and which is perceived as under the constant guidance of the Holy Spirit in the life of the church.[25] Yet, continuity, harmony, and basic identity with the ancient faith, practices, life, and mentality

of the church are equally necessary. To maintain the unity of the
church is to maintain its unity not only with a present living bishop,
not only with all presently living Orthodox bishops and faithful, not
only with the Orthodox teaching of the church, nor alone with the
local Eucharistic community, nor with the uniform practice
(homoiomorphia) of the church in its canons and its ethical life; it is to
be in unity with the whole scriptural, patristic, conciliar, sacramental,
canonical, and ethical tradition. Respect for that ongoing tradition
joins together the facets of the jewel of the Orthodox vision of the
unity of the church. Professor Bratiotes was able to find in this one
fact the distinctive characteristic of the "Orthodox Ethos."[26] What
Maximos the Confessor wrote thirteen centuries ago still holds true
for the Orthodox today:

> Let us guard the great and first remedy of our salvation (I am
> referring to the beautiful heritage of the faith). Let our soul and
> our mouth confess it with assurance, as the fathers have taught
> us.[27]

A sense of identity with the *consensus patrum* is an essential for the
Orthodox vision of the visible unity of the church. To separate one's
self from that tradition is to separate one's self from unity with the
church's own inner bond. However, since that tradition is apostolic,
scriptural, charismatic, mystical, experiential, and ultimately a reflection of man's destiny to live in communion with the Triune God so as
to achieve a destiny of "divinization" or *theosis*, the identity with the
tradition is dynamic and alive and capable of development.[28] Let it be
said, however, that one can still distinguish in that tradition much that
is neither uniform nor essential to unity. Thus, as we have seen, in the
Anglican-Orthodox history of relationships the Orthodox were prepared to distinguish issues into those which require conformity, those
which need clarification, and those which are indifferent.

The Orthodox vision of the visible unity of the church is thus like a
multi-faceted jewel, whose beauty is complex and whose lustrous bril-
liance consists of interpenetrating rays of light refracted and reflected
from facet to facet in a whole, which has yet to find an adequate
description, least of which is this effort.

3. A View on the Past, Present and Future of Orthodox-Anglican Relations

Orthodox and Anglicans met in Moscow in 1976 and in Thessalonike
in 1977. Uppermost on their minds was the question of the ordination

of women. In the Moscow meeting some discussion and agreement was reached on the *filioque* clause and upon questions related to inspiration of scripture and revelation. However, the issue of the ordination of women figured very prominently in their discussions. The Orthodox concern was serious. They declared "that if the Anglican Churches proceed to the ordination of women to the priesthood and the episcopate, this will create a very serious obstacle to the development of our relations in the future."[29] The relationships of the Orthodox Archbishop of London (Thyateira) with the Anglican Church have become increasingly strained.[30] Archbishop Athenagoras at a press conference at Lambeth Palace in October of 1977 said that "the Orthodox had been optimistic in the last ten years about the movement toward unity, and all of a sudden the question of the ordination of women appears"! At another meeting, at Corpus Christi College, Cambridge, in August of 1977, the Orthodox representatives opined that the "future of the (Anglican-Orthodox) dialogue will depend on the resolutions of the Lambeth Conference" on the question of the ordination of women.[31] Earlier, in April, Donald Coggan, Archbishop of Canterbury, visited Patriarch Demetrios in Istanbul. The patriarch's message was warm, friendly, and supportive of continued theological dialogue between the two churches. But he spoke directly and negatively to the women's ordination issue, asking rather that the western churches increase the honor paid to the Theotokos (Mary, the Mother of God).[32] Characteristic of the Orthodox response to the ordination of women in the Episcopal Church, U.S.A. was a *London Times* headline: "Disillusion of Orthodoxy with Anglicanism."[33] Other similar phrases used by some Orthodox included "betrayal," "appalling," "disappointing."

In the light of the two previous sections of this paper, I wish to propose what seems to me the cause of this overwhelming negative response on the part of the Orthodox. I suggest it is the fact that the Orthodox suddenly realized that their chief presupposition in their "special relationship" with the Anglicans was proven to be illusory by the women's ordination issue. In the history of the dialogue the Orthodox knew that there were serious differences of faith, that the question of Holy Orders was far from clear, that discipline and ethics were often in conflict, and that sacramental convergence was far in the future. Yet none of these ever elicited the disappointment and disillusionment which arose from the women's ordination issue.

It is interesting that the issue itself has not received the theological attention from the Orthodox point of view which one might have expected. Just a few relatively short studies have appeared in America, for instance. One by Maximos Aghiorgoussis[34] and another by Thomas Hopko[35] may be noted. Both approach the issue on the substantive question, casting the problem in terms of Christ as a male figure.

Yet, this is not where the weight of the Orthodox reaction rests. The major reactions saw this action as a denial of the tradition, a rejection of identity with the tradition of the One, Holy, Catholic, and Apostolic Church. Thus, Patriarch Demetrios casts his response in terms of "full reverence and faithfulness" to the apostolic tradition of the church.[36] Archbishop Athenagoras is said to have noted that "the Anglican Communion appears to have taken decisions without sufficient reference to the Catholic conscience of the Orthodox and Roman Catholics. . . . The Church has no right to abandon anything it has received from Christian antiquity. . . . 'We did not receive the Ordination of women.'"[37] And Aghiorgoussis judges that "The Episcopal Church in the United States can no longer be considered as a community of 'catholic' tradition. With (this) decision, the Episcopal Church proved itself to be as liberal as all those liberal Protestant communities, which do not have the traditional Priesthood with Apostolic succession, and which thus feel free to appoint women as ministers." In the same work Father Maximos concludes his treatment on the male character of the priesthood with these words:

> I am confident that the above statement reflects the doctrine of the Apostolic Tradition and Church. I have no doubts that it also reflects the feelings of all those Christians who are attached to this Tradition, and who are not willing to accept any other Gospel but that given to them by this great Tradition of the Holy Spirit.[38]

The obvious focus of these statements coincides with that of the Vatican's *Declaration on the Question of the Admission of Women to the Ministerial Priesthood* which titles its first section "The Church's Constant Tradition" and begins, "The Catholic Church has never held that priestly or episcopal Ordination can be validly conferred on women. A few heretical sects in the first centuries, especially Gnostic ones, entrusted the exercise of the priestly ministry to women: this innovation was immediately noted and condemned by the Fathers, who considered it as unacceptable in the Church."[39] A similar focus was displayed by the forces at the 1976 General Convention of the Episcopal Church U.S.A. in Minneapolis that were opposed to the vote permitting the ordination of women. Their news story reporting the vote of the bishops was entitled "96 Bishops Reject the Tradition," and the lead sentence read, "The final vote in the House of Bishops

Wednesday afternoon disclosed that 96 Bishops were willing, if not anxious to abandon the faith once delivered to the Saints in Christ Jesus almost 2000 years ago in the fullness of time."[40]

These statements, journalistic-sounding as they may be, indicate what appears to be—for the Orthodox—the crucial issue: identification with and loyalty to the catholic, patristic and unified tradition of the church. With reluctance, dismay, and shock, the Orthodox have come to the conclusion that their cherished assumption about the "special relationship" of the Anglicans and Orthodox was built upon an Orthodox misconception. Together with the Anglicans, the Orthodox felt that they shared a basic and common identity with, and respect for, the importance of the tradition. This is what made all the difference. In spite of the obvious differences and in spite of the difficulties experienced in pinpointing agreements, the assumption of a common allegiance and identity with the tradition made it worth the effort to pursue with intensity and seriousness the visible unity of the Anglican and Orthodox Churches. It is safe to say that the women's ordination issue has shattered that presupposition.

If the Anglicans are interested in resuming the dialogue, it would appear that it can take two courses, should the Orthodox decide to continue in it as well. The first course would require that the Anglican-Orthodox dialogue assume a new posture, renouncing the "special relationship" assumptions which it has had in the past. The dialogues will become no more than "friendly conversations" with the hope that in some small way the conversations will contribute to "undestanding." A second, more difficult course of action will be for Anglicans and Orthodox to seek to rebuild that "special relationship." I do not have any suggestions at this time how that can be accomplished.

The Orthodox vision of the visible unity of the church is multifaceted. Respect for and identity with the apostolic and historic tradition of the church seems to hold its many facets together. It appears that it was precisely this which inspired the expectations of both Orthodox and Anglicans in the past. Whether the ordination of women to the priesthood has in fact disposed of this fundamental presupposition for good, only the future will tell. However, the Orthodox vision of the visible unity of the church will always consider it as central and essential.

NOTES

1. Basil Istavrides, "Anglicanism and Orthodoxy" (Greek) in *Ethike kai Threskevtike Engyklopaideia* (Athens, Martinos).
2. These from an Orthodox perspective. There may have been moments of

history of weakened relations because of Orthodox actions with which I am not familiar.

3. Th. Lathbury, *History of the Non-Jurors, Their Controversies and Writings, with Remarks on Some of the Rubrics in the Book of Common Prayer* (London, 1845), pp. 309–318, 343–4. J. H. Overton, *The Non-Jurors, Their Lives, Principles, and Writings* (London, 1902), pp. 451–66.

4. Methodios Fouyas, *Orthodoxy, Roman Catholicism and Anglicanism* (London: Oxford University Press, N.Y., 1972), pp. 35–50.

5. J. Robert Wright, "Anglican Comprehensiveness and the Limits of Conscience." *Ecumenical Trends*, 6, 11 (December 1977), p. 169.

6. Fouyas, *op. cit.*, p. 45.

7. Basil Istavrides, *op. cit.*, column 203.

8. John Rinne, *Unity and Common Practice in the Church* (Greek) (Thessalonike: Epistemonike Epiteris Theologikes Scholes, Parartema, volume 15, 1971).

9. E.g., Rom. 5:6, 10:4, 14:9, 1 Cor. 1:23–24, 15:3, 15:12–17, 2 Cor. 6:15, Gal. 3:13, Eph. 5:2, Col. 2:8.

10. 2 Cor. 11:13, 2 Peter 2:1, Eph. 4:14, 1 Tim. 1:3.

11. 1 Tim. 6:1.

12. Titus 1:9, 2:1.

13. Revelation 2:14–15.

14. Jaroslav Pelikan, *The Christian Tradition: A History of the Development of Doctrine, Vol. 2: The Spirit of Eastern Christendom (600–1700)*. (Chicago: University of Chicago Press, 1974), p. 137. Pelikan is here quoting Theodore the Studite.

15. *Synodical Epistle*, PG 87:3149–52.

16. Pelikan, *op. cit.*, p. 22.

17. John Zizioulas, *The Unity of the Church in the Eucharist and the Bishop During the First Three Centuries* (Greek) (Athens: 1965), p. 190.

18. Stanley S. Harakas, "The Local Church: An Eastern Orthodox Perspective," *The Ecumenical Review*, 29, (April 1977), p. 143.

19. *Commentary on John*, Homily 85,3.

20. Romans 6.

21. Acts 2:1.

22. John Meyendorff, *Byzantine Theology: Historical Trends and Doctrinal Themes* (New York: Fordham University Press, 1974), p. 209.

23. Rom. 6:6, Eph. 4:22, Col. 3:9.

24. Pelikan, *op. cit.*, p. 23, quoting Maximos the Confessor, *Disputation with Pyrrhus*, PG 91:352.

25. Georges Florovsky, *The Body of the Living Christ: An Orthodox Interpretation of the Church* (Greek) (Thessalonike: Patriarchal Institute of Patristic Studies, 1972).

26. See his essay in *The Orthodox Ethos*, ed. Angelos Phillips (Oxford: Holywell Press, 1964).

27. *Epistles*, 12, PG 91:465.

28. Meyendorff, *op. cit.*, pp. 224–25.

29. William A. Norgren, "Anglican-Orthodox Parley in Moscow Seen Most Important in Recent Years," *Religious News Service*, Monday, August 16, 1976.

30. Archbishop Athenagoras of Thyateira and Great Britain, *Introduction to the Theological Dialogue of Anglicans and Orthodox* (Athens, 1967).

31. Jack Allen, "Resumption of Anglican-Orthodox Dialogue Hinges on Lambeth Vote on Women Priests," *Religious News Service*, Wednesday, October 26, 1977.
32. *Episkepsis*, 8, 168 (May 15, 1977), pp. 2–5.
33. *The Times*, London, March 21, 1977.
34. *Women Priests?* (Brookline, Mass.: Holy Cross Orthodox Press, 1978).
35. "On the Male Character of the Priesthood," *St. Vladimir's Theological Quarterly*, 19, 3 (1975), pp. 147–73.
36. *Episkepsis, op. cit.,* p. 4.
37. Allen, *op. cit.,* p. 2.
38. Aghiorgoussis, *op. cit.* I have used a mimeographed first draft for these quotations.
39. *Ibid.,* p. 5.
40. *Episcopalians United,* Issue No. 5, Thursday, Sept. 16, 1976, p. 1.

The Concordat Relationships
William A. Norgren

The "concordat" is not merely a theoretical model, but an actual means by which visible unity has been established between the Churches of the Anglican Communion and certain other Churches.[1] Concordats exist, four in number, with the Old Catholic Churches of the Union of Utrecht, the Lusitanian Church of Portugal and the Spanish Reformed Episcopal Church, the Philippine Independent Church, and the Mar Thoma Syrian Church of Malabar. What can be learned from experience of these concordat relationships about visible unity?

The word "concordat" means agreement. According to the Oxford English Dictionary it is used today for an agreement between church and state, but in earlier use the word was applied in canon law to a compact between ecclesiastical personages. Our present use, perhaps stemming from this earlier use, means an agreement between ecclesiastical bodies.

The word expresses the *fact* of agreeing or being in harmony. To be in concord is to be agreeing, consistent, correspondent. In our use, therefore, a concordat is a recognition of harmony between churches; it attests to an existing unity without any constitutional provision or other special act of union. The concordat may in turn open the way for further developments, because it imposes no contractual limitations save independence (autocephaly).

To clarify the concordat model and process, we shall examine briefly the historical origin, the precise relationship, and subsequent experience in each of the four cases. Then we shall compare and examine the development of the idea of a larger episcopal unity and its relationship to the Lambeth Conference of the Anglican Communion. Lastly we shall reflect on the possibility of a more diverse communion of Churches.

1. *The Old Catholic Churches*
The Old Catholic Churches of the Union of Utrecht were formed following the dogmatic pronouncement of the Roman Catholic Church in 1870 on Papal Infallibility. The Church of Utrecht in the Nether-

lands, which had been isolated from Rome since the Jansenist controversy in the 17th century, had retained the ancient catholic order and life, and so became the metropolitan see for national Churches of the Netherlands, Germany, Switzerland, Austria, Czechoslovakia, the Polish National Catholic Church of America, Poland, and Croatia (Yugoslavia). These autonomous national churches subscribe to the Declaration of Utrecht (1889)[2] and are in communion with the Archbishop of Utrecht, who is *ex officio* president of the International Conference of Old Catholic Bishops. An Old Catholic Congress meets periodically. Total membership is about 500,000.

These churches attracted the attention of Anglicans and visits were arranged between several Churches of the Anglican Communion and Old Catholic Churches. During the 1930 Lambeth Conference of bishops, meetings were held of a committee of Anglican and Old Catholic bishops, which took note of the recognition of Anglican orders by the Old Catholic Church of the Netherlands in 1925 and endorsement of this recognition by the Conference of Old Catholic Bishops later that year. The committee "agreed that there was nothing in the terms of that Declaration (of Utrecht) which might be an impediment to union between the Church of England and the Old Catholic Church." Following a resolution of the 1930 Lambeth Conference, the Archbishops of Canterbury and Utrecht appointed a joint doctrinal commission representing the Anglican Communion and the Old Catholic Churches. This commission met in Bonn on July 2, 1931, and, in what appears to have been a remarkable day's work, signed the following statement known as the Bonn Agreement:

1. Each Communion recognises the catholicity and independence of the other and maintains its own.
2. Each Communion agrees to admit members of the other Communion to participate in the Sacraments.
3. Intercommunion does not require from either Communion the acceptance of all doctrinal opinion, sacramental devotion, or liturgical practice characteristic of the other but implies that each believes the other to hold all the essentials of the Christian faith.[3]

The report of the commission's work includes a letter of commentary by the Anglican chairman, the Bishop of Gloucester (Headlam), which tells us that topics discussed included the authority of the Lambeth Conference, the position of "parties" in the Church of England, the authority of the Thirty-Nine Articles, and the meaning and interpretation of the Declaration of Utrecht, particularly on the authority of Scripture and tradition, the General Councils, the interpretation of the Eucharist, and the significance of "the five commonly called sacraments." According to the letter, the Bonn Agreement was drafted in this way:

> We took as our basis a statement which had been prepared by Mr. Graham-Brown, but it was pointed out how undesirable it would be that we should attempt in any way to make a new creed, and therefore any statements of doctrine contained in it were omitted. It was suggested by the Old Catholics that we should begin by recognizing mutually the catholicity and independence of the two Churches. It was then decided that what was required on both sides was an admission to Sacraments in the two Churches. If that admission was granted, then admission to other ordinances would naturally follow. In order to remove all misconception, a statement was further added that nothing in this agreement implied that either Church would necessarily adopt the customs or habits of devotion of the other. It was felt that this statement was quite sufficient for our purpose.[4]

The principle set forth in the Bonn Agreement is the mutual recognition in each of catholicity and independence. This means not only eucharistic fellowship, which was actually being realized in some places before this, but above all mutual participation in the episcopal consecrations. The third article draws out some of the meaning of indepencence, the "essentials" having been carefully weighed. Although the article does not mention it, no fusion of organization, no joint and authoritative synod, is contemplated. The deeper unity lies in catholicity, wherein is implied the recognition of continuity with the ancient Church. In this catholicity lies the conclusion that each party is convinced that the other possesses the wholeness of the Church in doctrine, ministry, and sacrament. In practice, this means that ministers of both communions can exchange with each other everywhere and in everything—subject to canonical disciplinary decisions and agreements. It means that when bishops of one communion take part in the consecration of bishops of the other communion they solemnly acknowledge the duty of mutual care and concern which exists between sister Churches in the communion of the one Church.

The Bonn Agreement was ratified by the Old Catholics in 1931 and the Church of England in 1932, and subsequent concordats in the same terms as the Bonn Agreement have been signed by the Churches of the Anglican Communion. The Episcopal Church in the U.S. ratified the Bonn Agreement in 1934, and reiterated its action in 1940. In 1943 a report to General Convention made it clear that the Bonn Agreement established full communion as well with the Polish

National Catholic Church in the U.S., which was already a part of the Old Catholic Union. The PNCC took action in 1946.

Since the Bonn Concordat, the Church of England and the Old Catholic Churches of Europe have held frequent joint theological conferences. At a 1947 conference on the relation of jurisdictions of the Church of England and the Old Catholic Church of the Netherlands, the following principles were adopted:[5]

1. Each communion has the right to provide its own ministrations for its own people, whatever they may be, i.e., the Church of England to send its clergy and build churches, etc., in Holland, the Rhineland, Switzerland, and elsewhere, for its own people, and *vice versa,* the Old Catholic Communion to send its clergy and build churches in England for its own people. A clergyman of one Communion when ministering in the church of the other is under the jurisdiction of his own Ordinary and of the Ordinary of the church where he is ministering.
2. It is desirable that, where the two Communions are working in the same locality, their congregations should as far as possible maintain their own distinct life, with their own clergy and liturgy, working in close contact with one another.

On the subject of the practical relations in Holland arising from communion, the conference agreed:

1. That Anglicans wishing to receive Communion in an Old Catholic Church should, if possible, carry a letter of introduction from their own priests.
2. That Anglicans residing in Holland should normally attend their own church.
3. That Anglicans temporarily residing in Holland who are out of reach of their own Church ministrations and wish to receive regular ministrations in an Old Catholic Church should be inscribed in the church in question in accordance with Old Catholic custom.

In 1958, another kind of conference was officially noted by a 1958 Lambeth Conference resolution which "welcomes suggestions made by a meeting between some Anglicans and Old Catholics in Holland, that the two Churches should co-operate in practical action to meet the spiritual needs of Dutch-speaking Christians who wish to resort to Anglican Churches in that country."[6]

Today, bishops of the Old Catholic Churches are not invited to the

Lambeth Conferences, although these churches are invited to send observers along with observers from Churches not in a relationship of
full communion. The Old Catholic Churches are not, however, invited
to meetings of the Anglican Consultative Council.[7] Relations between
the Old Catholic Churches and the Anglican Communion have, therefore, remained mainly regional: Old Catholic Churches of Europe
with the Church of England and the Polish National Catholic Church
with the Episcopal Church in the U.S.

Yet movement of people has produced a situation now where Anglicans from Canada, the United States, Australia, and many other nations are in Europe for shorter or longer periods, as well as people
from England. The need to minister to this "diaspora" has increased
the importance of work with English-speaking and other Anglicans in
Europe. At the same time it is necessary that Anglican congregations
and chaplaincies exercise their ministry in close contact with native
local churches, particularly the Old Catholic Churches with which
they are in full communion, and support their mission. This suggests
the need for wider regional European relationships than now exist,
certainly to include the bishops in full communion, as members of a
college of bishops, regularly meeting and coordinating mission.

In the United States and Canada, both the Polish National Catholic
Church and the two Anglican Churches are native local churches.
The PNCC was constituted between 1897 and 1907 by Polish people
dissatisfied with their position in the Roman Catholic Church in the
U.S., who later undertook a mission in Poland itself.[8] Today the PNCC
has five dioceses and reports about 250,000 members in the United
States and Canada (as well as congregations in Brazil). A number of
Roman Catholic priests joined the PNCC at its beginning, but the first
bishop was not consecrated until 1907 by the Old Catholic Church in
the Netherlands. In recent years, some Anglican and PNCC bishops
and parishes have consulted and cooperated, with some liturgical
sharings, but many Anglican and PNCC people are not aware of the
Concordat and its significance.

In 1976, an earlier "Intercommunion Council" was revived to help
these two Churches move into a more dynamic relationship. A project
to update earlier "Regulations as to Intercommunion" (1947), however, was set aside when, after the decision of the Episcopal Church to
permit ordination of women, the Prime Bishop suspended communion, and the 1978 General Synod of the PNCC terminated sacramental intercommunion. Under the earlier regulations:

> It was agreed that each Church would furnish the other with
> lists of clergy and of parishes. Notices of depositions or suspen-

sions will be sent by the authorities of each Church to the Prime Bishop or to the Presiding Bishop of the other Church.

There was unanimous agreement that at every General Synod of either Church an official representative of the other Church be invited to attend and to bring a message of brotherly greeting. A similar invitation at Diocesan Synods is also desirable. It was also recommended that on such occasions opportunity should be given if possible for intercelebration, a Bishop or priest of the other Church being invited to celebrate at the altar. It was explained that the Diocesan Synods of the Polish National Catholic Church meet every five years, and the General Synod every ten years, the next one being in 1956; while in the Episcopal Church, Diocesan Conventions meet annually and the General Convention every three years, the next being in 1949.

Particular care, it was agreed, must be taken by each Church to respect the disciplinary actions of the other Church, both as to clergy and as to laity. In the case of mixed marriages, the conditions required by both Churches shall be observed.

It was unanimously the view of both Committees that this closer relationship should lead in both Churches to a strengthening of loyalty. Thus it is expected that requests for transfer of membership would need to be considered only rarely, under very special conditions. In the case of clergy, transfer would be permissible only for one in good standing, and then only with the full agreement of the respective Bishops of both Churches. In the case of lay persons, the request should first be submitted to the Bishop of the Church to which that family belongs for his official approval; no pastor should receive members of the other Church without prior notice of such approval by the applicant's Bishop.

The relationship between the Churches, it was agreed, is one of *inter*communion—that is, sacramental communion between two autonomous Churches, each respecting the independence and jurisdiction of the other, and avoiding any actions that would tend to weaken the faith or loyalty of those in its sister Church, while seeking to cultivate all suitable means for increasing mutual acquaintance and fellowship. This is clearly stated in the terms of the Bonn Agreement, which is the basis on which both Churches have entered into the new relationship. In all doubtful matters, the pastors shall seek the counsel of their diocesan Bishops and shall abide by their decisions.[9]

The two churches today, living side by side in North America, still have an opportunity to overcome their isolation and become an example of visible unity in diversity. Significant steps would have to be taken by the two churches, however, before a single college of bishops could become an expression of visible unity and the duty of mutual care and concern be taken seriously. As in Europe, some wider regional North American relationship might be needed.

2. *The Lusitanian Church and the Spanish Reformed Episcopal Church*

These two small Churches in Portugal and Spain began with priests and laity dissatisfied with nineteenth-century developments in the Roman Catholic Church. Both churches view themselves as inheritors of the old peninsular pre-medieval Catholic tradition and of the Anglicanism they met in the nineteenth century. Their existence was brought to the attention of the General Convention of the Episcopal Church in 1883, 1889, and 1892, and their affairs concerned the Lambeth Conferences of 1878, 1888, 1897, and 1908.

Initially (1879), they were placed under the pastoral care of Episcopal Bishop Henry C. Riley of Mexico, but following disagreements with an American board of missions, he was forbidden to exercise episcopal functions in Spain and Portugal in 1883. Responsibility was assumed by a council of three bishops of the Church of Ireland. In 1894 Bishop Cabrera was consecrated the first bishop for the Spanish Church, and over the next twenty years he traveled extensively in Spain and also in Portugal. On his death in 1916 the Church of Ireland again took the two Churches under its guidance. Between 1884 and 1950 fourteen episcopal visitations were made to the two Churches, chiefly by bishops of the Irish Church. All ordinations and confirmations have been performed either by bishops of the Church of Ireland, or by Spanish and Portuguese bishops when these were available.

In recent years the early interest of the Episcopal Church in the affairs of the two Churches was resumed. In 1954 Bishop Keeler of Minnesota visited for confirmations and ordinations. In 1956 he, the Bishop of Northern Indiana, and the Bishop of Meath, Ireland, consecrated Bishop Molina for the Spanish Church. In 1958 Bishop Fiandor was consecrated the first bishop for the Portuguese Church by the bishop of Southwestern Brazil, the Bishop of Meath, and the Bishop of Massachusetts. Bishop Fiandor was succeeded by Bishop Pereira in 1958 and Bishop Molina by Bishop Taibo in 1967.

Local conditions discouraged growth of the two Churches, but they adhered unswervingly to the Anglican pattern of faith, order, worship, and discipline. The 1958 Lambeth Conference resolved that it was "entirely satisfied with reports received on the present doctrine and discipline" of the two Churches and "hopes that the desire of these Churches for the same relationship with Churches of the Anglican Communion as have the Old Catholic Churches will soon be fulfilled." In the same year the General Convention resolved to recognize the two

Churches and initiated discussions looking toward full communion. The 1961 General Convention then proceeded to apply the concordat principle to a new situation:

> RESOLVED, that the General Convention invites the General Synods of the Spanish Reformed Episcopal Church and of the Lusitanian Church, Catholic, Apostolic, Evangelical, to join with it in the following declaration, which shall be effective in each case when adopted by the General Synod of the respective Church:
>
> With gratitude to Almighty God for the blessings bestowed upon each of the Churches, and in appreciation of the fraternal relations which have long existed between them, the Churches recognize each other as a true part of the Holy Catholic Church and declare that they are in full communion with one another on the basis of mutual acceptance of the following Concordat:
>
> (1) Each Communion recognizes the catholicity and independence of the other and maintains its own.
>
> (2) Each Communion agrees to admit members of the other Communion to participate in the Sacraments.
>
> (3) Full Communion does not require from either Communion the acceptance of all doctrinal opinion, sacramental devotion, or liturgical practice characteristic of the other, but implies that each believes the other to hold all the essentials of the Christian Faith.
>
> And furthermore, the Churches pledge themselves to work together in brotherly harmony for the extension of the Gospel of our Lord Jesus Christ, and to give such mutual assistance as they are able.

The final paragraph of this resolution amounts, in effect, to a fourth point of the Bonn Agreement, for it recognizes that the relationship established by a concordat calls for "work together in brotherly harmony" and mutual assistance.

In 1963 the Church of England approved a Concordat with these same two Iberian Churches on the terms of the Bonn Agreement. The commission to examine the faith and order of these Churches reported the "present desire of both Churches not to be absorbed within the Anglican Communion, but to secure full recognition as sister Churches" which "would presumably be along the line of the agreement with the Old Catholics, which recognizes the possibility of local variations in belief and practice while maintaining their fundamental identity with us in Faith and Order."[10] This would be "in harmony with the true spirit of nationality on their own part" and "so far as the Anglican Communion is concerned, it would also accord with the purpose of the Diocese of Gibraltar, which is concerned primarily with shepherding our own people overseas and with maintaining friendly relations with the main Churches in the area in which its jurisdiction lies."

It is noteworthy that the report clearly recognizes that these Churches "struggle to foster and maintain a Church life of a *recognizably Anglican type*" (emphasis added), yet it is not proposed that they be recognized as fully part of the Anglican Communion. The situation of the two Iberian Churches thus differed from that of the Old Catholic Churches, the former being Anglican "type" and the latter being Old Catholic "type." Again, the two Iberian Churches received their episcopate from the Anglican Churches, whereas the Old Catholic Churches already had an episcopate. Lastly, these two Churches were isolated national Churches, and the Old Catholic Churches were a "world family of churches," though limited to ten nations of Europe and America.

The two Iberian Churches might have been admitted then to full membership in the Anglican Communion had it not been for the concern about preserving their own "nationality" and the concern about relations with the Roman Catholic Churches of Spain and Portugal. Matters have since altered in both respects, as will be noted later. Implicit recognition was, however, given to the fact that the two Churches were "Anglican" and isolated when a metropolitical authority was provided from an Irish, if not from an English source. Beginning from the consecration of Bishop Cabrera in 1894, a "provisional council" of bishops drawn from the Church of Ireland was responsible for safeguarding the Faith and Order of the two Churches. The original agreement was:[11]

> The Synod of each Church (in the Lusitanian Church called the Electoral Assembly) shall be pledged—
> (a) Not to permit the election or consecration of any bishop for the said Church without the written consent of the provisional council of bishops;
> (b) Not to alter or add to the doctrines, formularies, or discipline of the said Church without the previous approval of the provisional council.
> (c) To submit for the examination and sanction of the provisional council every resolution of a fundamental character that may be proposed for adoption by a future Synod.

This "provisional council" was to end at the date when there should be three bishops in each Church. It appears that substantial growth was expected, allowing each autonomous national Church to have its own house of bishops. It was left ambiguous whether at some future time these might become Anglican provinces. The 1963 report of the Church of England itself comments, "We consider that the Constitutions of both Churches sufficiently indicate their intention to maintain an ordered Church life recognizable within the Anglican pattern, though capable at some points of further clarification within the Constitutions themselves."

In 1964 the "(Provisional) Council of Bishops" was altered to provide wider contact between the two Iberian bishops and those of other Churches to help them share more fully in the universal Church. Members of the Council were now the Archbishop of Armagh (chairman); Bishops nominated by the English metropolitans, the Archbishop of Utrecht, and the Presiding Bishop of the Episcopal Church in the U.S.; the Bishop of Lebombo; the Obispo Maximo of the Philippine Independent Church; a bishop of the Brazilian Episcopal Church; and the Portuguese and Spanish bishops. This geographical dispersion has actually prevented the Council from functioning effectively, though its objects, agreed to by the Spanish and Portuguese Synods, are otherwise sound:[12]

(a) To ensure continuation of full communion between the Peninsular Churches and the others represented in the Council;

(b) To give advice to the peninsular bishops or their synods on all subjects that may be submitted or when "motu Proprio" they may deem it advisable to offer an opinion;

(c) To promote unity of procedure on all questions concerning the ecumenical movement;

(d) To voice an opinion on any alteration of Canons, Liturgy or Doctrine of the two Peninsular Churches;

(e) To ratify the election of Bishops in the said Churches and to make provision for their consecration, in agreement with the Church interested.

The two Iberian Churches signed a Concordat with the Old Catholic Churches at Vienna in 1965. In Europe today there is some coordination between Anglican work with English-speaking people and the Iberian Churches. The Episcopal Church in the U.S. provides small annual grants for the two Churches, and some dioceses in its Spanish-speaking Ninth Province have given support. The Spanish and Portuguese Church Aid Society in England maintains links and supports the two Churches. The two Churches are not permitted membership in the Anglican Consultative Council and their bishops are not invited to the Lambeth Conference, although both churches are invited to send observers.

Substantial change in Portugal and Spain has brought increased freedom of religion. The earlier danger that closer ties between the Portuguese and Spanish Churches with the churches of the Anglican

Communion "might conceivably give rise to criticism of a political character"[13] no longer exists. The close ecumenical relations between the two Churches themselves with the Roman Catholic Church in Spain and Portugal means the earlier danger that Church of England chaplaincy relations with the Roman Catholic Church would be affected no longer exists. The danger that Spanish and Portuguese "nationality" would be subordinated to English or any other "nationality" if the two Churches were to be part of the Anglican Communion is eliminated by the great variety of new nationalities now already in the Anglican Communion, including the Spanish-speaking Anglican dioceses in the Americas and the Portuguese-speaking Episcopal Church of Brazil.

Conditions are present for a further evolution in the incorporation of the Portuguese and Spanish Churches within the Anglican Communion. A consultation arranged by the Anglican Consultative Council in 1978 recommended full membership, and the 1978 Lambeth Conference responded positively. In Europe there is a collegial role which can be shared among the bishops of the Iberian local Churches, bishops of the Anglican chaplaincies to English-speaking people in Europe, and perhaps by bishops of the Old Catholic local Churches. Once again, greater regional European coordination of mission is indicated.

3. Philippine Independent Church

The origins of the Philippine Independent Church[14] are closely connected with the native revolt against Spanish rule that culminated in armed conflict during the late nineteenth century. Anti-clericalism was part of the revolt because the episcopate was exclusively Spanish and religious orders had become extensive and oppressive landowners. After the Spanish-American war and the purchase of the Philippines from Spain by the United States, the movement for an autonomous national catholic church led to the election of Filipino priests as bishops of new dioceses. Their hope for communion with Rome was not fulfilled.

After the Philippine Independent Church was established in 1902, Gregorio Aglipay began to make a number of innovations and it soon became apparent that some of the leaders were passing under strong Unitarian influence. Approaches to obtain the episcopate, made early in the century both to the Episcopal Church through its Philippine missionary district and to the Old Catholic Church of Switzerland, failed. Nevertheless Aglipay kept alive in his Church a sense of the defective nature of their orders and a desire to receive the apostolic succession.

After the election of Isabelo De Los Reyes as Obispo Maximo in 1946, a Declaration of Faith and Articles of Religion and a Constitution were adopted by the 1947 General Assembly. At the same meeting it was resolved to petition the Episcopal Church for the gift of apostolic succession. In the same year the House of Bishops of the Episcopal Church approved the petition and in 1948 the bishops of the Philippine Independent Church were consecrated and all the priests were episcopally ordained as deacons and then priests. In an account of these proceedings to the 1948 Lambeth Conference, it was emphasized that sole responsibility for the action rested with the House of Bishops of the Episcopal Church, but the hope was expressed that other steps would soon be taken for communion between the two Churches.

Close relations were established over the next ten years between the Episcopal missionary district in the Philippines and the Philippine Independent Church, and it was agreed that all clergy of the Independent Church would receive their theological training in the Episcopal seminary in Manila.

The 1958 Lambeth Conference passed a resolution expressing "its pleasure at the vigorous growth of the Philippine Independent Church" and welcoming "the progress being made between this Church and the Protestant Episcopal Church in the United States of America since the consecration of three bishops of the Philippine Independent Church . . ."

In 1960 the Independent Church made another move when the Supreme Council of Bishops proposed full communion with the Episcopal Church on the basis of the Bonn Agreement. This proposal was approved by the House of Bishops of the Episcopal Church later that year, supported by the Convention of the Philippine Episcopal Church in 1961, and finally approved by the 1961 General Convention of the Episcopal Church in a resolution containing this clause: "Whereas the Declaration of the Faith, the Articles of Religion, the Constitution, Canons, and other official formularies of the Iglesia Filipina Independiente embody and affirm adherence to principles of faith and order, discipline and worship that mark it as a true part of the One, Holy, Catholic, and Apostolic Church: Therefore be it Resolved . . ." Other Churches of the Anglican Communion have followed with concordats on similar lines.[15] A concordat between the Old Catholic Churches and the Independent Church was signed at Vienna in 1965.

The same 1961 General Convention of the Episcopal Church, with the concurrence of the Supreme Council of Bishops of the Independent Church, passed a "Resolution of Implementation" requesting the

Presiding Bishop and the Supreme Bishop, acting together, to establish and appoint a Joint Council of the Episcopal Church and the Philippine Independent Church with the Episcopal Bishop of the Philippines as chairman. The Council was to have equal representation of bishops, priests, and laity from the Philippine Episcopal Church and the Independent Church, two ex-offficio members from the U.S. Episcopal Church's ecumenical commissions, and the Executive Officer of the Anglican Communion (for liaison with the entire Anglican Communion). Grants were made from the Episcopal Church for a liaison officer between the two Churches and support of Joint Council personnel and program.

The next General Convention of the Episcopal Church in 1964 resolved these purposes for the Joint Council:

1. To promote mutual understanding between the two churches.
2. To direct a program which will assist the mutual growth and interdependence of these two Churches in the One, Holy, Catholic, and Apostolic Church.
3. To assist both the Philippine Independent Church and the Philippine Episcopal Church in matters crucial to their life and work, and
4. To direct and support joint projects of the Philippine Independent Church and the Philippine Episcopal Church.

The expansion and development of the work led the same Convention to reorganize the Joint Council to "advance the interests of mutual responsibility as between the two Churches" and aid in "the development and mission of the One, Holy, Catholic, and Apostolic Church in the Republic of the Philippines." This involved the addition of the Obispo Maximo and the Presiding Bishop as alternating chairmen of the Joint Council, and the appointment by the Presiding Bishop, with the approval of the Supreme Bishop, of an Executive Director of the Joint Council. As the Philippine Independent Church had been granted full membership in the (Anglican) Council of the Church of East Asia in 1963, provision was also made for this regional organization to appoint a member to the Joint Council. In the same Resolution, the Joint Council was instructed to concern itself primarily with Christian education, stewardship and evangelism, leadership-training programs, operation of schools and other institutions, and college work.

This was the most elaborate organizational mechanism yet invented between two concordat churches. In 1976 a Concordat Study Commission was authorized by the Joint Council to appraise past accomplishments and project future directions. Its 1977 report criticized the Joint Council as seeming independent of both Churches, its policies and decisions being made by a small group of leaders with implementation left to personnel of the Council, and funds coming directly from the Episcopal Church in the U.S. The report says the Joint Council has been called a "super church" and a "wedge" rather than a "bridge" between the two Churches. The Executive Director had power to allocate special funds to both Churches at his discretion and personnel of the Council could work in the field without coordination with the central offices of the two Churches or with the diocesan authority.

Actions have now been initiated to replace the Joint Council with a Concordat Council and to abolish the office of Executive Director. The senior bishop of the Philippine Episcopal Church replaces the Presiding Bishop as Episcopal chairman of the Council, finances are handled through the heads of the two Philippine Churches, and a coordinator of joint work is appointed by the two "head bishops." In a later phase of the reorganization, all structures except the Concordat Council, which is to become advisory, will be absorbed by the national offices of the two head bishops (of the Philippine Independent Church and of the Philippine Episcopal Church).

Substantial accomplishments of the Joint Council were nevertheless described in the 1977 Study Report, including the Council's witness to the commitment of the two Churches to seek and exploit opportunities for partnership in mission. The report says the terms of the Concordat itself, as well as the guidelines for their implementation by the Joint Council, not only promoted the understanding and practical manifestations of the *interdependence* of the two Churches but have clearly sought to preserve the *independence* of each as well. As to the future, the report calls attention to the endeavors of the Philippine Episcopal Church to become autonomous and its desire to keep open and in mind "the question of the affiliation of the PEC with other ecclesiastical bodies in the region, now loosely associated in the Council of the Church in East Asia." This "possible development will depend in large measure upon the needs of mission in the Philippines and in the wider region."

The section of the report on the needs of mission and their effect on the Concordat recognizes that both Churches have identified financial self-sufficiency as the top priority of and for mission in the Philippines. Each Church is developing its own plan based on its own needs, but the goal is the same. The obvious question is, "To what extent can the shared experience, goodwill and expertise of the churches in Concordat be utilized to assist both of them in the realization of a common end?" The answer: "If it is only in the realm or at the level of exchange of information and sharing of personnel, mutual assessment of procedures and results, shared advice and counsel, the conciliar patterns in general, and the envisaged Concordat Council in particular, should be of considerable help to PEC and PIC alike." A similar observation is made about other areas of common mission such as "human development." The future holds "insistent opportunity for sharing. The insistence may, in fact, be a divine imperative."

The report endorses the experience of exchange of priests as bringing the two Churches closer together, but asks for guidelines agreed by both Churches. A second example of mutual growth and interdependence is cited as being joint ministry in one congregation, but again guidelines are needed. Priests in joint ministries must presently keep two sets of registry books for the two Churches on baptism, marriage, burial, confirmation, and all sacramental services, and certificates should record the membership of the concerned parties. A third example of mutual growth is a common pension plan for the two Churches.

The report singles out conciliar relationships as a basic form of mutual growth and interdependence: "In council, whether formal or informal, representatives of both churches can get together to discuss common problems and plans of action on the regional, diocesan and parish levels. . . . It should be borne in mind that this relationship should not be simply in direct material assistance but also in consultation and exchange of new ideas for mutual growth and interdependence." The Joint Council is itself a conciliar relationship.

Ministry to the many Filipinos moving to the United States has also been studied and the Joint Council in the 1977 Report asked for agreed procedures to guide overseas ministries as the relationship between the two Churches evolves. Sometimes the Episcopal Church has assumed full responsibility to minister to members of the Philippine Independent Church in the U.S., while making every effort to be sensitive to uphold and preserve the integrity and uniqueness of the culture and tradition of the Philippine Independent Church. In other cases in the U.S., congregations established for Philippine Independent members have not been assumed to belong to the Episcopal Church, but to be part of the Philippine Independent Church, yet their care has been committed to the local Episcopal bishop by the Supreme Bishop. The Presiding Bishop of the Episcopal Church has suggested an annual visitation by the Supreme Bishop or his representative to meet the scattered flock of the Philippine Independent Church being ministered to by the Episcopal Church in the U.S.

The Philippine Independent Church is a developing Church and one which desires the closest relations with the whole Anglican Communion. At the same time it is a Church which maintains its own identity, which includes many traditions of Spanish-Filipino catholicism. In the Philippines "mutual growth and interdependence" of the Independent and Episcopal Churches is fostered in many ways, but particularly through the Joint Council, the one seminary, and the new order of Mass in English and Filipino dialects which is being adopted in many congregations of the 29 dioceses of the Independent Church and the three dioceses of the Episcopal Church. This Independent Church of two and a half million people is related to other Anglican Churches of the region through the Council of the Church in East Asia. Both it and the Philippine Episcopal Church, itself moving toward autonomy, may in future seek a closer partnership with these other Churches. In such ways the Philippine Independent Church shares more fully in the universal Church. At present, however, it is not permitted to be a member of the Anglican Consultative Council and its bishops are not invited to the Lambeth Conference, although it is invited to send observers.

4. *The Mar Thoma Syrian Church of Malabar*

The Mar Thoma Syrian Church of Malabar owes its independent and separate existence (1880) to a reform which took place in the Syrian Orthodox Church (Jacobite), partly under the influence of Anglican (Church Missionary Society) missionaries in Malabar in the nineteenth century. This Church is unique in preserving features of Eastern traditional forms of worship and Western reformation principles.[16]

In 1937 the Church of India, Burma, and Ceylon, having found no impediment in the Faith and Order of this Church, established limited and partial intercommunion with the Mar Thoma Church, and drew the attention of the other Churches of the Anglican Communion to this action. There had been a wide dispersion of members of the Mar Thoma Church of Malabar throughout India and beyond leading to the establishment of missions and congregations in several places. The 1948 Lambeth Conference committee on unity report suggested that the Church of India, Burma, and Ceylon and other dioceses concerned should feel at liberty to provide for episcopal supervision of these dispersed members on the request of the authorities of the Mar Thoma Church. A special note was added that "nothing should be done which is likely gravely to prejudice those wider relationships" with all the Eastern Churches.

Conversations between the two Churches began in 1957 with a view to revision and extension of the 1937 agreement. In 1960 the Church

of India, Pakistan, Burma and Ceylon, after notifying the Syrian Orthodox Churches in India, established a concordat with the Mar
Thoma Syrian Church and agreed on Rules of Comity:

1. On ecumenical occasions, and at other common gatherings
   when members of both Churches are present together at the
   Holy Communion, members of either Church may receive
   communion when the celebrant is of the other.
2. Persons seeking to change their membership from the Mar
   Thoma Church to the Anglican Church or vice versa shall be
   admitted to such new membership only after they produce a
   certificate signed both by the pastor of the congregation and by
   the Bishop of the Church to which they have belonged
   hitherto. Such certificate shall not ordinarily be issued until a
   period of at least three months has elapsed after it has been
   applied for. In a place where there is no parish priest of one of
   the Churches, the Bishop of the other shall inform the Metropolitan of the church whose member wishes to change his
   membership, before allowing him to be received.
3. The same procedure shall be followed in the case of those who
   may seek admission into the Anglican or Mar Thoma Church
   even from any other Church, if they were members of the
   Anglican or Mar Thoma Church at any period within three
   years before applying for such admission. In issuing certificates of admission the bishops will require information on this
   point.
4. Subject to rule (5) below, the Pastors of either Church shall
   have authority and discretion to admit to the Holy Communion communicant members of good standing in the other
   Church in places where they have no access to the ministrations of the Church to which they belong.
5. A pastor of either Church may require a certificate of good
   standing from a member of the other Church before admitting him regularly to Holy Communion. Such a certificate
   should be signed by a pastor of the Church of the member
   concerned.
6. Even in places where a member has access to the ministrations
   of his own Church he may on particular occasions be allowed
   to communicate in the other Church. In such cases the procedure laid down in rule 5 shall be followed, but the certificate to
   be produced in such cases must state not only that the member
   is a communicant of good standing in his own Church but also
   that his own Pastor approves of his being admitted to the Holy
   Communion in the other Church.
7. The existing rules obtaining between the two Churches regarding marriages (Deshakuri, Pasaram, etc.) shall continue to
   be observed until altered by mutual consent.
8. In the event of a member of the Mar Thoma Syrian Church
   taking up work in the sphere and jurisdiction of an Anglican
   diocese he may, with the approval of his Metropolitan, be

granted the status of membership of the Anglican Communion in that diocese by the Anglican Bishop concerned, during the period of his work there on the understanding that he does not cease to be a member of the Mar Thoma Syrian Church. At any particular time he can participate in the government of one Church only, by the exercise of vote and holding office.

9. Bishops of Provinces or of Missionary Dioceses of the Anglican Communion may be asked to exercise episcopal supervision over Clergy and Laity of the Mar Thoma Church at the request of the authorities of that Church (see Lambeth Conference Report 1948, Part II, p. 72).

In 1963 the Episcopal Synod of the Church of India, Pakistan, Burma and Ceylon passed the following resolution:

The Synod welcomes the desire of the Mar Thoma Syrian Church for mutual participation in Episcopal consecration and resolves that the Bishops of the C.I.P.B.C. may accept any invitation to such participation from the Mar Thoma Syrian Church subject to the permission of the Metropolitan, and that when convenient Mar Thoma Bishops be invited to take part in the consecration of C.I.P.B.C. Bishops.

The Anglican Consultative Council in 1973 encouraged "Churches of the Anglican Communion to enter into the same kind of relationship with the Mar Thoma Syrian Church as that which most of them already enjoy with the Old Catholics and other Churches in terms of the Bonn Agreement." The Episcopal Church responded in a resolution of the 1976 General Convention "that this Church, noting that the Mar Thoma Syrian Church of Malabar is a true part of the Church Universal holding the catholic faith and possessing the apostolic ministry of bishops, priests and deacons, enter into communion with that Church . . ." In this way, therefore, a concordat similar to but slightly different from the Bonn Agreement was established.

There have been a sufficient number of Mar Thoma Christians to form congregations outside India only in East Africa, the Persian Gulf, and Malaysia, but recent Indian immigration to the United States has led to the formation of several congregations here. Such overseas congregations are under the pastoral oversight of one of the Mar Thoma diocesan bishops in India. Discussion has begun about relating U.S. congregations to diocesan bishops of the Episcopal Church.

In India, the Mar Thoma Church is in full communion with the (united) Church of South India and the Church of North India. The three Churches are now taking steps which will lead to one national

Church in which their traditions will be maintained. The Mar Thoma Church is not a member of the Anglican Consultative Council and its bishops are not invited to the Lambeth Conference, although it is invited to send observers.

A Larger Episcopal Unity

Our examination has shown the distinctiveness of each concordat relationship, depending on the history and condition of the particular local churches. It has also shown elements common to them all. As a convenient measuring stick we use the signs of visible unity identified in the "Pillars of Light" report of the 1976 Anglican Consultative Council.[17]

	Old Cath.	Iberian Churches	Philippine Independent	Mar Thoma
The confession of a common faith	X	X	X	X
Mutual recognition of membership	X	X	X	X
Interchangeability of ministries	X	X	X	X
Complete eucharistic fellowship	X	X	X	X
Sharing of resources		X	X	
Streamlining of structures			X	
Maintenance and development of such diversity as enriches the whole church	X	X	X	X

The four concordats are based on the presence of catholic plenitude in each church, in doctrine, ministry, and sacraments, and they witness to this unity through sacramental communion. Two of the four witness to this unity through common action (sharing resources) and only one has produced alteration of structures (streamlining). We may say that the Churches of the Anglican Communion and the four concordat Churches have recognized their deeper unity in continuity of doctrine, ministry, and sacraments with the ancient church before any break or schism, but they have not really recognized their deeper unity in continuity with the ancient church in apostolic mission nor witnessed to this unity through common action. For this a Church would need to maintain "sustained and sustaining relationships with her sister churches, expressed in conciliar gatherings whenever required for the development of their common calling."[18]

It has usually been assumed that visible unity is to be sought for the sake of mission. Experience with the concordats seems to show that mission is not simply a consequence of visible unity, but is itself a sign of unity and may lead to unity.

A significant feature of the concordat is that the agreement is one of a series, pivotal to be sure, of events and developments which precede and follow. One further development has, in part, arisen from experience of the concordats, the idea of a larger episcopal unity to give expression to the mutual care and aid which should be expressed between sister churches.

A resolution of the 1948 Lambeth Conference welcomed the fact that Anglican Churches were already in full communion with the Old Catholic Churches and looked forward to the time when Anglicans would be in communion "with other parts of the Catholic Church not definable as Anglican," and therefore desired that "Churches thus linked together should express their common relationship in common counsel and mutual aid." It therefore recommended that "bishops of the Anglican Communion and bishops of other Churches which are, or may be, in communion with them should meet together from time to time as an episcopal conference, advisory in character, for brotherly counsel and encouragement."

The Lambeth bishops also had in mind the Churches of Sweden, Finland, Latvia, and Estonia, loyal to the Lutheran Confession and members of the Lutheran World Federation, but sharing the historic episcopate and having a limited intercommunion with certain Churches of the Anglican Communion. The report of the 1948 Lambeth committee on unity (the reports do not have the same authority as resolutions) viewed a wider conference of bishops as a way to grow together and develop a common conciliar life. They recognized that the number of bishops would be few but said "the time may come when other episcopal Churches—the Eastern Orthodox, the Lesser Eastern Churches, and Churches formed perhaps on lines resembling the Church of South India, will send their delegates too."

Nothing happened, so a resolution of the 1958 Lambeth Conference strongly recommended that within the next five years the Archbishop of Canterbury should "invite to a conference representative bishops from each Province of the Anglican Communion, together with representative bishops from each Church possessing the historic episcopate with which Churches and Provinces of the Anglican Communion are in full communion or in a relationship of intercommunion."[19]

From the 1958 Lambeth committee report on unity we learn that the bishops now were concerned for bishops in those parts of the Anglican Communion which might join united Churches such as the Church of South India then recently inaugurated, and saw the risk of new united Churches "becoming isolated from the main stream of Catholic tradition and the life of the Church Universal." The commit-

tee made a "radical" recommendation, which the Lambeth Conference referred to the consideration of the Archbishop of Canterbury
and the Consultative Body, that when a Church belonging to the
Anglican Communion decides, with the encouragement of the Lambeth Conference, to join a united Church, the bishops, or representative bishops, of the united Church should be invited to attend the
Lambeth Conferences as members.

Next, a meeting of 39 bishops took place in 1964 at Canterbury,
constituting what was called the Wider Episcopal Fellowship. These
bishops were from the concordat Churches, the four Lutheran
Churches, and the (united) Church of South India. Bishops of the
Church of South India were not, however, invited to be members of
the next Lambeth Conference.

The 1968 Lambeth Conference, taking a slightly different line, resolved to recommend that a General Episcopal Consultation (drawn
from many countries) be held in the near future, expressing the hope
that the Archbishop of Canterbury would take the initiative in sending
invitations "primarily" to those Churches in full communion or intercommunion. It also recommended that Regional Episcopal Consultations should be held on a wider basis of representation than that
suggested for the General Episcopal Consultation.

Nothing happened. The goal of some kind of larger episcopal conference to be a sign of the episcopate as a center of unity has continued
to be set forth, but the variety of ways proposed to do this is a sign of
the ambiguity of attitudes towards it. The confusion arises because
two distinct purposes have been mixed: (1) a "larger" episcopal conference of Anglicans and other bishops in full communion, and (2) a still
"wider" episcopal conference to include bishops not in communion
with Anglicans. Today we would wish to have the "widest" episcopal
conference, including Roman Catholic bishops. Yet as long as the conference is "advisory," for "brotherly counsel and encouragement," and
has only representative bishops of the several traditions, this "widest"
episcopal conference is possible and deserves exploration with other
Churches. It could be a major contribution to the ecumenical
movement.

The first purpose, a conference of bishops of Churches in full
communion with each other as a college of bishops, is more urgent. A
resolution of Lambeth 1968 recommended that "the principle of collegiality should be a guiding principle in the growth of relationships
between the provinces of the Anglican Communion and those
Churches with which we are or shall be in full communion." According to this advice, bishops in full communion ought to attend Lambeth

(or its successor) as members. What fundamental difference would there be between such a larger episcopal conference and the present Lambeth Conference?

The first Lambeth Conference took place in response to a letter of invitation from Archbishop Longley of Canterbury in 1867. The invitation specified the attendance "not only of our Home and Colonial Bishops, but of all who are avowedly in communion with our Church." Eucharistic communion with the United Church of England and Ireland, the see of Canterbury at its head, was the principle that determined membership, but in practice only Anglican bishops were in communion with Canterbury. At the Conference the question of the nature and authority of the new gathering was explored. Synodical authority was rejected: "Its decisions could only possess the authority which might be derived from the moral weight of such united counsels and judgments, and from the voluntary acceptance of its conclusions by any of the Churches there represented." The consultative nature of the Conference and its moral authority, as well as the voluntary acceptance of its conclusions, have been reaffirmed by successive Conferences.

At Lambeth in 1897, the "well-being of the Church" was thought to call for meetings of the "Bishops of the whole Anglican Communion" to consider "questions that may arise affecting the Church of Christ." In a committee report we see growing awareness of "the expansion and consequent importance of our duty to maintain and develop the unity and coherence of the Anglican Communion." The conference resolved that resolutions should be "formally communicated" to the churches "for their consideration, and for such action as may seem to them desirable." However, it also resolved that the conditions of membership of the Lambeth Conferences should remain unaltered from the Encyclical Letter of 1878 (substantially the same in the Letter of 1888): "Archbishops, Bishops Metropolitan and other bishops of the Holy Catholic Church, in full communion with the Church of England . . . all exercising superintendence over Dioceses, or lawfully commissioned to exercise Episcopal functions therein . . ."

The 1930 Lambeth Conference took another step when it defined the nature and status of the Anglican Communion:

> The Anglican Communion is a fellowship, within the One Holy Catholic and Apostolic Church, of those duly constituted Dioceses, Provinces or Regional Churches in communion with the See of Canterbury, which have the following characteristics in common:
> (a) They uphold and propagate the Catholic and Apostolic faith

(b)   and order as they are generally set forth in the Book of Common Prayer as authorized in their several Churches;

(b)   They are particular or national Churches, and, as such, promote within each of their territories a national expression of Christian faith, life and worship; and

(c)   They are bound together not by a central legislative and executive authority, but by mutual loyalty sustained through the common counsel of the Bishops in conference.

The committee report on the Anglican Communion also spoke of the ideal of the "Catholic Church in its entirety" and of the Anglican Communion in its present character as "transitional." In 1948 the Lambeth Conference committee on the Anglican Communion looked forward to the time "when the Anglican Communion itself will once again become part of a reunited Christendom."

Recent Lambeth Conferences add nothing fundamental to our understanding of their membership, nature, and authority. They remain advisory and consultative, their authority is moral and spiritual, and their membership is theoretically all bishops in communion with Canterbury but practically it is only Anglican type bishops, a contradiction which remains to be resolved.

A More Diverse Communion of Churches

The Anglican Communion has existed as such only since the second half of the nineteenth century. As it grew and extended it became more diverse. As early as 1930 a Lambeth Conference report stated that "the term 'Anglican' is no longer used in the sense it originally bore. The phrase 'Ecclesia Anglicana' in the Magna Carta had a purely local connotation. Now its sense is ecclesiastical and doctrinal, and the Anglican Communion includes not merely those who are racially connected with England, but many others whose faith has been grounded in the doctrines and ideals for which the Church of England has always stood." Today Anglican native local churches are found throughout the world, in Africa, Asia, Spanish America, and French-speaking areas, as well as in the British Isles, North America, and Australia. Despite diverse languages, nations, cultures, and liturgies, all are of the historic Anglican "type."[20]

Anglicans have grown accustomed to the term "sister churches," meaning families of Churches such as the Anglican reconciled with one another in faith, sacrament, and ministry, maintaining and developing their theological approaches, liturgical expressions, spiritual and devotional traditions, and canon laws, and meeting with other Churches as required. True ecumenism does not desire the destruction of Christian cultures and their assimilation into one; rather it glories in diversity, provided that there be charity and the spirit of truth, unity, and concord, to govern the whole. To realize in full communion the truth of our baptismal unity would seem to be a proper ecumenical aim.

The form of unity specific to the Church is communion. It is not something we achieve by human effort but is God's gift to us. Communion does not mean one Church will absorb the other or that they will both be absorbed by a bigger Church. The aim is not a new political structure with a new constitution. Each type of Church will retain and develop its own identity, character, ethos, and distinctive qualities. We know, however, that communion should mean a broader *koinonia* than simply recognizing each other's sacraments and offering each other access to them. It means a sharing of spiritual activity and resources. Studies of "conciliar fellowship" by the World Council of Churches, and the 1976 report on unity from the Anglican Consultative Council point in the direction of some form of conciliar arrangement (not synods) between Churches in full communion in order to express the binding common purpose of witness and service. Finding ways for dioceses and Churches in full communion to move into such a partnership with one another ought to have high priority in the Anglican Communion. It offers a way of viewing the movement toward unity of all Churches.

It will be essential in this task, however, to concentrate primarily on the mission of episcopal Churches which share the Eucharist, rather than on organization or hierarchy or administrative jurisdiction. The episcopate is peculiarly suited to this task as "an extension of the apostolic office and function in both time and space," not only as guardian of the faith and father of the people, but also as "the driving force of mission."

> The principle underlying *collegiality* is that the apostolic calling, responsibility, and authority are an inheritance given to the whole body or college of bishops. Every individual bishop has a responsibility both as a member of this college and as chief pastor in his diocese. In the former capacity he shares with bishops throughout the world a concern for the well being of the whole Church.[21]

The Anglican Communion can act on this belief. The Lambeth Conference and Anglican Consultative Council could initiate study and action which will lead to inviting all bishops (or representative bishops) in communion with the see of Canterbury to the next Lambeth Conference (or its successor): Old Catholic type, Philippine Independent type, Mar Thoma type, "united" type. What witness of catholicity this would make!

The bishops prepare the community for its mission of evangelization and service to the world, but mission involves the complementary activity of the entire Church, laity and clergy. Study and action should, therefore, lead to the Anglican Consultative Council including in its membership representatives of Churches in full communion with·Anglican Churches. The ACC has already managed to include the "united" Churches of South India, North India, and Pakistan, which are not Anglican, though they incorporate former dioceses of the Anglican Communion. As the Council is responsible for "promoting the unity, renewal, and mission of Christ's Church," the inclusion of the Old Catholic, Philippine Independent, and Mar Thoma Churches seems theologically imperative.

In appropriate regions of the world, too, partnership with concordat Churches can be intensified or established. There is need for autonomy and independence in matters affecting the internal life or structure of each Church, but there is also the necessity of a common mind, expressed through conclusions of the bishops and others meeting in conferences or council in matters of common and general concern.

In Europe, the Old Catholic Churches, native to seven nations, and the Iberian (Anglican type) Churches in Spain and Portugal are in communion, but have no regular conciliar means for partnership, consultation, and coordination. The existing small College of Bishops in Europe, composed of bishops of the English and American jurisdictions for English-speaking people in Europe, and the small Anglican Advisory Council in Europe, with clergy and lay members, are bodies where native and English-speaking Churches could share common problems while maintaining independence. If they became participants, it could lead to such further steps as cooperation through the national or regional archdeaconries and ultimately perhaps to a grouping modeled on the Council of the Church in East Asia. Europe is a dynamic region, has many important centers of Christianity, is passing through great change, and receives people from many parts of the world, and these are all mission concerns.

In North America, the Polish National Catholic Church and the Anglican Churches have need of partnership in mission and conciliar relationships, perhaps through the Intercommunion Council with the Episcopal Church, perhaps through a renewed regional "Anglican Council of North America."

In the Philippines, partnership between the Philippine Independent Church and the Philippine Episcopal Church has grown since the concordat. Membership of the Independent Church in the (Anglican) Council of East Asia is a model for Europe and North America.

In India, the Mar Thoma Church is seeking partnership through conciliar relations with the (united) Church of South India and the Church of North India. Though the united Churches have the burden of relating equally to the Reformed and Methodist as well as to the Anglican world families of Churches, their bishops could be invited to the Lambeth Conference (or its successor) and partnership in mission could be developed with the Anglican Churches. The same is true of the (united) Churches of Pakistan and Bangladesh.

In such ways these churches—and the Anglican Churches—may all share more fully in the universal Church. The emphasis in this paper on the future possibilities of universal, regional, and national collegiality and partnership should not, however, leave the impression that concordats have no impact on the local churches. Significant examples of local partnership can be cited in the Philippines, in help to Old Catholics in Europe to rebuild after World War II, and in other places. The point is that partnership in mission can and should increase locally, nationally, regionally, and universally. Granted that every expression of visible unity has an element of provisionality, the concordat is a model as well as a means of visible unity with considerable potential.

NOTES

1. A concordat in which Anglicans are not involved in the Leunenberg Agreement, or Statement of Concord, completed in 1973 and signed by most of the Lutheran and Reformed Churches in Europe along with the Union Churches that grew out of them, and the related pre-Reformation Churches, the Waldensian Church and the Church of the Czech Brethren. Further see *Lutheran World*, vol. 20, no. 4, 1973, pp. 347–353; and vol. 21, no. 4, 1974, pp. 328–348.
2. *Report of the Meeting of the Commission of the Anglican Communion and the Old Catholic Churches* held at Bonn on Thursday, July 2, 1931, p. 37.
3. *Ibid.*, p. 7. Further on the Bonn Agreement, see *Journal of the General Convention*, 1940, pp. 236–237; C. B. Moss, *The Old Catholic Movement—Its Origins and History* (London: SPCK, 1964), pp. 340–351; Andreas Rinkel, "Intercommunion: Its Basis, Content, and Consequences," in *Anglican Theological Review* 38 (1956), pp. 54–70; and G. K. A. Bell, *Documents on Christian Unity: Third Series 1930–48* (London, 1948), pp. 60–62. Further on concordats generally, see Stephen F. Bayne, Jr., "Concordats and Companionship," in *Anglican World*, vol. 1 (June/July 1961), pp. 9–11, 67; reprinted in Bayne, *An Anglican Turning-Point* (Austin, 1964), pp. 290–296.
4. *Report of the Meeting*, p. 10.

5. *The Lambeth Conference* 1948 (London: SPCK, 1948), pp. 73–74.

6. *Lambeth Conference* 1958, p. 1.40 f. and 2.53.

7. A 1972 meeting in Trier of Anglican, Lusitanian, Old Catholic, and Spanish Reformed Episcopal bishops recommended that Old Catholic and Iberian bishops should be represented on The Anglican Consultative Council. This recommendation was referred to the latter body in 1973, which welcomed the developing collaboration and fellowship between these Churches in Europe, but felt the invitation would need to be further extended to the Philippine Independent Church, and that the Council "needed some time to find its feet and consider its role before it was ready to take so decisive a step . . . in further extending its membership beyond the Anglican Communion." In the case of the united Churches in India and Pakistan, "which are already members of the ACC, the Council thought the position was somewhat different, as the united Churches incorporated the former Anglican Churches in those countries." The Council declined to accept the recommendation "at the present moment, but . . . in a few years' time it should be considered again" (*Partners in Mission: Anglican Consultative Council, Report of the Second Meeting, Dublin, 1973*, pp. 65–66). At the next meeting in 1976, a request from Archbishop Kok that the Old Catholic Church participate in ACC meetings was denied on the ground that "as to admit one such Church must involve admitting several, the whole nature of the ACC would be changed" and it was decided that "such participation would not in fact be permissible under the ACC Constitution" (*Anglican Consultative Council, Report of the Third Meeting, Trinidad, 1976*, p. 68).

8. Further see Theodore Andrews, *The Polish National Catholic Church in America and Poland* (London: SPCK, 1953); Warren C. Platt, "The Polish National Catholic Church: An Inquiry into Its Origins," in *Church History* 46:4 (1977), pp. 474–489; and Laurence Orzell, *Rome and the Validity of Orders in the Polish National Catholic Church* (Scranton, 1977).

9. Bell, *Documents: Third Series 1930–48*, pp. 62–63.

10. *The Faith and Order of the Lusitanian and Spanish Reformed Episcopal Churches*, Report of the Commission appointed by the Archbishop of Canterbury (London: Church Information Office, 1963). Further see Louis Haselmeyer, "The Lusitanian Church of Portugal," in *Historical Magazine of the Protestant Episcopal Church*, vol. xix (1950), pp. 242–263; and H. E. Noyes, *Church Reform in Spain and Portugal. A Short History of the Reformed Episcopal Churches of Spain and Portugal, from 1868 to the Present Time.* (London, 1897).

11. *Faith and Order of the Lusitanian and Spanish Reformed Episcopal Churches*, p. 5.

12. Correspondence from C. M. Gray-Stack, 1965. National and World Mission Archives, Episcopal Church Center, 815 Second Avenue, New York City.

13. *Lambeth Conference* 1948, p. 77.

14. Further see Lewis B. Whittemore, *Struggle for Freedom: History of the Philippine Independent Church* (Greenwich, Conn.: Seabury, 1961); Francis H. Wise, *The History of the Philippine Independent Church* (Manila, 1965); Isabelo de los Reyes, Jr., *The Iglesia Filipina Independiente in the World* (Manila, 1966); and Pedro S. de Achútegui, *Religious Revolution in the Philip-*

pines, 2nd ed. (Manila, 1961). The following from *Studies in Philippine Church History,* ed. Gerald H. Anderson (Ithaca: Cornell University Press, 1969), are also of considerable importance: *"Iglesia Filipina Independiente:* The Revolutionary Church" by Sister Mary Dorita Clifford (pp. 223–55), "The Liturgy of the Philippine Independent Church," by H. Ellsworth Chandlee (pp. 256–76), and also the bibliographical references on pp. 404–5.

15. See *The Faith and Order of the Philippine Independent Church,* Report of the Commission appointed by the Archbishop of Canterbury, (London: Church Information Office, 1963)

16. Further see *The Indian Churches of St. Thomas* by C. P. Mathew and M. M. Thomas (Delhi: ISPCK, 1967); *Christianity in India: A History in Ecumenical Perspective,* ed. H. C. Perumalil and E. R. Hambye (Alleppey, S. India, 1972); and Juhanon Mar Thoma, *Christianity in India and a Brief History of the Mar Thoma Syrian Church* (Madras: K. M. Cherian, rev. ed. 1968). Also of importance is Thomas P. George, "The Mar Thoma Congregations in the United States of America" (New York: General Theological Seminary, S.T.M. thesis, 1979).

17. *Anglican Consultative Council, Report of the Third Meeting, Trinidad, 1976,* p. 14 ff.

18. *What Kind of Unity: Report of the Faith and Order Meeting at Salamanca in 1974,* p. 121.

19. The 1958 Lambeth Conference endorsed the use of the term "full communion" where a Church of the Anglican Communion has "unrestricted *communio in sacris,* including the mutual recognition of ministries with a church outside our communion," and urged that where "varying degrees of relation other than full communion" are established by agreement between two such Churches the appropriate term is intercommunion (*Lambeth Conference* 1958, pp. 2, 23–24).

20. *Documents on Anglican-Roman Catholic Relations,* 1972, p. 32ff.

21. *Lambeth Conference* 1968, *Report on Renewal in Unity,* p. 137.

·III·

TO WHAT ARE WE ALREADY COMMITTED?

Documents

The Episcopal Church's Vision of Visible Unity:
Changing and Unchanging
edited by
William A. Norgren and J. Robert Wright

In order to assess the ecumenical posture of the Episcopal Church and con-sider its ecumenical goals, a review of previous Episcopal and Anglican official statements on visible unity is required. The goal of visible unity remains con-stant, but the Church's perception of the goal may change in light of the changing human and ecclesiastical environment in which she lives and carries out her mission.

This is not a complete collection of documents related to Christian unity, still less a history of the Episcopal Church's ecumenical participation and leader-ship. The documents selected are those significantly related to the visible unity of the Church and approved either by the Lambeth Conferences of Anglican bishops or the General Conventions of the Episcopal Church. The documents tell their own story, so commentary is kept to a minimum.

It must be emphasized that resolutions* of the Lambeth Conference, which has no juridical authority, are formally communicated to the various member churches of the Anglican Communion for their consideration and such action as may seem to them desirable. The Lambeth Conference has substantial moral, spiritual, and practical authority in the Anglican Communion, but the General Convention alone may decide for the Episcopal Church.

Each document is numbered, followed by its source, followed by a descriptive title. The documents are grouped in two categories: A. The Unity of the Angli-can Communion, showing what has been learned from the Anglican experience. B. The Anglican Ecumenical Stance, including the goal and models of visible unity, faith and order statements, endorsement of agreements, communion disci-pline, limited ecclesial recognition, cooperation, councils of churches, coalitions and clusters, and collaboration and strategy around limited issues. Omitted

---

* The Lambeth Conference as a whole is responsible only for the formal resolutions passed after discussion. Committee reports have the authority only of the sections by which they were prepared and presented.

from the collection are authorizations of dialogues and consultations with no goal stated, actions establishing ecumenical committees, appreciations, greetings, and statements of councils of churches not endorsed by Lambeth or Convention.

A. *Documents on the Unity of the Anglican Communion*

1. Lambeth I, 1867: Nature and Stance of the Anglican Communion

In a preamble to the formal resolutions of the first Lambeth Conference, an historic expression of the unity of the Anglican Communion, the bishops described in general terms the standpoint taken by the Anglican Church:

We, Bishops of Christ's Holy Catholic Church in visible Communion with the United Church of England and Ireland, professing the faith delivered to us in Holy Scripture, maintained by the Primitive Church and by the Fathers of the English Reformation, now assembled, by the good providence of God, at the Archiepiscopal Palace of Lambeth, under the presidency of the Primate of all England, desire: —*First,* to give hearty thanks to Almighty God for having thus brought us together for common counsels and united worship; *Secondly,* we desire to express the deep sorrow with which we view the divided condition of the flock of Christ throughout the world, ardently longing for the fulfilment of the prayer of our Lord, 'That all may be one, as Thou, Father, art in Me, and I in Thee, that they also may be one in us, that the world may believe that Thou has sent Me' and, *Lastly,* we do here solemnly record our conviction that unity will be most effectually promoted by maintaining the Faith in its purity and integrity, as taught in the Holy Scriptures, held by the Primitive Church, summed up in the Creeds, and affirmed by the undisputed General Councils, and by drawing each of us closer to our common Lord, by giving ourselves to much prayer and intercession, by the cultivation of a spirit of charity, and a love of the Lord's appearing.

This statement was affirmed by the House of Bishops at the General Convention of 1868.

2. Lambeth II, 1878: Maintaining Union Among the Various Churches of the Anglican Communion

1.—In considering the best mode of maintaining union among the various Churches of our Communion, the Committee, first of all, recognise, with deep thankfulness to Almighty God, the essential and evident unity in which the Church of England and the Churches in visible communion with her have always been bound together. United under One Divine Head in the fellowship of the One Catholic and Apostolic Church, holding the One Faith revealed in Holy Writ, defined in the Creeds, and maintained by the Primitive Church, receiving the same Canonical Scriptures of the Old and New Testaments as containing all things necessary to salvation—these Churches teach the same Word of God, partake of the same divinely-ordained Sacraments, through the ministry of the same Apostolic orders, and worship one God and Father through the same Lord Jesus Christ, by the same Holy and Divine Spirit, Who is given to those that believe, to guide them into all truth.

2.—Together with this unity, however, there has existed among these Churches that variety of custom, discipline, and form of worship which necessarily results from the exercise by each "particular or national Church" of its right "to ordain, change, and abolish ceremonies or rites of the Church ordained only by man's authority, so that all things be done to edifying." We gladly acknowledge that there is at present no real ground for anxiety on account of this diversity; but the desire has of late been largely felt and expressed, that some practical and efficient methods should be adopted, in order to guard against possible sources of disunion in the future, and at the same time further to manifest and cherish that true and substantial agreement which exists among these increasingly numerous Churches.

3.—The method which first naturally suggests itself is that which, originating with the inspired Apostles, long served to hold all the Churches of Christ in one undivided and visible communion. The assembling, however, of a true General Council, such as the Church of England has always declared her readiness to resort to, is, in the present condition of Christendom, unhappily but obviously impossible. The difficulties attending the assembling of a Synod of all the Anglican Churches, though different in character and less serious in nature, seem to us nevertheless too great to allow of our recommending it for present adoption.

4.—The experiment, now twice tried, of a Conference of Bishops called together by the Archbishop of Canterbury, and meeting under his presidency, offers at least the hope that the problem, hitherto unsolved, of combining together for consultation representatives of Churches so differently situated and administered, may find, in the providential course of events, its own solution. Your Committee would, on this point, venture to suggest that such Conferences, called together from time to time by the Archbishop of Canterbury, at the request of, or in consultation with, the Bishops of our Communion, might with advantage be invested in future with somewhat larger liberty as to the initiation and selection of subjects for discussion. For example, a Committee might be constituted, such as should represent, more or less completely, the several Churches of the Anglican Communion; and to this Committee it might be entrusted to draw up, after receiving communications from the Bishops, a scheme of subjects to be discussed.

5.—Meanwhile, there are certain principles of Church order which, your Committee consider, ought to be distinctly recognised and set forth, as of great importance for the maintenance of union among the Churches of our Communion.

(1.) First, that the duly-certified action of every national or particular Church, and of each ecclesiastical Province (or Diocese not included in a Province), in the exercise of its own discipline, should be respected by all the other Churches, and by their individual members.

(2.) Secondly, that when a Diocese, or territorial sphere of administration, has been constituted by the authority of any Church or Province of this Communion within its own limits, no Bishop or other clergyman of any other Church should exercise his functions within that Diocese without the consent of the bishop thereof.

(3.) Thirdly, that no Bishop should authorise to officiate in his Diocese a clergyman coming from another Church or Province, unless such clergyman present letters testimonial, countersigned by the Bishop of the Diocese from which he comes; such letters to be, as nearly as possible, in the form adopted by such Church or Province in the case of the transfer of a clergyman from one Diocese to another.

3. Lambeth IV, 1897: The Diocese the Center of Unity
21. That due care should be taken to make the Diocese the centre of unity, so that, while there may be contained in the same area under one Bishop various races and languages necessitating many modes of administration, nothing shall be allowed to obscure the fact that many races form but one Church.

4. Lambeth V, 1908: Church Membership Not Limited to Particular Languages, Races, or Peoples

20. All races and peoples, whatever their language or conditions, must be welded into one Body, and the organisation of different races

living side by side into separate or independent Churches, on the basis of race or colour, is inconsistent with the vital and essential principle of the unity of Christ's Church.

5. Lambeth V, 1908: The Principle of One Bishop for One Area
22. This Conference reaffirms Resolution 24 of the Conference of 1897 and further resolves that, though it may be desirable to recognise, in some cases and under certain special circumstances, the episcopal care of a Bishop for his own countrymen within the jurisdiction of another Bishop of the Anglican Communion, yet the principle of one Bishop for one area is the ideal to be aimed at as the best means of securing the unity of all races and nations in the Holy Catholic Church.

6. Lambeth VII, 1930: Race No Barrier to Eucharistic Fellowship
22. The Conference affirms its conviction that all communicants without distinction of race or colour should have access in any church to the Holy Table of the Lord, that no one should be excluded from worship in any church on account of colour or race. Further, it urges that where, owing to diversity of language or custom, Christians of different races normally worship apart, special occasions should be sought for united services and corporate communion in order to witness to the unity of the Body of Christ.

7. Lambeth VII, 1930: Fellowship of Anglican Communion Itself to Promote Union
47. The Conference calls upon all members of the Anglican Communion to promote the cause of union by fostering and deepening in all possible ways the fellowship of the Anglican Communion itself, so that by mutual understanding and appreciation all may come to a fuller apprehension of the truth as it is in Jesus, and more perfectly make manifest to the world the unity of the Spirit in and through the diversity of His gifts.

8. Lambeth VII, 1930: Nature and Status of the Anglican Communion
48. The Conference affirms that the true constitution of the Catholic Church involves the principle of the autonomy of particular churches based upon a common faith and order, and commends to the faithful those sections of the Report of Committee IV which deal with the ideal and future of the Anglican Communion.

The sections referred to are as follows:

1. The Anglican Communion has frequently been discussed at meetings of the Lambeth Conference, but we believe that to-day it has become a subject of quite paramount importance, and raises far-reaching questions of principle which demand consideration. This is partly due to its expansion. Our Communion has come to occupy a large place in the thought of the Christian world, and provokes questionings as a world-wide institution. But the development has not only been in numbers. Flourishing young Churches are now in existence, conscious of themselves, and conscious of the world outside them, where half a century ago there were but struggling Missions or possibly no Christian work at all.

2. For their sake, then, as for our own, the time has come for us to make some explicit statement of the ideal before us and of the future to which we look forward.

Our ideal is nothing less than the Catholic Church in its entirety. Viewed in its widest relations, the Anglican Communion is seen as in some sense an incident in the history of the Church Universal. It has arisen out of the situation caused by the divisions of Christendom. It has indeed been clearly blessed of God, as we thankfully acknowledge; but in its present character we believe that it is transitional, and we forecast the day when the racial and historical connections which at present characterise it will be transcended, and the life of our Communion will be merged in a larger fellowship in the Catholic Church. But in order to expound this ideal it is necessary to glance at the principle which, as we believe, underlies the constitution of the Church.

3. That principle is clear to us. There are two prevailing types of ecclesiastical organisation: that of centralised government, and that of regional autonomy within one fellowship. Of the former, the Church of Rome is the great historical example. The latter type, which we share with the Orthodox Churches of the East and others, was that upon which the Church of the first centuries was developing until the claims of the Roman Church and other tendencies confused the issue. The Provinces and Patriarchates of the first four centuries were bound together by no administrative bond: the real nexus was a common life resting upon a common faith, common Sacraments, and a common allegiance to an Unseen Head. This common life found from time to time an organ of expression in the General Councils.

4. The Anglican Communion is constituted upon this principle. It is a fellowship of Churches historically associated with the British Isles. While these Churches preserve apostolic doctrine and order they are independent in their self-government, and are growing up freely on their own soil and in their own environment as integral parts of the Church Universal. It is after this fashion that the characteristic endowment of each family of the human race may be consecrated, and so make its special contribution to the Kingdom of God.

5. The bond which holds us together is spiritual. We desire emphatically to point out that the term "Anglican" is no longer used in the sense it originally bore. The phrase "Ecclesia Anglicana" in Magna Carta had a purely local connotation. Now its sense is ecclesiastical and doctrinal, and the Anglican Communion includes not merely those who are racially connected with England, but many others whose faith has been grounded in the doctrines and ideals for which the Church of England has always stood.

6. What are these doctrines? We hold the Catholic faith in its entirety: that is to say, the truth of Christ, contained in Holy Scripture; stated in the Apostles' and Nicene Creeds; expressed in the Sacraments of the Gospel and the rites of the Primitive Church as set forth in the Book of Common Prayer with its various local adaptations; and safeguarded by the historic threefold Order of the Ministry.

And what are these ideals? They are the ideals of the Church of Christ. Prominent among them are an open Bible, a pastoral Priesthood, a common worship, a standard of conduct consistent with that worship, and a fearless love of truth. Without comparing ourselves with others, we acknowledge thankfully as the fruits of these ideals within our Communion, the sanctity of mystics, the learning of scholars, the courage of missionaries, the uprightness of civil administrators, and the devotion of many servants of God in Church and State.

7. While, however, we hold the Catholic Faith, we hold it in freedom. Every Church in our Communion is free to build up its life and development upon the provisions of its own constitution. Local Churches (to quote the words of Bishop Creighton) "have no power to change the Creeds of the Universal Church or its early organisation. But they have the right to determine the best methods of setting forth to their people the contents of the Christian faith. They may regulate rites, ceremonies, usages, observances and discipline for that purpose, according to their own wisdom and experience and the needs of the people." (Creighton, *Church and Nation*, p. 212. See also Article XXXIV.)

8. This freedom naturally and necessarily carries with it the risk of divergence to the point even of disruption. In case any such risk should actually arise, it is clear that the Lambeth Conference as such could not take any disciplinary action. Formal action would belong to the several Churches of the Anglican Communion individually; but the advice of the Lambeth Conference, sought before executive action is taken by the constituent Churches, would carry very great moral weight. And we believe in the Holy Spirit. We trust in His power working in every part of His Church as the effective bond to hold us together.

9. The freedom of each separate Church thus resembles, both in its scope and in its limitations, the freedom of a member in a living organism. It performs its distinctive functions under the direction of the Head, and for the benefit of the whole body. If it

functions in separation from the other members, or in imperfect
correspondence with the will of Christ, it is not necessarily separated from the body, but its own life is impoverished, and the
whole body is weakened and distracted.

10. From this survey of the character and mutual relations of
the Churches comprised in the Anglican Communion we turn to
the future. We have already referred to the racial and historical
associations which at present characterise us; but already the racial bond has begun to disappear. The Churches growing up in
China, Japan, India and other parts of the world, are joined to us
solely by the tie of common beliefs and common life; and the
historical connection whereby they owe their existence in the first
instance to Anglican missionaries is receding into the past. The
future is big with further possibilities. We are to-day in friendly
relations with Churches altogether foreign to us in race and different in traditions. Those relations may ripen; and we know not
what the future has in store. It is clear to us, however, that the
development of unity with them will be something other than the
expansion of the Anglican Communion as we have known it. But
we hope that, even though in some instances, and for the time, the
bond may be loose, there will nevertheless emerge in principle an
instalment of the final unity of the Catholic Church.

11. And we dare to look further still. We humbly believe that
when in God's good providence the Church Universal now divided is finally brought together in the unity which is His will, the
foundation of this unity will be the freedom based upon common
fundamental beliefs which has ever been our heritage: and that if
ever in the days to come a council of the whole Church were to be
called together, it would be assembled on a plan of autonomy and
fellowship similar to that which is the basis of our Conference
to-day.

49. The Conference approves the following statement of the nature
and status of the Anglican Communion, as that term is used in its
Resolutions:

The Anglican Communion is a fellowship, within the One Holy
Catholic and Apostolic Church, of those duly constituted Dioceses,
Provinces or Regional Churches in communion with the See of Can-
terbury, which have the following characteristics in common:—

(a) they uphold and propagate the Catholic and Apostolic faith and
order as they are generally set forth in the Book of Common
Prayer as authorised in their several Churches;

(b) they are particular or national Churches, and, as such, promote
within each of their territories a national expression of Christian
faith, life and worship; and

(c) they are bound together not by a central legislative and executive authority, but by mutual loyalty sustained through the common counsel of the Bishops in conference.

The Conference makes this statement praying for and eagerly awaiting the time when the Churches of the present Anglican Communion will enter into communion with other parts of the Catholic Church not definable as Anglican in the above sense, as a step towards the ultimate reunion of all Christendom in one visibly united fellowship.

9. Lambeth VII, 1930: Organization of Dioceses into Provinces

52. Saving always the moral and spiritual independence of the Divine Society, the Conference approves the association of Dioceses or Provinces in the larger unity of a "national Church," with or without the formal recognition of the Civil Government, as serving to give spiritual expression to the distinctive genius of races and peoples, and thus to bring more effectually under the influence of Christ's Religion both the process of government and the habit of society.

53. (a) In view of the many advantages of the organisation of Dioceses into Provinces and the difficulties and dangers of isolation, the formation of Provinces should everywhere be encouraged.

(b) The minimum organisation essential to provincial life is a College or Synod of Bishops which will act corporately in dealing with questions concerning the faith, order and discipline of the Church.

(c) The minimum number of Dioceses suitable to form a Province is four.

(d) The balance between provincial authority and diocesan autonomy may vary from province to province according to the constitutions agreed upon in each case.

10. Lambeth VIII, 1948: The Book of Common Prayer a Bond of Unity

78. (1) The Conference holds that the Book of Common Prayer has been, and is, so strong a bond of unity throughout the whole Anglican Communion that great care must be taken to ensure that revisions of the Book shall be in accordance with the doctrine and accepted liturgical worship of the Anglican Communion.

11. Lambeth IX, 1958: Revision of the Book of Common Prayer

73. The Conference welcomes the contemporary movement towards unanimity in doctrinal and liturgical matters by those of differing

traditions in the Anglican Communion as a result of new knowledge gained from Biblical and liturgical studies, and is happy to know of parallel progress in this sphere by some Roman Catholic and Reformed theologians. It commends the Report of the subcommittee on the Book of Common Prayer on this subject to the careful study of all sections of the Anglican Communion.

74. The Conference, recognizing the work of Prayer Book Revision being done in different parts of the Anglican Communion,

(a) calls attention to those features in the Books of Common Prayer which are essential to the safeguarding of our unity: i.e. the use of the Canonical Scriptures and the Creeds, Holy Baptism, Confirmation, Holy Communion, and the Ordinal;
(b) notes that there are other features in these books which are effective in maintaining the traditional doctrinal emphasis and ecclesiastical culture of Anglicanism and therefore should be preserved;
(c) and urges that a chief aim of Prayer Book Revision should be to further that recovery of the worship of the Primitive Church which was the aim of the compilers of the first Prayer Books of the Church of England.

75. The Conference commends to the study of the whole Anglican Communion the counsel on Prayer Book Revision given in the Report of the sub-committee on the Book of Common Prayer.

An example from the sub-committee Report follows:

. . . Our unity exists because we are a federation of Provinces and Dioceses of the One, Holy, Catholic, and Apostolic Church, each being served and governed by a Catholic and Apostolic Ministry, and each believing the Catholic faith. These are the fundamental reasons for our unity.

At a less profound level we experience a unity based on the consciousness of having a common history and deriving from a common root. Of this history, the Prayer Book in its various forms is probably the most powerful symbol. The use of its forms for sacrament and worship enables us to live the life of the Catholic Church. But the special character and quality of these forms and the theological and liturgical principles upon which they are based, impart to Anglican worship everywhere a distinct ecclesiastical culture. This common culture undoubtedly aids the widely separated provinces and dioceses of our Communion in their task of living and worshipping in godly union and concord with each other. Only in this secondary sense can the Book of Common Prayer be said to possess "features which are essential to the safeguarding of the unity of the Anglican Communion."

12. General Convention, 1967: Constitution, Preamble Defining the Episcopal Church

The Protestant Episcopal Church in the United States of America, otherwise known as The Episcopal Church (which name is hereby recognized as also designating the Church), is a constituent member of the Anglican Communion, a Fellowship within the One, Holy, Catholic, and Apostolic Church, of those duly constituted Dioceses, Provinces, and regional Churches in communion with the See of Canterbury, upholding and propagating the historic Faith and Order as set forth in the Book of Common Prayer.

13. Lambeth X, 1968: Anglican Consultative Council: Functions

1. To share information about developments in one or more provinces with the other parts of the communion and to serve as needed as an instrument of common action.
2. To advise on inter-Anglican, provincial, and diocesan relationships, including the division of provinces, the formation of new provinces and of regional councils, and the problems of extra-provincial dioceses.
3. To develop as far as possible agreed Anglican policies in the world mission of the Church and to encourage national and regional Churches to engage together in developing and implementing such policies by sharing their resources of manpower, money, and experience to the best advantage of all.
4. To keep before national and regional Churches the importance of the fullest possible Anglican collaboration with other Christian Churches.
5. To encourage and guide Anglican participation in the Ecumenical Movement and the ecumenical organizations; to co-operate with the World Council of Churches and the world confessional bodies on behalf of the Anglican Communion; and to make arrangements for the conduct of pan-Anglican conversations with the Roman Catholic Church, the Orthodox Churches, and other Churches.
6. To advise on matters arising out of national or regional church union negotiations or conversations and on subsequent relations with united Churches.

7. To advise on problems of inter-Anglican communication and to help in the dissemination of Anglican and ecumenical information.
8. To keep in review the needs that may arise for further study and, where necessary, to promote inquiry and research.

14. Lambeth XI, 1978: Consultation on Issues of Concern, and the Question of Authority

11. The Conference advises member Churches not to take action regarding issues which are of concern to the whole Anglican Communion without consultation with a Lambeth Conference or with the episcopate through the Primates Committee, and requests the primates to initiate a study of the nature of authority within the Anglican Communion.

15. Lambeth XI, 1978: International Meetings and Anglican Primates

12. The Conference asks the Archbishop of Canterbury, as President of the Lambeth Conference and President of the Anglican Consultative Council, with all the primates of the Anglican Communion, within one year to initiate consideration of the way to relate together the international conferences, councils, and meetings within the Anglican Communion so that the Anglican Communion may best serve God within the context of the one, holy, catholic, and apostolic Church.

16. Lambeth XI, 1978: Lambeth Conference and Episcopal Collegiality

13. In order that the guardianship of the faith may be exercised as a collegial responsibility of the whole episcopate, the Conference affirms the need for Anglican bishops from every diocese to meet together in the tradition of the Lambeth Confererence and recommends that the calling of any future Conference should continue to be the responsibility of the Archbishop of Canterbury, and that he should be requested to make his decision in consultation with the other primates. While recognizing the great value which many set on the link with Canterbury, we believe that a Conference could well be held in some other province.

17. Lambeth XI, 1978: Women in the Priesthood and the Unity of the Anglican Communion

1. The Conference notes that since the last Lambeth Conference in 1968, the diocese of Hong Kong, the Anglican Church of Canada,

the Episcopal Church in the United States of America, and the Church of the Province of New Zealand have admitted women to the presbyterate, and that eight other member Churches of the Anglican Communion have now either agreed or approved in principle or stated that there are either no fundamental or no theological objections to the ordination of women to the historic threefold ministry of the Church.

We also note that other of its member Churches have not yet made a decision on the matter. Others again have clearly stated that they do hold fundamental objections to the ordination of women to the historic threefold ministry of the Church.

2. The Conference acknowledges that both the debate about the ordination of women as well as the ordinations themselves have, in some Churches, caused distress and pain to many on both sides. To heal these and to maintain and strengthen fellowship is a primary pastoral responsibility of all, and especially of the bishops.

3. The Conference also recognizes
   a. The autonomy of each of its member Churches, acknowledging the legal right of each Church to make its own decision about the appropriateness of admitting women to Holy Orders;
   b. That such provincial action in this matter has consequences of the utmost significance for the Anglican Communion as a whole.

4. The Conference affirms its commitment to the preservation of unity within and between all member Churches of the Anglican Communion.

5. The Conference therefore:
   a. Encourages all member Churches of the Anglican Communion to continue in communion with one another, notwithstanding the admission of women (whether at present or in the future) to the ordained ministry of some member Churches;
   b. In circumstances in which the issue of the ordination of women has caused, or may cause, problems of conscience, urges that every action possible be taken to ensure that all baptized members of the Church continue to be in communion with their bishop and that every opportunity be given for all members to work together in the mission of the Church irrespective of their convictions regarding this issue;
   c. Requests the Anglican Consultative Council
      i. to use its good offices to promote dialogue between those

member Churches which ordain women and those which do not, with a view to exploring ways in which the fullest use can be made of women's gifts within the total ministry of the Church in our Communion; and

   ii. to maintain, and wherever possible extend, the present dialogue with Churches outside the Anglican family.

6. Consistent with the foregoing, this Conference
   a. declares its acceptance of those member Churches which now ordain women, and urges that they respect the convictions of those provinces and dioceses which do not.
   b. declares its acceptance of those member Churches which do not ordain women, and urges that they respect the convictions of those provinces and dioceses which do;
   c. with regard to women who have been ordained in the Anglican Communion being authorized to exercise their ministry in provinces which have not ordained women, we recommend that, should synodical authority be given to enable them to exercise it, it be exercised only
      i. where pastoral need warrants and
      ii. where such a ministry is agreeable to the bishop, clergy, and people where the ministry is to be exercised and where it is approved by the legally responsible body of the parish, area or institution where such a ministry is to be exercised.

7. We recognize that our accepting this variety of doctrine and practice in the Anglican Communion may disappoint the Roman Catholic, Orthodox and Old Catholic Churches, but we wish to make it clear
   a. that the holding together of diversity within a unity of faith and worship is part of the Anglican heritage;
   b. that those who have taken part in ordinations of women to the priesthood believe that these ordinations have been into the historic ministry of the Church as the Anglican Communion has received it; and
   c. that we hope the dialogue between these other Churches and the member Churches of our Communion will continue because we believe that we still have understanding of the truth of God and his will to learn from them as together we all move towards a fuller catholicity and a deeper fellowship in the Holy Spirit.

8. This Conference urges that further discussions about the ordinations of women be held within a wider consideration of theological issues of ministry and priesthood.

18. Lambeth XI, 1978: Women in the Episcopate
22. While recognizing that a member Church of the Anglican Communion may wish to consecrate a woman to the episcopate, and accepting that such member Church must act in accordance with its own constitution, the Conference recommends that no decision to consecrate be taken without consultation with the episcopate through the primates and overwhelming support in any member Church and in the diocese concerned lest the bishop's office should become a cause of disunity instead of a focus of unity.

19. Lambeth XI, 1978: Common Structure for the Eucharist a Factor in Church Unity
23. The Conference welcomes and commends the adoption of a common structure for the Eucharist as an important unifying factor in our Communion and ecumenically. We ask provincial liturgical committees to continue to keep in touch with one another by circulating work in progress to the chairmen of the other liturgical committees through the good offices of the Secretary General of the Anglican Consultative Council.

20. Lambeth XI, 1978: Common Lectionary a Factor in Church Unity
24. The Conference recommends a common lectionary for the Eucharist and the Offices as a unifying factor within our Communion and ecumenically; and draws attention to the experience of those Provinces which have adopted the three-year Eucharistic lectionary of the Roman Catholic Church.

21. Lambeth XI, 1978: Inter-Anglican Theological and Doctrinal Advisory Commission
25. The Conference endorses the proposal suggested in resolution 8 of the third (Trinidad, 1976) meeting of the Anglican Consultative Council, to set up an Inter-Anglican Theological and Doctrinal Advisory Commission, and asks the Standing Committee of the ACC to establish the Commission with the advice of the primates, and the primates and Provinces, by whatever means they feel best, to review its work after a period of not more than five years.

B. *Documents on the Anglican Ecumenical Stance*

1. Lambeth II, 1878: Principles of Union

In response to the promulgation of papal infallibility by the first Vatican Council, the bishops of the Lambeth Conference outlined the position which the

Anglican Church should assume toward "Old Catholics" and others in Europe who "have renounced their allegiance to the Church of Rome, and who are desirous of forming some connection with the Anglican Church, either English or American."

The principles on which the Church of England has reformed itself are well known. We proclaim the sufficiency and supremacy of the Holy Scriptures as the ultimate rule of faith and commend to our people the diligent study of the same. We confess our faith in the words of the ancient Catholic creeds. We retain the Apostolic order of Bishops, Priests, and Deacons. We assert the just liberties of particular or national Churches. We provide our people, in their own tongue, with a Book of Common Prayer and Offices for the administration of the Sacraments, in accordance with the best and most ancient types of Christian faith and worship. These documents are before the world, and can be known and read of all men. We gladly welcome every effort for reform upon the model of the Primitive Church. We do not demand a rigid uniformity; we deprecate needless divisions; but to those who are drawn to us in the endeavour to free themselves from the yoke of error and superstition we are ready to offer all help, and such privileges as may be acceptable to them and are consistent with the maintenance of our own principles as enunciated in our formularies.

2. General Convention, 1886: The Chicago Quadrilateral

The Muhlenberg Memorial, addressed to the House of Bishops as "a College of Catholic and Apostolic Bishops" at the General Convention of 1853, called attention to the "divided and distracted state of our American Protestant Christianity, the new and subtle forms of unbelief" and "the consolidated forces of Romanism bearing with renewed skill and activity against the Protestant faith, and as more or less the consequence of these, the utter ignorance of the Gospel." The memorial proposed to the bishops "some ecclesiastical system, broader and more comprehensive than that which you now administer, surrounding and including the Protestant Episcopal Church as it now is, leaving that Church untouched, identical with that Church in all its great principles, yet providing for as much freedom in opinion, discipline and worship as is compatible with the essential Faith and order of the Gospel. To define and act upon such a system, it is believed, must sooner or later be the work of an American Catholic Episcopate."

The House of Bishops appointed five of its number to report back in 1856, when it appointed a Commission on Church Unity which reported to the bishops periodically thereafter.

In 1886 the House of Bishops adopted the Chicago version of the Quadrilat-

eral. Although not enacted by the House of Deputies, it was referred for study and action to a newly created Joint Commission on Christian Unity. The Quadrilateral was originally suggested in 1870 by William Reed Huntington in The Church Idea.* *The lengthy preamble referred to the Muhlenberg Memorial and to an 1880 declaration of the House of Bishops "to the effect that, in virtue of the solidarity of the Catholic Episcopate, in which we have part, it was the right and duty of the Episcopates of all National Churches holding the primitive Faith and Order, and of the several Bishops of the same, to protect in the holding of that Faith, and in the recovering of that Order, those who have been wrongfully deprived of both; and this without demanding a rigid uniformity, or the sacrifice of the national traditions of worship and discipline, or of their rightful autonomy." Then the bishops said:*

Whereas, many of the faithful in Christ Jesus among us are praying with renewed and increasing earnestness that some measures may be adopted at this time for the re-union of the sundered parts of Christendom:

Now, Therefore, in pursuance of the action taken in 1853 for the healing of the divisions among Christians in our own land, and in 1880 for the protection and encouragement of those who had withdrawn from the Roman Obedience, we Bishops of the Protestant Episcopal Church in the United States of America, in Council assembled as Bishops in the Church of God, do hereby solemnly declare to all whom it may concern, and especially to our fellow-Christians of the different Communions in this land, who, in their several spheres, have contended for the religion of Christ:

1. Our earnest desire that the Saviour's prayer, "That we all may be one," may, in its deepest and truest sense, be speedily fulfilled;

2. That we believe that all who have been duly baptized with water, in the name of the Father, and of the Son, and of the Holy Ghost, are members of the Holy Catholic Church;

3. That in all things of human ordering or human choice, relating to modes of worship and discipline, or to traditional customs, this Church is ready in the spirit of love and humility to forego all preferences of her own;

4. That this Church does not seek to absorb other Communions, but rather, co-operating with them on the basis of a common Faith and Order, to discountenance schism, to heal the wounds of the Body of Christ, and to promote the charity which is the chief of Christian graces and the visible manifestation of Christ to the world;

* Further see John F. Woolverton, "Huntington's Quadrilateral: A Critical Study," in *Church History*, vol. 39 (June 1970), pp. 198–211.

But furthermore, we do hereby affirm that the Christian unity now so earnestly desired by the memorialists can be restored only by the return of all Christian communions to the principles of unity exemplified by the undivided Catholic Church during the first ages of its existence; which principles we believe to be the substantial deposit of Christian Faith and Order committed by Christ and his Apostles to the Church unto the end of the world, and therefore incapable of compromise or surrender by those who have been ordained to be its stewards and trustees for the common and equal benefit of all men. As inherent parts of this sacred deposit, and therefore as essential to the restoration of unity among the divided branches of Christendom, we account the following, to wit:

1. The Holy Scriptures of the Old and New Testament as the revealed word of God.
2. The Nicene Creed as the sufficient statement of the Christian Faith.
3. The two Sacraments—Baptism and the supper of the Lord—ministered with unfailing use of Christ's words of institution and the elements ordained by Him.
4. The Historic Episcopate, locally adapted in the methods of its administration to the varying needs of the nations and peoples called of God into the unity of His Church.

Furthermore, Deeply grieved by the sad divisions which affect the Christian Church in our own land, we hereby declare our desire and readiness, so soon as there shall be any authorized response to this Declaration, to enter into brotherly conference with all or any Christian Bodies seeking the restoration of the organic unity of the Church, with a view to the earnest study of the conditions under which so priceless a blessing might happily be brought to pass.

3. Lambeth III, 1888: The Lambeth Quadrilateral

By action of the Lambeth Conference in 1888 and subsequent meetings, the second set of four points of the Chicago Quadrilateral of 1886 became the platform of the whole Anglican Communion in its approaches to reunion. Point 1 on the Holy Scriptures was revised to read "as being the rule and ultimate standard of faith." Lambeth also added "the Apostles' Creed as the Baptismal symbol" to point 2, leaving the third and fourth points in the Chicago form. The General Convention has frequently reaffirmed the Chicago-Lambeth Quadrilateral, first in 1892 and most recently in 1976.

11. That, in the opinion of this Conference, the following Articles supply a basis on which approach may be by God's blessing made towards Home Reunion:—

(A) The Holy Scriptures of the Old and New Testaments, as "containing all things necessary to salvation," and as being the rule and ultimate standard of faith.

(B) The Apostles' Creed, as the Baptismal Symbol; and the Nicene Creed, as the sufficient statement of the Christian faith.

(C) The two Sacraments ordained by Christ Himself—Baptism and the Supper of the Lord—ministered with unfailing use of Christ's words of Institution, and of the elements ordained by Him.

(D) The Historic Episcopate, locally adapted in the methods of its administration to the varying needs of the nations and peoples called of God into the Unity of His Church.

12. That this Conference earnestly requests the constituted authorities of the various branches of our Communion, acting, so far as may be, in concert with one another, to make it known that they hold themselves in readiness to enter into brotherly conference (such as that which has already been proposed by the Church in the United States of America) with the representatives of other Christian Communions in the English-speaking races, in order to consider what steps can be taken, either towards corporate Reunion, or towards such relations as may prepare the way for fuller organic unity hereafter.

4. Lambeth III, 1888: On Dissemination of Information as an Aid to Reunion

13. That this Conference recommends as of great importance, in tending to bring about Reunion, the dissemination of information respecting the standards of doctrine and the formularies in use in the Anglican Church; and recommends that information be disseminated, on the other hand, respecting the authoritative standards of doctrine, worship, and government adopted by the other bodies of Christians into which the English-speaking races are divided.

5. Lambeth III, 1888: The Scandinavian Churches

14. That, in the opinion of this Conference, earnest efforts should be made to establish more friendly relations between the Scandinavian and Anglican Churches; and that approaches on the part of the Swedish Church, with a view to the mutual explanation of differences, be most gladly welcomed, in order to the ultimate establishment, if possible, of intercommunion on sound principles of ecclesiastical polity.

6. Lambeth III, 1888: The Old Catholic Churches

15. (A) That this Conference recognises with thankfulness the dignified and independent position of the Old Catholic Church of Hol-

land, and looks to more frequent brotherly intercourse to remove many of the barriers which at present separate us.

(B) That we regard it as a duty to promote friendly relations with the Old Catholic Community in Germany, and with the "Christian Catholic Church" in Switzerland, not only out of sympathy with them, but also in thankfulness to God Who has strengthened them to suffer for the truth under great discouragements, difficulties, and temptations; and that we offer them the privileges recommended by the Committee under the conditions specified in its Report.

(C) That the sacrifices made by the Old Catholics in Austria deserve our sympathy, and that we hope, when their organisation is sufficiently tried and complete, a more formal relation may be found possible.

(D) That, with regard to the reformers in Italy, France, Spain, and Portugal, struggling to free themselves from the burden of unlawful terms of communion, we trust that they may be enabled to adopt such sound forms of doctrine and discipline, and to secure such Catholic organisation as will permit us to give them a fuller recognition.

The privileges referred to in (B) are specified in the Report:

We see no reason why we should not admit their Clergy and faithful Laity to Holy Communion on the same conditions as our own Communicants, and we also acknowledge the readiness which they have shown to offer spiritual privileges to members of our own Church.

7. Lambeth III, 1888: The Eastern Orthodox Church

17. That this Conference, rejoicing in the friendly communications which have passed between the Archbishops of Canterbury and other Anglican Bishops, and the Patriarchs of Constantinople and other Eastern Patriarchs and Bishops, desires to express its hope that the barriers to fuller communion may be, in course of time, removed by further intercourse and extended enlightenment. The Conference commends this subject to the devout prayers of the faithful, and recommends that the counsels and efforts of our fellow-Christians should be directed to the encouragement of internal reformation in the Eastern Churches, rather than to the drawing away from them of individual members of their Communion.

8. Lambeth III, 1888: Recognition of Newly Constituted Churches in Non-Christian Lands

19. That, as regards newly-constituted Churches, especially in non-Christian lands, it should be a condition of the recognition of them as

in complete intercommunion with us, and especially of their receiving from us Episcopal Succession, that we should first receive from them satisfactory evidence that they hold substantially the same doctrine as our own, and that their Clergy subscribe Articles in accordance with the express statements of our own standards of doctrine and worship; but that they should not necessarily be bound to accept in their entirety the Thirty-nine Articles of Religion.

9. Lambeth IV, 1897: Avoidance of Division in the Foreign Mission Field

27. That in the Foreign Mission Field of the Church's work, where signal spiritual blessings have attended the labours of Christian Missionaries not connected with the Anglican Communion, a special obligation has arisen to avoid, as far as possible without compromise of principle, whatever tends to prevent the due growth and manifestation of that "unity of the Spirit," which should ever mark the Church of Christ.

10. Lambeth IV, 1897: Visible Unity as a Fact of Revelation

34. That every opportunity be taken to emphasise the Divine purpose of visible unity amongst Christians, as a fact of revelation.

11. Lambeth IV, 1897: Intercession for the Unity of the Church

35. That this Conference urges the duty of special intercession for the unity of the Church in accordance with our Lord's own prayer.

12. Lambeth V, 1908: Correlation and Co-operation of Missionary Agencies

23. The Conference commends to the consideration of the Church the suggestions of the Committee on Foreign Missions, contained in their Report, for correlation and co-operation between Missions of the Anglican Communion and those of other Christian bodies.

13. Lambeth V, 1908: Reunion of the Whole of Christendom

38. This Conference reaffirms the resolution of the Conference of 1897 that "Every opportunity should be taken to emphasise the Divine purpose of visible unity amongst Christians as a fact of revelation." It desires further to affirm that in all partial projects of reunion and intercommunion the final attainment of the divine purpose should be kept in view as our object; and that care should be taken to do what will advance the reunion of the whole of Christendom, and to abstain from doing anything that will retard or prevent it.

14. Lambeth V, 1908: The Eastern Orthodox Church

The unilateral action of this resolution that members of the Orthodox Church should be admitted to communion in cases of special need was never approved by the Orthodox Churches, although the practice was informally countenanced in some places in the past.

62. The Conference is of opinion that it should be the recognised practice of the Churches of our Communion: (1) at all times to baptize the children of members of any Church of the Orthodox Eastern Communion in cases of emergency, provided that there is a clear understanding that baptism should not be again administered to those so baptized; (2) at all times to admit members of any Church of the Orthodox Eastern Communion to communicate in our churches, when they are deprived of the ministrations of a priest of their own Communion, provided that (a) they are at that time admissible to Communion in their own Churches, and (b) are not under any disqualification so far as our own rules of discipline are concerned.

15. Lambeth V, 1908: The Ancient Eastern Churches

The next Lambeth Conference of 1920, having received a report on the present doctrinal position of the Ancient Eastern Churches, expressed the opinion that "any errors . . . have at any rate now passed away," and repeated the proposal of "occasional intercommunion." The steps outlined in this 1908 resolution, however, have not been taken by the Anglican and the Ancient Eastern Churches, although in some places the Ancient Churches have encouraged their members to communicate with Anglicans in cases of special need.

63. The Conference would welcome any steps that might be taken to ascertain the precise doctrinal position of the ancient separate Churches of the East with a view to possible intercommunion, and would suggest to the Archbishop of Canterbury the appointment of Commissions to examine the doctrinal position of particular Churches, and (for example) to prepare some carefully framed statement of the faith as to our Lord's Person, in the simplest possible terms, which should be submitted to each of such Churches, where feasible, in order to ascertain whether it represents their belief with substantial accuracy. The conclusions of such Commissions should in our opinion be submitted to the Metropolitans or Presiding Bishops of all the Churches of the Anglican Communion.

64. In the event of doctrinal agreement being reached with such separate Churches, the Conference is of opinion that it would be right (1) for any Church of the Anglican Communion to admit individual

communicant members of those Churches to communicate with us when they are deprived of this means of grace through isolation, and conversely, for our communicants to seek the same privileges in similar circumstances; (2) for the Churches of the Anglican Communion to permit our communicants to communicate on special occasions with these Churches, even when not deprived of this means of grace through isolation, and conversely, that their communicants should be allowed the same privileges in similar circumstances.

65. We consider that any more formal and complete compact between us and any such Church, seeing that it might affect our relations with certain other Churches, should not take place without previous communication with any other Church which might be affected thereby.

16. Lambeth V, 1908: Mixed Marriages with Roman Catholics
67. We desire earnestly to warn members of our Communion against contracting marriages with Roman Catholics under the conditions imposed by modern Roman canon law, especially as these conditions involve the performance of the marriage ceremony without any prayer or invocation of the divine blessing, and also a promise to have their children brought up in a religious system which they cannot themselves accept.

17. Lambeth V, 1908: The Old Catholic Churches
68. The Conference desires to maintain and strengthen the friendly relations which already exist between the Churches of the Anglican Communion and the ancient Church of Holland and the Old Catholic Churches, especially in Germany, Switzerland, and Austria.

69. With a view to the avoidance of further ecclesiatical confusion, the Conference would earnestly deprecate the setting up of a new organised body in regions where a Church with apostolic ministry and Catholic doctrine offers religious privileges without the imposition of uncatholic terms of communion, more especially in cases where no difference of language or nationality exists; and, in view of the friendly relations referred to in the previous Resolution, it would respectfully request the Archbishop of Canterbury, if he thinks fit, to bring this Resolution to the notice of the Old Catholic Bishops.

18. Lambeth V, 1908: Unitas Fratrum
70. For the sake of unity, and as a particular expression of brotherly affection, we recommend that any official request of the *Unitas Fratrum* for the participation of Anglican Bishops in the consecration of Bishops of the *Unitas* should be accepted, provided that

(i)   Such Anglican Bishops should be not less than three in number,
      and should participate both in the saying of the Prayers of Con-
      secration and in the laying on of hands, and that the rite itself is
      judged to be sufficient by the Bishops of the Church of our Com-
      munion to which the invited Bishops belong;
(ii) The Synods of the *Unitas* (a) are able to give sufficient assurance of
      doctrinal agreement with ourselves in all essentials (as we believe
      that they will be willing and able to do); and (b) are willing to
      explain its position as that of a religious community or missionary
      body in close alliance with the Anglican Communion; and (c) are
      willing to accord a due recognition to the position of our Bishops
      within Anglican Dioceses and jurisdictions; and (d) are willing to
      adopt a rule as to the administration of Confirmation more akin to
      our own.

71. After the conditions prescribed in the preceding Resolution
have been complied with, and a Bishop has been consecrated in accordance with them, corresponding invitations from any Bishop of the
Unitas Fratrum to an Anglican Bishop and his Presbyters to participate
in the ordination of a Moravian Presbyter should be accepted, provided that the Anglican Bishop should participate both in the saying
of the prayers of ordination and in the laying on of hands, and that
the rite itself is judged to be sufficient by the Bishops of the Church of
our Communion to which the invited Bishop belongs.

72. Any Bishop or Presbyter so consecrated or ordained should be
free to minister in the Anglican Communion with due episcopal
license; and, in the event of the above proposals—i.e. Resolutions 1
and 2—being accepted and acted upon by the Synods of the *Unitas,*
during the period of transition some permission to preach in our
churches might on special occasions be extended to Moravian Ministers by Bishops of our Communion.

19. Lambeth V, 1908: Reunion with Presbyterians or Other Non-episcopal Churches

75. The Conference receives with thankfulness and hope the Report
of its Committee on Reunion and Intercommunion, and is of opinion
that, in the welcome event of any project of reunion between any
Church of the Anglican Communion and any Presbyterian or other
non-episcopal Church, which, while preserving the Faith in its integrity and purity, has also exhibited care as to the form and intention of
ordination to the ministry, reaching the stage of responsible official
negotiation, it might be possible to make an approach to reunion on

the basis of consecrations to the episcopate on lines suggested by such precedents as those of 1610. Further, in the opinion of the Conference, it might be possible to authorise arrangements (for the period of transition towards full union on the basis of episcopal ordination) which would respect the convictions of those who had not received episcopal Orders, without involving any surrender on our part of the principle of Church order laid down in the Preface to the Ordinal attached to the Book of Common Prayer.

20. Lambeth V, 1908: Cooperation in Social and Moral Welfare

76. Every opportunity should be welcomed of co-operation between members of different Communions in all matters pertaining to the social and moral welfare of the people.

21. Lambeth V, 1908: Meetings to Promote Mutual Understanding

77. The members of the Anglican Communion should take pains to study the doctrines and position of those who are separated from it and to promote a cordial mutual understanding; and, as a means towards this end, the Conference suggests that private meetings of ministers and laymen of different Christian bodies for common study, discussion, and prayer should be frequently held in convenient centres.

22. General Convention, 1910: Proposal for a World Conference on Faith and Order

Resolved, the House of Bishops concurring, That a Joint Committee, consisting of seven Bishops, seven Presbyters, and seven Laymen, be appointed to take under advisement the promotion by this Church of a Conference following the general method of the World's Missionary Conference, to be participated in by representatives of all Christian bodies throughout the world which accept our Lord Jesus Christ as God and Saviour, for the consideration of questions pertaining to the Faith and Order of the Church of Christ, and that such Committee, if it deem such a conference feasible, shall report to this Convention.

23. Lambeth VI, 1920: An Appeal to All Christian People

We, Archbishops, Bishops Metropolitan, and other Bishops of the Holy Catholic Church in full communion with the Church of England, in Conference assembled, realizing the responsibility which rests upon us at this time and sensible of the sympathy and the prayers of many, both within and without our own Communion, make this appeal to all Christian people.

We acknowledge all those who believe in our Lord Jesus Christ, and have been baptized into the name of the Holy Trinity, as sharing with us membership in the universal Church of Christ which is His Body. We believe that the Holy Spirit has called us in a very solemn and special manner to associate ourselves in penitence and prayer with all those who deplore the divisions of Christian people, and are inspired by the vision and hope of a visible unity of the whole Church.

I. We believe that God wills fellowship. By God's own act this fellowship was made in and through Jesus Christ, and its life is in His Spirit. We believe that it is God's purpose to manifest this fellowship, so far as this world is concerned, in an outward, visible, and united society, holding one faith, having its own recognized officers, using God-given means of grace, and inspiring all its members to the world-wide service of the Kingdom of God. This is what we mean by the Catholic Church.

II. This united fellowship is not visible in the world today. On the one hand there are other ancient Episcopal Communions in East and West, to whom ours is bound by many ties of common faith and tradition. On the other hand there are the great non-Episcopal Communions, standing for rich elements of truth, liberty and life which might otherwise have been obscured or neglected. With them we are closely linked by many affinities, racial, historical and spiritual. We cherish the earnest hope that all these Communions, and our own, may be led by the Spirit into the unity of the Faith and of the knowledge of the Son of God. But in fact we are all organized in different groups, each one keeping to itself gifts that rightly belong to the whole fellowship, and tending to live its own life apart from the rest.

III. The causes of division lie deep in the past, and are by no means simple or wholly blameworthy. Yet none can doubt that self-will, ambition, and lack of charity among Christians have been principal factors in the mingled process, and that these, together with blindness to the sin of disunion, are still mainly responsible for the breaches of Christendom. We acknowledge this condition of broken fellowship to be contrary to God's will, and we desire frankly to confess our share in the guilt of thus crippling the Body of Christ and hindering the activity of His Spirit.

IV. The times call us to a new outlook and new measures. The Faith cannot be adequately apprehended and the battle of the Kingdom cannot be worthily fought while the body is divided, and is thus unable to grow up into the fullness of the life of Christ. The time has come, we believe, for all the separated groups of Christians to agree in forgetting the things which are behind and reaching out towards the goal of a reunited Catholic Church. The removal of the barriers which have arisen between them will only be brought about by a new comradeship of those whose faces are definitely set this way.

The vision which rises before us is that of a Church genuinely Catholic, loyal to all Truth, and gathering into its fellowship all "who profess and call themselves Christians," within whose visible unity all the treasures of faith and order, bequeathed as a heritage by the past to the present, shall be possessed in common, and made serviceable to the whole Body of Christ. Within this unity Christian Communions now separated from one another would retain much that has long been distinctive in their methods of worship and service. It is through a rich diversity of life and devotion that the unity of the whole fellowship will be fulfilled.

V. This means an adventure of goodwill and still more of faith, for nothing less is required than a new discovery of the creative resources of God. To this adventure we are convinced that God is now calling all the members of His Church.

VI. We believe that the visible unity of the Church will be found to involve the whole-hearted acceptance of:—

The Holy Scriptures, as the record of God's revelation of Himself to man, and as being the rule and ultimate standard of faith; and the Creed commonly called Nicene, as the sufficient statement of the Christian faith, and either it or the Apostles Creed as the Baptismal confession of belief;

The divinely instituted sacraments of Baptism and the Holy Communion, as expressing for all the corporate life of the whole fellowship in and with Christ;

A ministry acknowledged by every part of the Church as possessing not only the inward call of the Spirit, but also the commission of Christ and the authority of the whole body.

VII. May we not reasonably claim that the Episcopate is the one means of providing such a ministry? It is not that we call in question for a moment the spiritual reality of the ministries of those Communions which do not possess the Episcopate. On the contrary, we thankfully acknowledge that these ministries have been manifestly blessed and owned by the Holy Spirit as effective means of grace. But we submit that considerations alike of history and of present experience justify the claim which we make on behalf of the Episcopate. Moreover, we would urge that it is now and will prove to be in the future the best instrument for maintaining the unity and continuity of the Church. But we greatly desire that the office of a Bishop should be everywhere exercised in a representative and constitutional manner, and more truly express all that ought to be involved for the life of the Christian Family in the title of Father-in-God. Nay more, we eagerly look forward to the day when through its acceptance in a united Church we may all share in that grace which is pledged to the members of the whole body in the apostolic rite of the laying-on-of-hands, and in the joy and fellowship of a Eucharist in which as one Family we may together, without any doubtfulness of mind, offer to the one Lord our worship and service.

VIII. We believe that for all the truly equitable approach to union is by the way of mutual deference to one another's consciences. To this end, we who send forth this appeal would say that if the authorities of other Communions should so desire, we are persuaded that, terms of union having been otherwise satisfactorily adjusted, Bishops and clergy of our Communion would willingly accept from these authorities a form of commission or recognition which would commend our ministry to their congregations, as having its place in the one family life. It is not in our power to know how far this suggestion may be acceptable to those to whom we offer it. We can only say that we offer it in all sincerity as a token of our longing that all ministries of grace, theirs and ours, shall be available for the service of our Lord in a united Church.

It is our hope that the same motive would lead ministers who have not received it to accept a commission through episcopal ordination, as obtaining for them a ministry throughout the whole fellowship.

In so acting no one of us could possibly be taken to repudiate his past ministry. God forbid that any man should repudiate a past experience rich in spiritual blessings for himself and others. Nor would any of us be dishonouring the Holy Spirit of God, whose call led us all to our several ministries, and whose power enabled us to perform them. We shall be publicly and formally seeking additional recognition of a new call to wider service in a reunited Church, and imploring for ourselves God's grace and strength to fulfill the same.

IX. The spiritual leadership of the Catholic Church in days to come, for which the world is manifestly waiting, depends upon the readiness with which each group is prepared to make sacrifices for the sake of a common fellowship, a common ministry, and a common service to the world.

We place this ideal first and foremost before ourselves and our own people. We call upon them to make the effort to meet the demands of a new age with a new outlook. To all other Christian people whom our words may reach we make the same appeal. We do not ask that any one Communion should consent to be absorbed in another. We do ask that all should unite in a new and great endeavor to recover and to manifest to the world the unity of the Body of Christ for which He prayed.

24. Lambeth VI, 1920: Counsel Bearing Upon Problems of Reunion

12. The Conference approves the following statements as representing the counsel which it is prepared to give to the Bishops, Clergy and other members of our own Communion on various subjects which bear upon the problems of reunion, provided that such counsel is not to be regarded as calling in question any Canons or official declarations of any Synod or House of Bishops of a national, regional, or provincial Church which has already dealt with these matters.

(A) In view of prospects and projects of reunion—

(i) A Bishop is justified in giving occasional authorization to ministers, not episcopally ordained, who in his judgement are working towards an ideal of union such as is described in our Appeal, to preach in churches within his Diocese, and to clergy of the Diocese to preach in the churches of such ministers:

(ii) The Bishops of the Anglican Communion will not question the action of any Bishop who, in the few years between the initiation and the completion of a definite scheme of union, shall countenance the irregularity of admitting to Communion the baptized but unconfirmed Communicants of the non-episcopal congregations concerned in the scheme:

(iii) The Conference gives its general approval to the suggestions contained in the report of the Sub-Committee on Reunion with Non-Episcopal Churches in reference to the status and work of ministers who may remain after union without episcopal ordination.*

---

* *The appropriate extract from the report referred to in (A,iii):*

(a) Ministers of both the uniting Communions should be at once recognized as of equal status in all Synods and Councils of the United Church.

(b) The terms of union should not confer on non-episcopally ordained ministers the right to administer the Holy Communion to those congregations which already possess an episcopal ministry, but they should include the right to conduct other services and to preach in such churches, if licensed thereto by the Bishop.

(c) All other matters might well be left to the decision of the Provincial or General Synods of the United Church, in full confidence that these Synods will take care not to endanger that fellowship with the universal Church which is our common ultimate aim.

(B) Believing, however, that certain lines of action might imperil both the attainment of its ideal and the unity of its own Communion, the Conference declares that—

(i) It cannot approve of general schemes of intercommunion or exchange of pulpits:

(ii) In accordance with the principle of Church order set forth in the Preface to the Ordinal attached to the Book of Common Prayer, it cannot approve the celebration in Anglican churches of the Holy Communion for members of the Anglican Church by ministers who have not been episcopally ordained; and that it should be regarded as the general rule of the Church that Anglican communicants should receive Holy Communion only at the hands of ministers of their own Church, or of Churches in communion therewith.

(C) In view of doubts and varieties of practice which have caused difficulties in the past, the Conference declares that—

(i) Nothing in these Resolutions is intended to indicate that the rule of Confirmation as conditioning admission to the Holy Communion must necessarily apply to the case of baptized persons who seek Communion under conditions which in the Bishop's judgement justify their admission thereto.

(ii) In cases in which it is impossible for the Bishop's judgement to be obtained beforehand the priest should remember that he has no canonical authority to refuse Communion to any baptized person kneeling before the Lord's Table (unless he be excommunicate by name, or, in the canonical sense of the term, a cause of scandal to the faithful); and that, if a question may properly be raised as to the future admission of any such person to Holy Communion, either because he has not been confirmed or for other reasons, the priest should refer the matter to the Bishop for counsel or direction.

25. Lambeth VI, 1920: The Church of Sweden

24. The Conference welcomes the Report of the Commission appointed after the last Conference entitled, "The Church of England and the Church of Sweden," and, accepting the conclusions there maintained on the succession of the Bishops of the Church of Sweden and the conception of the priesthood set forth in its standards, recommends that members of that Church, qualified to receive the Sacrament in their own Church, should be admitted to Holy Communion in ours. It also recommends that on suitable occasions permission should be given to Swedish ecclesiastics to give addresses in our Churches.

If the authorities of any Province of the Anglican Communion find local irregularities in the order or practice of the Church of Sweden outside that country, they may legitimately, within their own region, postpone any such action as is recommended in this Resolution until they are satisfied that these irregularities have been removed.

25. We recommend further that in the event of an invitation being extended to an Anglican Bishop or Bishops to take part in the consecration of a Swedish Bishop, the invitation should, if possible, be accepted, subject to the approval of the Metropolitan. We also recommend that, in the first instance, as an evident token of the restoration of closer relations between the two Churches, if possible more than one of our Bishops should take part in the Consecration.

26. Lambeth VI, 1920: Councils Representing All Christian Communions

13. The Conference recommends that, wherever it has not already been done, Councils representing all Christian Communions should be formed within such areas as may be deemed most convenient, as centres of united effort to promote the physical, moral, and social welfare of the people, and the extension of the rule of Christ among all nations and over every region of human life.

27. Lambeth VII, 1930: The Malines Conversations with Roman Catholics

32. Believing that our Lord's purpose for His Church will only be fulfilled when all the separated parts of His Body are united, and that only by full discussion between the Churches can error and misunderstanding be removed and full spiritual unity attained, the Conference expresses its appreciation of the courage and Christian charity of Cardinal Mercier in arranging the Malines Conversations, unofficial and not fully representative of the Churches though they were, and its regret that by the Encyclical, *Mortalium animos*, members of the Roman Catholic Church are forbidden to take part in the World Conference on Faith and Order and other similar Conferences.

28. Lambeth VII, 1930: The Eastern Orthodox Church

33. (b) The Conference requests the Archbishop of Canterbury to appoint representatives of the Anglican Communion and to invite the Ecumenical Patriarch to appoint representatives of the Patriarchates and Autocephalous Churches of the East to be a Doctrinal Commission, which may, in correspondence and in consultation, prepare a joint statement on the theological points about which there is difference and agreement between the Anglican and the Eastern Churches.

(c) The Conference not having been summoned as a Synod to issue any statement professing to define doctrine, is therefore unable to issue such a formal statement on the subjects referred to in the *Résumé* of the discussions between the Patriarch of Alexandria with the other Orthodox Representatives and Bishops of the Anglican Communion, but records its acceptance of the statements of the Anglican Bishops contained therein as a sufficient account of the teaching and practice of the Church of England and of the Churches in communion with it, in relation to those subjects.

29. Lambeth VII, 1930: The Old Catholic Churches
35. (b) The Conference requests the Archbishop of Canterbury to appoint representatives of the Anglican Communion, and to invite the Archbishop of Utrecht to appoint representatives of the Old Catholic Churches to be a Doctrinal Commission to discuss points of agreement and difference between them.

(c) The Conference agrees that there is nothing in the Declaration of Utrecht inconsistent with the teaching of the Church of England.

30. Lambeth VII, 1930: The Ancient Eastern Churches
36. (c) The Conference welcomes the development of closer relations between the Anglican Communion and the Separated Churches of the East which is recorded in its Committee's Report, and earnestly desires that these relations may be steadily strengthened, in consultation with the Orthodox Church, in the hope that in due course full intercommunion may be reached.

31. Lambeth VII, 1930: South India
40. (a) The Conference has heard with the deepest interest of the proposals for Church union in South India now under consideration between the Church of India, Burma and Ceylon, the South India United Church and the Wesleyan Methodist Church of South India, and expresses its highest appreciation of the spirit in which the representatives of these Churches have pursued the long and careful negotiations.

(b) The Conference notes with warm sympathy that the project embodied in the Proposed Scheme for Church Union in South India is not the formation of any fresh Church or Province of the Anglican Communion under new conditions, but seeks rather to bring together the distinctive elements of different Christian Communions, on a basis of sound doctrine and episcopal order, in a distinct Province of the Universal Church, in such a way as to give the Indian expression of the spirit, the thought and the life of the Church Universal.

(c) We observe further, as a novel feature in the South Indian Scheme, that a complete agreement between the uniting Churches on certain points of doctrine and practice is not expected to be reached before the inauguration of the union; but the promoters of the scheme believe that unity will be reached gradually and more securely by the interaction of the different elements of the united church upon one another. It is only when the unification resulting from that interaction is complete that a final judgment can be pronounced on the effect of the present proposals. Without attempting, therefore, to pronounce such judgment now, we express to our brethren in India our strong desire that, as soon as the negotiations are successfully completed, the venture should be made and the union inaugurated. We hope that it will lead to the emergence of a part of the Body of Christ which will possess a new combination of the riches that are His. In this hope we ask the Churches of our Communion to stand by our brethren in India, while they make this experiment, with generous good will.

(d) The Conference thinks it wise to point out that, after the union in South India has been inaugurated, both ministers and lay people of the united Church, when they are outside the jurisdiction of that Church, will be amenable to the regulations of the Province and Diocese in which they desire to officiate or to worship, and it must be assumed that those regulations will be applied to individuals in the same manner as they would now be applied to similarly circumstanced individuals, unless any Province takes formal action to change its regulations.

(e) The Conference, fully assured in the light of the Resolutions of the General Council of the Church of India, Burma and Ceylon adopted in February, 1930, that nothing will be done to break the fellowship of the Churches of the Anglican Communion, confidently leaves in the hands of the Bishops of that Church the task of working out in detail the principles which are embodied in the Proposed Scheme.

(f) The Conference gives its general approval to the suggestions contained in the Report of its Committee with regard to the Proposed Scheme for Church Union in South India, and commends the Report to the attention of the Episcopal Synod and General Council of the Church of India, Burma and Ceylon.

32. Lambeth VII, 1930: Intercommunion

42. The Conference, maintaining as a general principle that intercommunion should be the goal of, rather than a means to, the restoration of union, and bearing in mind the general rule of the Anglican

Churches that "members of the Anglican Churches should receive the Holy Communion only from ministers of their own Church," holds nevertheless, that the administration of such rule falls under the discretion of the Bishop, who should exercise his dispensing power in accordance with any principles that may be set forth by the national, regional or provincial authority of the Church in the area concerned. The Bishops of the Anglican Communion will not question the action of any Bishop who may, in his discretion so exercised, sanction an exception to the general rule in special areas, where the ministrations of an Anglican Church are not available for long periods of time without travelling great distances, or may give permission that baptized communicant members of Churches not in communion with our own should be encouraged to communicate in Anglican churches, when the ministrations of their own Church are not available, or in other special or temporary circumstances.

The Conference adopted the following explanatory note:

In view of the dangers of misconception, we think it desirable to say that in recognising that a Bishop of the Anglican Communion may under very strict regulations and in very special circumstances permit individual communicants to join with members of other Christian bodies in their Services of the administration of the Lord's Supper, we felt bound to consider the difficulties created by present conditions, especially in some parts of the Mission Field. But we would point out that the very special circumstances and the very strict regulations specified in this Resolution of themselves show that we are not departing from the rule of our Church that the minister of the Sacrament of Holy Communion should be a priest episcopally ordained.

33. Lambeth VII, 1930: Paramount Duty to Seek Unity in Every Direction

45. In view of the various schemes of Re-union and other projects and advances towards union and intercommunion which have been the subject of discussion or negotiation, the Conference reminds the Church that it is a paramount duty to seek unity among Christians in every direction, and assures all who are working for this end of its cordial support in their endeavours; it also reminds the Church that until full and final schemes are set out and terms of intercommunion are definitely arranged, the expression of final judgments on individual schemes is premature.

34. Lambeth VII, 1930: Evangelism and Unity

46. Meanwhile the Conference urges the desirability of organising and participating in efforts of Evangelism in co-operation with Christians of other Communions, both as a means of bearing effective witness to the multitudes who are detached from all forms of organised Christianity, and as a means of expressing and strengthening that sense of unity in the Gospel which binds together in spiritual fellowship those who own allegiance to different Churches.

35. General Convention, 1934: Ratification of Bonn Agreement

In accordance with the request of the Lambeth Conference of 1930, a Joint Doctrinal Commission was appointed by the Archbishop of Canterbury and the Archbishop of Utrecht. It met at Bonn in July, 1931, and adopted a statement showing an agreement between representatives of the Old Catholic Church and the Churches of the Anglican Communion. This was ratified by the Episcopal Synod of the Old Catholic Churches in 1931 and accepted by the Convocations of the Church of England in 1932.

Resolved, that the terms of Intercommunion drawn up by the Joint Commission of Anglicans and Old Catholics, we hereby accept and ratify them. Furthermore, we agree to the establishment of Intercommunion between the Protestant Episcopal Church and the Old Catholics of the Utrecht Convention on these terms.

36. General Convention, 1937: Proposal for Organic Union with the Presbyterian Church in the U.S.A.

Resolved, That the General Convention of the Protestant Episcopal Church in the United States of America, acting with full realization of the significance of its proposal, hereby invites the Presbyterian Church in the United States of America to join with it in accepting the following declaration:

The two Churches one in the faith of the Lord Jesus Christ, the Incarnate Word of God, recognizing the Holy Scriptures as the supreme rule of faith, accepting the two Sacraments ordained by Christ, and believing that the visible unity of Christ's Church is the will of God, hereby formally declare their purpose to achieve organic union between their respective churches.

Upon the basis of these agreements the two churches agree to take immediate steps toward the framing of plans whereby this end may be achieved.

37. General Convention, 1940: Ratification of the Bonn Agreement

Resolved, that this General Convention of the Protestant Episcopal Church approves the following statements agreed on between the representatives of the Old Catholic Churches and the Churches of the Anglican Communion at a Conference held at Bonn, on July 2, 1931:

a. Each communion recognises the catholicity and independence of the other and maintains its own.
b. Each communion agrees to admit members of the other communion to participate in the sacraments.
c. Intercommunion does not require from either communion the acceptance of all doctrinal opinion, sacramental devotion, or liturgical practice characteristic of the other, but implies that each believes the other to hold all essentials of the Christian faith.

and on these terms the General Convention agrees to the establishment of intercommunion between the Protestant Episcopal Church and the Old Catholic Churches which are in communion with the See of Utrecht.

In 1943 a report to the General Convention made it clear that the resolutions of 1934 and 1940 established intercommunion as well with the Polish National Catholic Church in the U.S., which was already a part of the Old Catholic Union. The PNCC ratified the Bonn Agreement in 1946, and the General Convention in 1946 reaffirmed its action to make it clear that the Bonn Agreement established communion with the PNCC. The Lambeth Conference of 1948 welcomed and subscribed to the Bonn Agreement and recommended it to other churches of the Anglican Communion. Thus a precedent was set for formal association between Churches which recognize each other's ministries and doctrine. (Further see William A. Norgren, "The Concordat Relationships," pp. 184–211 of this volume.)

38. General Convention, 1940: Constituent Member of the World Council of Churches

Whereas, These terms have been incorporated in the constitution drawn up and adopted at Utrecht in May, 1938, and
Whereas, The official invitation to become a constituent member of the World Council of Churches is now before this Convention, issued by the Committee of Fourteen appointed for this purpose by the Oxford and Edinburgh Conferences, therefore, be it
Resolved, That the General Convention of the Protestant Episcopal Church hereby accepts the invitation to become a constituent member of the World Council of Churches; and further

Resolved, That the appointment of representatives from this Church to the Assembly of the World Council, should such appointment be necessary before the next General Convention, be made by the Presiding Bishop on nomination by the Commission on Faith and Order.

39. General Convention, 1940: Member of the Federal Council of Churches

Resolved, That this Church hereby become a member of the Federal Council of the Churches of Christ in America, and that the National Council of this Church be and hereby is instructed to appoint such representatives as may be required to make that membership effective.

40. Lambeth VIII, 1948: Cooperation in Christian Action

40. The Conference believes that it is the duty of the Church to bear united witness to God's redeeming grace in Jesus Christ, to do battle against the powers of evil, and to seek the glory of God in all things. It therefore appeals to Christians in all Communions, whatever the differences which may separate them in Church order and doctrine, to join in Christian action in all parts of the world irrespective of political party for the application of the principles of the Christian religion to all departments of national and international life.

41. Lambeth VIII, 1948: World Council of Churches

76. The Conference cordially welcomes the formation of the World Council of Churches and desires to place on record its deep appreciation of the valuable services already rendered to the cause of Christian unity by the officers and members of its Provisional Committee, and sends its good wishes to the Council for its first Assembly at Amsterdam and prays that God may guide and direct all its deliberations. The Conference hopes that the results of the Assembly at Amsterdam may be made widely known throughout the Anglican Communion, and that an active interest in the World Council of Churches may be encouraged in all dioceses and parishes.

42. Lambeth VIII, 1948: The Church of South India

52. We

(a) endorse generally the paragraphs in the Report of our Committee on Unity which refer to South India;

(b) give thanks to God for the measure of unity locally achieved by the inauguration of the Church of South India, and we pledge ourselves to pray and work for its development into an even more perfect fulfillment of the will of God for His Church; and we

(c) look forward hopefully and with longing to the day when there shall be full communion between the Church of South India and the Churches of the Anglican Communion.

43. Lambeth VIII, 1948: The Anglican Communion and the Church of South India

54. In the sphere of immediate and practical action, the Conference recommends:

(a) That former Anglicans, clerical or lay, who are now members of the Church of South India, and also Anglicans who hereafter join it, should be accepted and allowed full privileges of ministry and communion in any Church, Province, or Diocese of the Anglican Communion, subject to the regulations of the responsible authorities in the area concerned.

(b) That members, whether clerical or lay, of the Churches of the Anglican Communion, who may go to South India, should not be subject to censure if they join the Church of South India or take work of any kind in it.

(c) That clerical or lay members of the Churches of the Anglican Communion visiting the territory of the Church of South India should not be subject to censure if they accept the hospitality of that Church for the performance of priestly functions or the receiving of Holy Communion, subject to the regulations of the Churches, Provinces, or Dioceses to which they belong.

(d) That ministers of the Church of South India who have not been episcopally ordained should not be regarded as having acquired any new rights or status in relation to the Anglican Communion as a whole solely by reason of the fact that they are ministers of that Church.

(e) In regard to the bishops, presbyters, and deacons consecrated or ordained in the Church of South India at or after the inauguration of that Church, the Conference is unable to make one recommendation agreed to by all. It therefore records the two following views:

(1) One view (held by a majority) that such bishops, presbyters, and deacons should be acknowledged as true bishops, presbyters, and deacons in the Church of Christ and should be accepted as such in every part of the Anglican Communion, subject only to such regulations as are normally made in all such cases by the responsible authorities in each area;

(2) Another view (held by a substantial minority) that it is not yet possible to pass any definite judgement upon the precise status of such bishops, presbyters, and deacons in the Church of Christ or to recommend that they be accepted in the Anglican Communion as bishops, presbyters, or deacons.

The Conference records the fact that no member of the Conference desires to condemn outright or to declare invalid the episcopally consecrated and ordained ministry of the Church of South India. It recognizes that there will be differences in the attitude of Churches, Provinces, or Dioceses regarding the status of the bishops, presbyters, and deacons of the Church of South India, but it expresses the unanimous hope that such differences may never in any part of the Anglican Communion be made a ground for condemnation of action taken by any Church, Province, or Diocese.

(f) That lay communicants who in the Church of South India have received episcopal confirmation should, in Churches of the Anglican Communion, be received as communicants, subject to the approval of responsible authority, but should not thereby acquire any new status or rights in relation to the Anglican Communion as a whole; and

(g) That other recognized communicants of the Church of South India should, in Churches of the Anglican Communion, subject to the approval of responsible authority and to any such regulations as may locally obtain, be admissible to communion by an exercise of the principle of "economy."

44. Lambeth VIII, 1948: Further Approaches to Reunion

56. The Conference calls upon all the Churches of the Anglican Communion to seek earnestly by prayer and by conference the fulfilment of the vision "of a Church, genuinely Catholic, loyal to all truth, and gathering into its fellowship 'all who profess and call themselves Christians' within whose visible unity all the treasures of faith and order, bequeathed as a heritage by the past to the present, shall be possessed in common and made serviceable to the whole body of Christ." It recognizes that "within this unity Christian Communions now separated from one another would retain much that has long been distinctive in their methods of worship and service."

In the hope of setting forward the fulfillment of this vision, the Conference recalls the principles set forth in the Appeal to All Christian People, and the relevant Resolutions of the Lambeth Conference of 1920 on the Reunion of Christendom, and records certain counsels and considerations which it believes should guide the Churches of our Communion in future approaches to reunion:

(a) The theological issues, especially those concerning the Church and the ministry, should be faced at the outset, and to this end the negotiating Churches should obtain the help of theologians in framing schemes for reunion or intercommunion.

(b) The unification of the ministry in a form satisfactory to all the bodies concerned, either at the inauguration of the union or as soon as possible thereafter, is likely to be a prerequisite to success in all future proposals for the reunion of the Churches.

(c) The integral connexion between the Church and the ministry should be safeguarded in all proposals for the achievement of intercommunion through the creation of a mutually recognized ministry.

(d) The goal in any steps towards a united Church within a given area should always be a Church with which the Anglican Churches could eventually be in full communion.

(e) Because the Anglican Communion is itself a treasured unity with a special vocation, a part of our Communion contemplating a step which would involve its withdrawal from the Anglican family of Churches should consult the Lambeth Conference or the Provinces and member Churches of this family of Churches before final commitment to such a course.

45. Lambeth VIII, 1948: Proposals for Organic Union
57. The Conference has heard with satisfaction and hope of proposals for organic union in various areas, and, while calling the attention of those concerned in such schemes to the warnings contained in the Report of the Committee on Unity, believes that schemes of this type have undoubted advantages.

Separate resolutions dealt specifically with proposals in Ceylon, North India, Iran, and Nigeria.

46. Lambeth VIII, 1948: Schemes for the Provision of a Mutually Recognized Ministry
58. The Conference has heard with interest and sympathy of proposals for the provision of a mutually recognized ministry in advance of any explicit plans for organic union. In spite of the disadvantages attaching to such schemes, which are noted in the Report of the Committee on Unity, the Conference is not prepared to discourage

further explorations along this line, if they are linked with provisions for the growing together of the Churches concerned and with the definite acceptance of organic union as their final goal.

47. Lambeth VIII, 1948: A Wider Episcopal Unity

74. The Conference, welcoming the fact that some of the Churches of the Anglican Communion are already in intercommunion with the Old Catholic Churches, looking forward to the time when they will enter into communion with other parts of the Catholic Church not definable as Anglican, and desiring that Churches thus linked together should express their common relationship in common counsel and mutual aid, recommends that bishops of the Anglican Communion and bishops of other Churches which are, or may be, in communion with them should meet together from time to time as an episcopal conference, advisory in character, for brotherly counsel and encouragement.

This was reaffirmed by Lambeth IX, 1958, Resolution 16.

48. Lambeth VIII, 1948: Friendship Between Christians

77. The Conference recognizes that work of great value for the cause of reunion has been accomplished by the cultivation of personal friendships between Christians of different denominations; it believes that such friendships assist the growth of mutual understanding and of intercession; and it encourages members of the Anglican Communion to cultivate such friendships.

49. General Convention, 1949: Statement of Faith and Order

At the request of the General Convention of 1946, a Statement of Faith and Order was prepared by the Joint Commission on Approaches to Unity for the Lambeth Conference of 1948 and the General Convention of 1949. Lambeth 1948 declared it to be "in entire harmony with the Lambeth Quadrilateral, and may be used in negotiations of the Protestant Episcopal Church with any interested Christian body." The 1949 General Convention resolved likewise "that the Statement on Faith and Order may be used with any interested Christian body."

I. INTRODUCTION

. . . In accordance with the foregoing directive, the Joint Commission on Approaches to Unity presents this statement of Faith and Order as a basis for intercommunion, looking toward organic federation with other Christian bodies.

Intercommunion between two churches is understood as meaning that members of either church shall be permitted to receive Holy Communion in the other, and that ministers of either church shall be competent to celebrate the Holy Communion in the other.

One example of intercommunion now actually in effect is that between the Anglican and Old Catholic churches in Europe and America. The Bonn Agreement, which is the basis of this intercommunion though not necessarily normative for all future agreements, reads:

"1. Each communion recognizes the Catholicity and independence of the other, and maintains its own.

"2. Each communion agrees to admit members of the other communion to participate in the sacraments.

"3. Intercommunion does not require from either communion the acceptance of all doctrinal opinion, sacramental devotion, or liturgical practice characteristic of the other, but implies that each believes the other to hold all the essentials of the Christian faith."

Organic federation, which presupposes intercommunion, may take any one of several forms. It may be: (1) a federation, such as now exists among the churches of the Anglican Communion, with a council whose functions are purely advisory; (2) a federation which has an advisory council as in (1), and in addition merges administrative and missionary agencies, the autonomy of the uniting churches being not affected; (3) a federation which merges administrative and missionary agencies as in (2), and in addition has an overall legislative body with limited delegated powers . . .

II. THE QUADRILATERAL

A. The Holy Scriptures

The Holy Scriptures are the inspired record of God's self-revelation to man and of man's response to that revelation. This is the primary ground of the authority of the Scriptures.

The fact that the Church under the guidance of the Holy Spirit has accepted the Bible as canonical invests it as a whole with an authoritative character for all Christians. Its authority is further validated by the continuing experience of Christian people.

The Bible has an inner unity as the record of the special preparation for Christ, and of His redemption of man through His Life, Death, Resurrection, and Ascension, and through the gift of the Holy Ghost. Both in the Old and in the New Testaments the Kingdom of God is proclaimed and everlasting life is offered to mankind in Christ, the only Mediator between God and Man.

The Bible has been and is for the Christian Church the ultimate criterion of its teaching and the chief source of guidance for its life. It contains all doctrine required for salvation through faith in Jesus Christ.

The reading and preaching of the Word of God is indispensable for the life and worship of the Church.

B. The Creeds

The Apostles' Creed rehearses the mightly acts of God in creation, redemption, and sanctification as recorded in the Holy Scriptures. Upon these, the life of the Church is based. As a declaration of allegiance to the Triune God the Apostles' Creed is a profession of faith appropriate to Holy Baptism.

The Nicene Creed likewise witnesses to the faith of the historic Church in its assertion of fundamental Christian truths and its denial of fundamental errors and is appropriate to Holy Communion.

While liberty of interpretation may be allowed, the Christian faith as set forth in these two creeds ought to be received and believed by all Christian people.

The recitation of the Creeds in public worship is to be commended, though their invariable use in such fashion is not essential to the unity or the life of the Church.

C. The Sacraments

Baptism with water and with the Spirit, in the Name of the Father and of the Son and of the Holy Ghost, is a divinely instituted sacrament whereby we are made children of grace and incorporated into the Church, and receive forgiveness of sin and a new birth unto righteousness. The requirements for baptism are repentance and faith, declared by the recipient or on his behalf by his sponsors.

The Supper of the Lord, ministered with unfailing use of Christ's words of institution and the elements ordained by Him, is the supreme act of sacramental worship in the Christian Church. This Sacrament is a corporate act of the Church towards God, wherein it is united with its Lord, victorious and triumphant, Himself both Priest and Victim in the sacrifice of the Cross. In it the faithful continue a perpetual memory of the precious death of Christ who is their Advocate with the Father and the propitiation for their sins, according to His precept, until His coming again. For first they offer the sacrifice of praise and thanksgiving; then next they plead and represent before the Father the sacrifice of the Cross, and by it they confidently entreat remission of sins and all other benefits of the Lord's passion for all the whole Church; and lastly they offer the sacrifice of themselves to the Creator of all things which they have already signified by the oblations of the bread and wine which are His creatures. In the Supper of the Lord the faithful receive and partake, spiritually, of the Body and Blood of Christ; and thus enter into communion with Christ Himself and with one another in His Life.

In addition to the sacraments of Baptism and the Supper of the Lord, the Church recognizes sacramental rites or mysteries, namely, Confirmation, Absolution, the Marriage Blessing, Holy Orders and the Unction of the Sick.

D. The Historic Episcopate

1. *The Ministry.* The fundamental Christian ministry is the ministry of Christ. There is no Christian priesthood or ministry apart from His. His priestly and ministerial function is to reconcile the world to God in and through Himself, by His Incarnation and by His "one sacrifice once offered" and by the gift of the Holy Spirit, delivering men from the power of sin and death.

The Church as the Body of Christ, sharing His Life, has a ministerial function derived from that of Christ. In this function every member has his place and share according to his different capabilities and calling. The Church is set before us in the New Testament as a body of believers having within it, as its recognized focus of unity, of teaching and of authority, the Apostolate, which owed its origin to the action of the Lord Himself. There was not first an Apostolate which gathered a body of believers about itself; nor was there a completely structureless collection of believers which gave authority to the Apostles to speak and act on its behalf. From the first there was the fellowship of believers finding its unity in the Twelve. Thus the New Testament bears witness to the principle of a distinctive ministry, as an original element, but not the sole constitutive element, in the life of the Church.

2. *The Episcopate.* Anglican formularies deal with the episcopate as a fact rather than a doctrine. It is, however, a fact deeply rooted in history. The Lambeth Quadrilateral is, accordingly, employing a defining phrase when it speaks of the "historic episcopate." Acceptance of episcopacy as a basis of reunion necessarily means acceptance of it not as a bare fact, but a fact accompanied by its historical meaning.

The maintenance of a ministerial succession, by way of ordination with the laying-on-of-hands, is a familiar fact in the life of most Christian communions. All such ministerial successions are in some sense historic, differing from one another, however, in form and in the degree to which succession is continuous in history. Anglican formularies pronounce no judgments on other ministerial successions. They do claim, however, for the churches of the Anglican Communion for which they speak, that these churches have preserved both the form and the succession which traces back to the "Apostles' time," and they make the preservation of this succession a matter of scrupulous discipline. They define ministers within this historic stream as "Ministers of Apostolic Succession."

It should be clear, therefore, that while acceptance of the "historic episcopate" may not involve acceptance of any one formulation of the doctrine of the ministry, it does involve acceptance, in the form of a fact, of the three-fold ministry of bishops, priests, and deacons, and the acceptance of it also as accompanied by the claim that it is a ministerial succession tracing back to the "Apostles' time."

The Lambeth Conference Report of 1930 enlarges upon this claim as follows:

> When we speak of the Historic Episcopate, we mean the Episcopate as it emerged in the clear light of history from the time when definite evidence begins to be available. . . . Without entering into the discussion of theories which divide scholars, we may affirm shortly that we see no reason to doubt the statement made in the Preface to our Ordinal that 'from the Apostles' time there have been these Orders of Ministers in Christ's Church: Bishops, Priests and Deacons.' Whatever variety of system may have existed in addition to the earlier age, it is universally agreed that by the end of the second century episcopacy had no effective rival. Among all the controversies of the fourth and fifth centuries the episcopal ministry was never a subject of dispute. . . . If the Episcopate, as we find it established universally by the end of the second century, was a result of a process of adaptation and growth in the organism of the Church, that would be no evidence that it lacked divine authority, but rather that the life of the Spirit within the Church had found it to be the most appropriate organ for the functions which it discharged. In the course of time the Episcopate was greatly affected by secular forces, which bent it to many purposes alien to its true character and went far to obscure its spiritual purpose. . . . The Historic Episcopate as we understand it goes behind the perversions of history to the original conception of the Apostolic Ministry.

The concept of the episcopate can, accordingly, receive definition as an historical fact. It can also receive clarification from a description of its functions.

To quote from the Lambeth Report of 1930: "When we say that we must insist on the Historic Episcopate but not upon any theory or interpretation of it, we are not to be understood as insisting on the office apart from the functions. What we uphold is the Episcopate, maintained in successive generations by continuity of succession and consecration, as it has been throughout the history of the Church from the earliest times, and discharging those functions which from the earliest times it has discharged."

When we refer to the historic episcopate we are concerned with the essentials and purposes of the office of bishop and not with the incidental attributes of the office or the details of the administration of the Church, which have changed from time to time and may continue to change.

The most obvious function of the "historic episcopate"—the one which in the course of its varied history, has been most scrupulously guarded—is its vocation of transmitting the ministerial succession. The bishop is thus the organ of ministerial continuity. He is also the personal organ of the Church's unity. The very name bishop (episcopos) implies the function of pastoral care, of oversight. He is addressed in the Church's traditional liturgies as Father-in-God. He is also addressed as the Church's Shepherd. He represents the Church catholic to his flock, as the localized minister cannot do. Expressive of the Bishop's function of ministering the Word and of pastoral oversight is the opening prayer of the Anglican Form of Ordaining or Consecrating a Bishop.

> Almighty God, who by thy Son Jesus Christ didst give to thy holy Apostles many excellent gifts, and didst charge them to feed thy flock; Give grace, we beseech thee, to all Bishops, the Pastors of thy Church, that they may diligently preach thy Word, and duly administer the godly Discipline thereof. . . .

The fourth point of the Lambeth Quadrilateral was rephrased by the Lambeth Conference of 1920, in its Appeal to All Christian People, as follows: "A ministry acknowledged by every part of the Church as possessing not only the inward call of the Spirit, but also the commission of Christ and the authority of the whole Body."

We close this section by further quoting from this Appeal:

> May we not reasonably claim that the Episcopate is the one means of providing such a ministry? It is not that we call in question for a moment the spiritual reality of the ministries of those Communions which do not possess the Episcopate. On the contrary, we thankfully acknowledge that these ministries have been manifestly blessed and owned by the Holy Spirit as effective means of grace. But we submit that considerations alike of history

and of present experience justify the claim which we make on behalf of the Episcopate. Moreover, we would urge that it is now and will prove to be in the future the best instrument for maintaining the unity and continuity of the Church. But we greatly desire that the office of a Bishop should be everywhere exercised in a representative and constitutional manner, and more truly express all that ought to be involved for the life of the Christian Family in the title of Father-in-God. Nay more, we eagerly look forward to the day when through its acceptance in a united Church we may all share in that grace which is pledged to the members of the whole body in the apostolic rite of the laying-on-of-hands, and the joy and fellowship of a Eucharist in which as one Family we may together, without any doubtfulness of mind, offer to the one Lord our worship and service.

3. *The Priesthood and the Diaconate.* The office of a priest (presbyter) is to minister to the people committed to his care; to preach the Word of God; to baptize; to celebrate the Holy Communion; to pronounce absolution, or remission of sins, and blessing in God's name. Thus he exercises part of the Apostolic office, and it is significant that in the Anglican Ordinals, as in the general practice of the Western Church, which is itself based on very early usage, priests are associated with the bishop in laying-on-of-hands at the ordination of priests.

The office of a deacon is to assist the priest in divine service, and in his other ministrations, under the direction of the bishop. In the early Church the diaconate represented the ministry of the Church to men's bodily needs, but not as though these were separable from their spiritual states. Though this function is still emphasized in Anglican Ordinals, the deacon today exercises his office almost entirely in spiritual activities.

4. *Laity.* To the whole Church of God and to every member of it belongs the duty and privilege of spreading the good news of the Kingdom of God and the message of salvation through Jesus Christ and of interceding for the brethren. All, according to their measure, share in the priesthood which the Church derives from Him. This is the meaning of the doctrine of the priesthood of all believers.

III. THE QUADRILATERAL AND THE CHURCH

We have confined our exposition to the Quadrilateral; its interpretation must be seen in the context of the scriptural doctrine of the Church. This involves more extended consideration than can be given in this statement. We can, however, join with other Christian bodies in the affirmation in the Edinburgh report on Faith and Order:

We are at one in confessing belief in the Holy Catholic Church. We acknowledge that through Jesus Christ, particularly through the fact of His resurrection, of the gathering of His disciples round their crucified, risen, and victorious Lord, and of the coming of the Holy Spirit, God's Almighty will constituted the Church on earth.

The Church is the people of the new covenant, fulfilling and transcending all that Israel under the old covenant foreshadowed. It is the household of God, the family in which the fatherhood of God and the brotherhood of man is to be realized in the children of His adoption. It is the body of Christ, whose members derive their life and oneness from their one living head; and thus it is nothing apart from Him, but is in all things dependent upon the power of salvation which God has committed to His Son.

The presence of the ascended Lord in the Church, His Body, is effected by the power of the one Spirit, who conveys to the whole fellowship the gifts of the ascended Lord, dividing to every man severally as He will, guides it into all the truth and fills it unto all the fulness of God.

We all agree that Christ is present in His Church through the Holy Spirit as Prophet, Priest, and King. As Prophet He reveals the divine will and purpose to the Church; as Priest He ever liveth to make intercession for us, and through the eternal sacrifice once offered for us on Calvary He continually draws His people to the Most High; and as King He rules His Church and is ever establishing and extending His Kingdom.

Christ's presence in the Church has been perpetual from its foundation, and this presence He makes effective and evident in the preaching of the Word, in the faithful administration of the Sacraments, in prayer offered in His name, and through the newness of life whereby He enables the faithful to bear witness to Himself. Even though men often prove faithless, Christ will remain faithful to the promise of His presence, and will so continue till the consummation of all things.

IV. CONCLUSION

The foregoing statement is not a complete formulation of the faith and order of the Church. It is an exposition of the background and chief implications of the Chicago-Lambeth Quadrilateral. It has been formulated, not as a final pronouncement to which literal subscription should be asked, but as a means of assuring a substantial agreement upon the basis of which formal schemes for Church Union with any other Church may later be drawn up. We hope that the document will form a useful instrument of further negotiation with those Christian bodies which may be willing to join with us in seeking a way into that unity to which our Lord is calling all Christian people.

50. Lambeth IX, 1958: Statement on Christian Unity

13. The Conference welcomes and endorses the Statement on Christian Unity contained in the Report of the Committee on Christianity and the Church Universal.

The Statement said, in part:

We believe in One, Holy, Catholic, and Apostolic Church, which takes its origin not in the will of man but in the will of our Lord Jesus Christ. All those who believe in our Lord Jesus Christ and have been baptized in the name of the Holy Trinity are incorporated into the Body of Christ and are members of the Church. Here is a unity already given.

We believe that the mission of the Church is nothing less than the remaking and gathering together of the whole human race by incorporation into Christ. In obedience to this mission we must continually pray and work for the visible unity of all Christian believers of all races and nations in a living Christian fellowship of faith and sacrament, of love and prayer, witness and service.

The recovery and manifestation of unity, which we seek, is the unity of the whole Church of Christ. This means unity in living Christian fellowship, in obedience to Christ in every department of human life, and plain for all men to see. There can be no limit to the range of such unity. We are working for unity with the nonepiscopal Churches in our own countries and elsewhere. We continue to seek for such complete harmony of spirit and agreement in doctrine as would bring unity with the Eastern Orthodox Church and other ancient Churches. We must hope and pray for such eventual agreement in faith and order as shall lead to the healing of the breach between ourselves and the Church of Rome . . .

Loyalty to the age-long tradition of the Church, and to our own experience, compels us to believe that a ministry to be acknowledged by every part of the Church can only be attained through the historic episcopate, though not necessarily in the precise form prevailing in any part of the Anglican Communion. This ministry we believe to have been given to the Church by Divine Providence from primitive Christian times with its traditional functions of pastoral care and oversight, ordination, leadership in worship, and teaching. We fully recognize that there are other forms of ministry than episcopacy in which have been revealed the gracious activity of God in the life of the universal Church. We believe that other Churches have often borne more effective witness, for example, to the status and vocation of the laity as spiritual persons and to the fellowship and discipline of congregational life than has been done in some of the Churches of our communion. It is our longing that all the spiritual gifts and insights by which the particular Churches live to his glory may find their full scope and enrichment in a united Church.

The unity between Christian Churches ought to be a living unity in the love of Christ which is shown in full Christian fellowship and in mutual service, while also, subject to sufficient agreement in faith and order, expressing itself in free interchange of ministries, and fullness of sacramental Communion. Such unity, while marked by the bond of the historic episcopate, should always include congregational fellowship, active participation both of clergy and laity in the mission and government of the Church, and zeal for evangelism.

Such is the vision we set before ourselves and our own people, calling them to regard the recovery and manifestation of the unity of the whole Church of Christ as a matter of the greatest urgency. We call upon our own Church members, under the leadership of the bishop and clergy of the diocese, in full loyalty to their own Church, to join with their fellow Christians in united prayer. And we urge them to do their utmost through national and local Councils of Churches, for common Christian witness and common service to their fellows. Only so can the world see the People of God giving united witness to the Lord Jesus Christ, and feeding, clothing, healing, and visiting the least of his brethren in his Name.

Finally we appeal to all our people to show a spirit of charity in their dealings with other Christians wherever they may be, to respect other Christian Churches, to refrain from harsh or unkind words about them, whether in speech or in writing, and to seek to understand both their life and their doctrine by common study and by personal contacts. Above all, we appeal to them to pray for Christian unity, privately, corporately, and together with members of other Christian communions, that all believers may be united "in the way Christ wills and by the means he chooses," and to remember always that the nearer we draw to Christ, the nearer we draw to one another.

51. Lambeth IX, 1958: Full Communion and Intercommunion

14. The Conference endorses the paragraph in the Report of the Committee on Church Unity and the Church Universal which refers to the use of the terms "full communion" and "intercommunion," and recommends accordingly that where between two Churches not of the same denominational or confessional family, there is unrestricted *communio in sacris,* including mutual recognition and acceptance of

ministries, the appropriate term to use is "full communion," and that where varying degrees of relation other than "full communion" are established by agreement between two such Churches the appropriate term is "intercommunion."

The paragraph endorsed is as follows:

The Committee has examined the use of the terms "full communion" and "intercommunion" in official documents in recent years. Although since 1931 the terminology used to describe various degrees of inter-Church relationship has been inconsistent and confusing, the most common usage has been that advocated by the Lund Faith and Order Conference in 1952, whereby the term "full communion" has been kept to describe the close relation which exists between Churches of the same denominational or confessional family, such as the Churches of the Anglican Communion, and of the Orthodox, Lutheran, or Reformed "families" of Churches; whereas the term "Intercommunion" has been used to describe varying degrees of relation between Churches of one communion with a Church or Churches of another. Thus, for example, various Provinces and Churches of the Anglican Communion enjoy unrestricted *communio in sacris* with the Old Catholic Churches. Such unrestricted *communio in sacris,* involving complete sacramental fellowship and the mutual recognition and acceptance of ministries, has been described as "full intercommunion". It has however been pointed out that, although there may be a logical satisfaction in distinguishing between the "full communion" which exists between Churches which have grown up within the same family, and the "full intercommunion" which has been established with Churches outside the family, there is no distinction so far as spiritual reality is concerned. In each case there is unrestricted *communio in sacris*.

The committee therefore has concluded that it would be less confusing and indeed more true to reality to use the term "full communion" in all cases where a Province of the Anglican Communion by agreement enters into a relation of unrestricted *communio in sacris,* including the mutual recognition of ministries, with a Church outside our Communion. This would mean, for example, that the relation already existing between Churches of our Communion with the Old Catholic Churches would henceforth be described as that of "full communion," rather than "full intercommunion". The term "intercommunion" could then be used to describe the varying degrees of relation other than full communion, which already exist, or may be established in the future, between Churches of the Anglican family with others outside this family.

52. Lambeth IX, 1958: The Scheme of Church Union in Ceylon and the Plan of Church Union in North India and Pakistan

20. The Conference endorses generally the paragraphs of the Committee on Church Unity and the Church Universal which refer to the Scheme of Church Union in Ceylon and the Plan of Church Union in North India and Pakistan, and gives thanks to God for manifest signs of the work of the Holy Spirit in the negotiations which have brought the Scheme and Plan to this stage.

21. The Conference advises that when Churches have united in such a way that the whole ministry of the United Church has been episcopally united, permission to visiting ministers, not episcopally ordained, of Churches in communion with the United Churches at the time of the union, to celebrate the Holy Communion occasionally when visiting a United Church, be not regarded as a bar to relations of full communion between the United Church and the Churches and Provinces of the Anglican Communion; provided that due constitutional provisions are made to safeguard the conscience of worshippers.

In separate resolutions the Conference advised Churches of the Anglican Communion that they should be willing to enter into full Communion with the Church of Lanka and the Church of North India and Pakistan on their inauguration. This advice was repeated in 1968 with the addition that they should "foster the relations of fellowship which this involves."

53. Lambeth IX, 1958: The Methodist Church

29. The Conference has heard with interest and sympathy of the conversations now proceeding between representatives of the Church of England and representatives of the Methodist Church in England, and between representatives of the Protestant Episcopal Church, and representatives of the Methodist Church in the U.S.A.

30. The Conference calls attention to the Report of the Committee on Unity; and encourages continuance of the conversations with a view to the making of concrete proposals, as offering a possible first step on the way to reunion in the particular historic situations in which the Churches concerned are placed; but on the understanding that organic union is definitely accepted as the final goal, and that any plans for the interim stage of intercommunion are definitely linked with provisions for the steady growing together of the Churches concerned.

54. Lambeth IX, 1958: West Africa

31. The Conference expresses its sincere thankfulness at the growing interest within the Province of West Africa in conversations on re-union, having had before it the proposed Scheme of Union for Nigeria and the Cameroons which is at present receiving the prayerful consideration of the dioceses of the Province of West Africa and of the Methodist and Presbyterian Churches in Nigeria and the Cameroons.

32. The Conference, while recognizing the weight to be attached to arguments in favour of retaining the model of the Church of South India and the policy of gradualness therein expressed, but aware also of the desire within the Province that from the outset full communion should be maintained between Churches of the Anglican Communion and any united Church which might be formed, strongly recommends to the Province of West Africa further consideration of the Ceylon Scheme as a model, since only so does it seem likely that the desired result will be achieved.

33. The Conference recommends that in any Reunion Scheme the Ceylon or North India/Pakistan statement as to the Faith of the Church should be followed.

55. Lambeth IX, 1958: The Roman Catholic Church

38. The Conference welcomes the permission given by Roman Catholic authority for contacts, discussions, and co-operation between Roman Catholics and other Christians, as contained in the document, *Instruction to Local Ordinaries on the Oecumenical Movement,* issued by the Supreme Sacred Congregation of the Holy Office in December 1949; and expresses the hope, first, that these permissions may be more widely and generously used, secondly, that they may be further extended in the interests of Christian understanding and fellowship, and thirdly, that Anglicans will make full use of these and all other available opportunities for promoting charitable understanding.

56. Lambeth IX, 1958: The Old Catholic Churches

47. The Conference welcomes the suggestions made by a meeting between some Anglicans and Old Catholics in Holland, that the two Churches should co-operate in practical action to meet the spiritual needs of Dutch-speaking Christians who wish to resort to Anglican Churches in that country. It is of the opinion that such practical action would not only be a valuable demonstration of the intercommunion which exists between the Anglican and Old Catholic Churches, but also a means of deepening the fellowship that exists between the members of those Churches.

57. Lambeth IX, 1958: The Spanish Reformed Episcopal Church and the Lusitanian Church

51. The Conference, being entirely satisfied with Reports received on the present doctrine and discipline of the Spanish Reformed Episcopal Church and the Lusitanian Church, welcomes the news of the consecration of Bishop Molina in Spain and of Bishop Fiandor in Portugal by bishops of the Episcopal Church of the United States and of the Church of Ireland, and prays that these Churches may be blessed by God in the service of his Kingdom. The Conference hopes that the desire of these Churches for the same relationship with Churches of the Anglican Communion as have the Old Catholic Churches will soon be fulfilled.

58. Lambeth IX, 1958: The Philippine Independent Church

53. The Conference records its pleasure at the vigorous growth of the Philippine Independent Church and welcomes the progress being made in the relations between this Church and the Protestant Episcopal Church in the United States of America since the consecration of three bishops of the Philippine Independent Church by bishops of the Protestant Episcopal Church in the United States of America in 1948. The Conference is gratified to learn that priests of the Philippine Independent Church are receiving their theological training at St. Andrew's Theological Seminary in Manila.

59. Lambeth IX, 1958: *Episcopi Vagantes*

54. The Conference draws attention to the fact that there are *Episcopi Vagantes* who call themselves either "Old Catholic" or "Orthodox," in combination with other names. It warns its members of the danger of accepting such persons at their own valuation without making further enquiries. The Conference reiterates the principle contained in Resolution 27 of the 1920 Lambeth Conference, that it cannot recognize the Churches of such *episcopi vagantes* as properly constituted Churches, or recognize the orders of their ministers, and recommends that any such ministers desiring to join an Anglican Church, who are in other respects duly qualified, should be ordained *sub conditione* in accordance with the provisions suggested in the Report of the relevant Committee of the 1920 Lambeth Conference.

60. Lambeth IX, 1958: World Council of Churches

55. The Conference records its thankfulness to Almighty God for the formation, growth, and achievements of the World Council of Churches, and urges all the Churches and Provinces of the Anglican

Communion to ensure that they are adequately represented in its counsels, take a full share in its work, and assume a just part of its financial responsibility.

61. Lambeth IX, 1958: Inter-Church Aid

56. The Conference commends to all members of the Anglican Communion the outstanding work of relief and reconciliation carried out by the World Council of Churches Department of Inter-Church Aid and Service to Refugees, in which they have gladly participated. It urges them to support it wholeheartedly and when possible, themselves to offer sanctuary and the deepest charity to those who, for whatever cause, have lost their home and citizenship.

62. Lambeth IX, 1958: Prayer for the Unity of Christ's People in the Way He Wills and by the Means He Chooses

57. The Conference wishes to emphasize the importance of widespread prayer for the unity of all Christian people, and commends to all Anglicans the observance of the Week of Prayer for Christian Unity in the spirit of the late Abbé Paul Couturier, who taught many to pray for the unity of Christ's people in the way he wills and by the means he chooses. It welcomes the remarkable growth of such prayer and commends the formation of local groups of Christians of different traditions for the purpose of promoting prayer for Christian unity.

63. General Convention, 1961: Consultation on Church Union

Whereas, The United Presbyterian Church in the United States of America in its General Assembly of May, 1961, adopted the following resolution:

"1. The 173d General Assembly of the United Presbyterian Church in the United States of America meeting in Buffalo, New York, May 17–24, 1961, being convinced that in obedience to the Lord Jesus Christ the unity of His Church should be made more fully manifest that it may be renewed by the Holy Spirit for its mission to our nation and to the world 'that the world may believe,' invites the Protestant Episcopal Church, meeting in General Convention in Detroit, Michigan, in this same year, to join us in an invitation to The Methodist Church and the United Church of Christ to explore the establishment of a united church truly Catholic, truly Reformed, and truly Evangelical.

"Each Church giving or accepting the invitation is asked to authorize by its own procedures a committee of nine persons to negotiate a plan of union and further to authorize these representatives in cooperation with those of the several negotiating Churches to invite other Churches to appoint representatives, either to join them in the development of the plan or to sit with them as observers and consultants as they do their work together.

"It is understood that each Church will review the progress of the work at each meeting of its plenary body and that when a plan of union is agreed upon by the joint negotiating Committee, each Church will then decide whether to adopt it. . . ."

Whereas, The Joint Commission on Approaches to Unity is mindful that it has been instructed by every General Convention since 1934 to explore possibilities for organic union with Presbyterians, Methodists, and other interested bodies, on the basis of the Chicago-Lambeth Quadrilateral; therefore be it

Resolved, The House of . . . concurring, that the General Convention of the Protestant Episcopal Church in the United States of America accepts the invitation of The United Presbyterian Church in the United States of America to join with it in inviting The Methodist Church and the United Church of Christ to explore possibilities for an eventual united church "truly Catholic, truly Reformed, and truly Evangelical"; with the understanding that any proposal shall be referred to the General Convention for its consideration and action; and be it further

Resolved, That the General Convention authorize the Joint Commission on Approaches to Unity to conduct these conversations on the basis of the Chicago-Lambeth Quadrilateral on behalf of the Protestant Episcopal Church; to determine the size and nature of any subcommittee which shall from time to time take part; to notify the Stated Clerk of The United Presbyterian Church in the United States of America of our readiness to participate; and regularly to report the results of these conversations to the General Convention for its consideration; and be it further

Resolved, That the General Convention direct the Joint Commission on Approaches to Unity to invite representatives of the Polish National Catholic Church, with whom we are in full communion in this country, as well as from time to time representatives of any Church with which this Church is in full communion, to participate in the conversations.

64. General Convention, 1961: Historic Position the Framework for All Conversations

Resolved, that the Joint Commission on Approaches to Unity be reminded of the various historic statements defining this Church's stand in the field of Christian reunion beginning with the Chicago version of the Quadrilateral in 1886 and including several statements by successive Lambeth Conferences, particularly the Faith and Order Statement prepared by the Commission itself for the Lambeth Conference of 1948 and the General Convention of 1949; and that the Joint Commission on Approaches to Unity be, and it hereby is, instructed to make the historic position of this Church as defined in these several statements the framework for all Church unity conversations in which it shall be engaged.

65. General Convention, 1961: The Lusitanian Church

Resolved, The House of Deputies concurring, that the General Convention invites the General Synods of the Spanish Reformed Episcopal Church and of the Lusitanian Church, Catholic, Apostolic, Evangelical, to join with it in the following declaration, which shall be effective in each case when adopted by the General Synod of the respective Church:

"With gratitude to Almighty God for the blessing bestowed upon each of the Churches, and in appreciation of the fraternal relations which have long existed between them, the Churches recognize each other as a true part of the Holy Catholic Church and declare that they are in full communion with another on the basis of mutual acceptance of the following Concordat:*

(1) Each Communion recognizes the catholicity and independence of the other and maintains its own.

(2) Each Communion agrees to admit members of the other Communion to participate in the Sacraments.

(3) Full Communion does not require from either Communion the acceptance of all doctrinal opinion, sacramental devotion, or liturgical practice characteristic of the other, but implies that each believes the other to hold all the essentials of the Christian Faith.

"And furthermore, the Churches pledge themselves to work together in brotherly harmony for the extension of the Gospel of our Lord Jesus Christ, and to give such mutual assistance as they are able."

66. General Convention, 1961: The Philippine Independent Church

Whereas, the Supreme Council of Bishops and the General Assembly of the Iglesia Filipina Independiente have passed resolutions proposing full communion with the Protestant Episcopal Church, and have agreed on the establishment of full communion on the basis of a

* Further on the term "concordat" see William A. Norgren, "The Concordat Relationships," pp. 184–211 of this volume.

mutually-accepted concordat similar to the Bonn Agreement existing between the Old Catholic and the Anglican Churches, and

Whereas, the House of Bishops of the Protestant Episcopal Church has received the resolution of the Iglesia Filipina Independiente with deep thanksgiving in Christ, and unanimously recommended that such a concordat be entered into; and,

Whereas, the Convention of the Philippine Episcopal Church has also recommended to the General Convention that this concordat be entered into; and

Whereas, the Declaration of the Faith, the Articles of Religion, the Constitution, Canons, and other official formularies of the Iglesia Filipina Independiente embody and affirm adherence to principles of faith and order, discipline and worship that mark it as a true part of the One, Holy, Catholic, and Apostolic Church; therefore be it

Resolved, that the Protestant Episcopal Church agrees to the establishment of a relation of full communion with the Iglesia Filipina Independiente on the basis of mutual acceptance of the following concordat:

(1) Each Communion recognizes the catholicity and independence of the other and maintains its own.

(2) Each Communion agrees to admit members of the other Communion to participate in the Sacraments.

(3) Full Communion does not require from either Communion the acceptance of all doctrinal opinion, sacramental devotion, or liturgical practice characteristic of the other, but implies that each believes the other to hold all the esentials of the Christian Faith.

Resolved, that this agreement shall be communicated to the Obispo Maximo, the Supreme Council of Bishops and the General Assembly of Iglesia Filipina Independiente with the assurance of our thanksgiving for the full measure of Christian fellowship thus achieved and our confident hope in Christ that the mission of the two Churches will be widened and strengthened in the future by the full communion now established.

67. General Convention, 1964: New Delhi Statement on Christian Unity

Resolved, that subject to the official teaching of this Church as expressed in its own formularies, this Convention give its approval to the following two paragraphs adopted by the New Delhi Assembly of the

World Council of Churches and commend them to the Church for use in ecumenical study and dialogue:

We believe that the unity which is both God's will and his gift to his Church is being made visible as all in each place who are baptized into Jesus Christ and confess Him as Lord and Saviour are brought by the Holy Spirit into one fully committed fellowship, holding the one Apostolic Faith, preaching the one gospel, breaking the one bread, joining in common prayer, and having a corporate life reaching out to witness and service to all; and who at the same time are united with the whole Christian fellowship in all places and ages in such wise that ministry and members are accepted by all and that all can act and speak together as occasion requires for the tasks to which God calls his people.

It is for such unity that we believe we must pray and work.

68. General Convention, 1967: The Visible Unity of the Whole Christian Fellowship

Whereas, This Church has, in the statement of the House of Bishops in Chicago, 1886, and in subsequent affirmations thereof, expressed its commitment to Church unity in the following terms:

(1) Our earnest desire that the Saviour's prayer "that we all may be one", may, in its deepest and truest sense, be speedily fulfilled;

(2) That we believe that all who have been duly baptized with water in the Name of the Father, and of the Son, and of the Holy Ghost, are members of the Holy Catholic Church;

(3) That in all things of human ordering or human choice, relating to modes of worship and discipline, or to traditional customs, this Church is ready in the spirit of love and humility to forego all preferences of her own;

(4) That this Church does not seek to absorb other Communions, but rather, co-operating with them on the basis of a common Faith and Order, to discountenance schism, to heal the wounds of the Body of Christ, and to promote the charity which is the chief of Christian graces and the visible manifestation of Christ to the world;

and

Whereas, The Consultation on Church Union, in *Principles of Church Union,* adopted in 1966, has declared: "The people of God exist as one people, and only one, of every nationality and race and tongue. They have been made so in Christ; and he wills that they make this unity evident"; and, in its Open Letter to the Churches, has said, "We recognize also that the united body proposed will still be far from the wholeness of the body of Christ . . . We have imagined this structure as best we could, to keep it open to all others who with ourselves seek a wider unity of catholic and evangelical traditions, alike reformed by every true obedience to God", now, therefore, be it

Resolved, the House of Deputies concurring, That this General Convention affirm that the object of this Church's ecumenical policy is to press toward the visible unity of the whole Christian fellowship in the faith and truth of Jesus Christ, developing and sharing in its various dialogues and consultations in such a way that the goal be neither obsured nor compromised and that each separate activity be a step toward the fullness of unity for which our Saviour prayed.

69. General Convention, 1967: Ecumenical Study and Prayer

Resolved, That Church people in parishes and dioceses be and they hereby are encouraged to study the reports and documents of the Consultation on Church Union, together with such significant ecumenical developments as Vatican II, Anglican-Orthodox Relations, and other movements toward understanding, co-operation, and unity among God's people; that such studies be undertaken in concert with members of other Churches as much as possible, and that the Executive Council be and it hereby is authorized to provide designs and materials for such programs of study; and be it further

Resolved, That members of this Church be asked to keep the cause of Christian unity constantly in their hearts and minds and to make it the subject of daily intercession, both public and private.

70. General Convention, 1967: Statement on Communion Discipline

Endorsed by the Convention, this statement affords theological principles to show who may receive Communion in the Episcopal Church. It indicates movement from the House of Bishops statement in 1952 (Journal of General Convention, 1952, p. 40), which allowed Christians of other churches to receive at special occasions of ecumenical significance, by adding "circumstances of individual spiritual need." The statement does not apply, of course, to members of Churches already in full communion or intercommunion with the Episcopal Church. Further see "Discipline of the Episcopal Church on Sharing of the Eucharist," Ecumenical Bulletin *No. 29, 1978.*

The Holy Communion must be seen in its proper context of the fellowship of committed Christians in the household of the Apostolic Faith, to which we are admitted by Baptism. In the historic tradition which the Episcopal Church maintains and practices, the baptized member completes his baptismal initiation by personal profession of faith and loyalty, and so proceeds to the blessing of Confirmation and participation in the Holy Eucharist.

In the historic Churches, Eastern and Western, the Bishop, as the center of unity of the Christian family, is active in the whole process—authorizing the administration of Baptism (usually by a priest, but sometimes by a deacon or a layman); confirming, either in person or (in some traditions) by delegation to a priest; ordaining the celebrant of the Eucharist, if he does not officiate at it himself.

The normative condition of the Church is union in one fellowship, at once of faith, sacramental practice, personal relations, and Church Order; and this is, therefore, the situation which the services and rules of the Prayer Book embody.

The anomalous situation of Christian division requires us to accept at the heart of our Christian experience the pain of its divisions which the present ecumenical renewal of the Church is beginning to over-come. Yet all who have been baptized in the Name of the Father, the Son, and Holy Spirit, have been made members of the Body of Christ.

Those who, in other Christian traditions than ours, have, by personal profession of faith and personal commitment affirmed their status as members of the Body, may, on occasion, be led by their Christian obedience to wish to receive Communion in our Church. We believe that such baptized persons may properly do so, where the discipline of their own Church permits, not only at special occasions of ecumenical gatherings specifically looking toward Church unity, but also in cir-cumstances of individual spiritual need; and that this does not require any rubrical or canonical changes, since this Statement does not authorize what is commonly known as "Open Communion."

We hope that such recognition of the deep significance of our basic fellowship and Baptism will help to speed the day when all the chil-dren of God will be able to join in fellowship around the Table of the Lord.

71. General Convention, 1967: Anglican–Roman Catholic Relations To Be Set in International Context

Whereas, The conversations of the Joint Commission on Ecumenical Relations with the official representatives of the Roman Catholic Church have moved significantly toward theological understanding and common Christian witness; now, therefore, be it

Resolved, That this dialogue be strongly endorsed and that the Joint Commission be instructed to continue explorations toward theological agreement and effective working relationships with the Roman Catholic Church; and be it further

Resolved, That the Joint Commission relate the conversations in the United States to the world-wide dialogue between the Roman Catholic Church and the Anglican Communion and include in its Report and recommendations to the next General Convention the developments from this wider consultation.

72. Lambeth X, 1968: The Lund Principle

44. (a) We believe that each bishop of the Anglican Communion should ask himself how seriously he takes the suggestion of the Lund Conference on Faith and Order that we should do together everything which conscience does not compel us to do separately. To do so immediately raises the need to review church structures (conduct of synods, budgets, areas of jurisdiction, etc.) to see where they can be altered to foster rather than hinder co-operation. It involves giving encouragement in this direction to all whom we can influence. It involves also the exploration of *responsible experiment* so that ecumenical work beyond the present limits of constitutional provision is encouraged to keep in touch with the common mind of the Church and not tempted to break away.

73. Lambeth X, 1968: Prior Attention to the Local Level

44. (b) We believe that prior attention in ecumenical life and action should be given to the local level, and point to local ecumenical action as the most direct way of bringing together the whole Christian community in any area.

74. Lambeth X, 1968: Goal of a Genuinely Universal Council

44. (c) We believe that as ecumenical work develops in local, national, and regional areas the need becomes more apparent for an ecumenical forum on the widest possible scale. We therefore endorse the hope expressed at the Uppsala Assembly that "the members of the World Council of Churches, committed to each other, should work for the time when a genuinely universal council may once more speak for all Christians".

Our interim confessional and ecumenical organizations should be tested by their capacity to lead in this direction.

75. Lambeth X, 1968: Admission of Non-Anglicans to Holy Communion

45. The Conference recommends that, in order to meet special pastoral needs of God's people, under the direction of the bishop Christians duly baptized in the name of the Holy Trinity and qualified to receive Holy Communion in their own Churches may be welcomed at the Lord's table in the Anglican Communion.

76. Lambeth X, 1968: Anglicans Communicating in Other Churches

46. The Conference recommends that, while it is the general practice of the Church that Anglican communicants receive the Holy Communion at the hands of ordained ministers of their own Church or of Churches in communion therewith, nevertheless under the general direction of the bishop, to meet special pastoral need, such communicants be free to attend the Eucharist in other Churches holding the apostolic faith as contained in the Scriptures and summarized in the Apostles' and Nicene Creeds, and as conscience dictates to receive the sacrament, when they know they are welcome to do so.

77. Lambeth X, 1968: Reciprocal Acts of Intercommunion

47. The Conference recommends that, where there is agreement between an Anglican Church and some other Church or Churches to seek unity in a way which includes agreement on apostolic faith and order, and where that agreement to seek unity has found expression, whether in a covenant to unite or in some other appropriate form, a Church of the Anglican Communion should be free to allow reciprocal acts of intercommunion under the general direction of the bishop; each province concerned to determine when the negotiations for union in which it is engaged have reached the stage which allows this intercommunion.

78. Lambeth X, 1968: The Church of South India

48. The Conference recommends:

(a) that when a bishop or episcopally ordained minister of the Church of South India visits a diocese of the Anglican Communion and exercises his ministry in Anglican Churches there should now be no restriction on the exercise of his ministry in other Churches with which the Church of South India is in communion.

(b) that Churches and Provinces of the Anglican Communion re-examine their relation to the Church of South India with a view to entering into full communion with the Church.

79. Lambeth X, 1968: Anglican–Methodist Unity in Great Britain

51. The Conference welcomes the proposals for Anglican-Methodist unity in Great Britain and notes with satisfaction the view expressed in the report of Section III that the proposed Service of Reconciliation is theologically adequate to achieve its declared intentions of reconciling the two Churches and integrating their ministries.

80. Lambeth X, 1968: Anglican–Roman Catholic Relations

52. The Conference welcomes the proposals made in the report of Section III which concern Anglican relations with the Roman Catholic Church.

An excerpt from the above-mentioned report follows:

In the "Common Declaration," signed in Rome on 24 March 1966, the Pope and the Archbishop of Canterbury gave thanks to Almighty God for the new atmosphere of Christian fellowship now existing between the two Churches, and declared their intention of inaugurating "a serious dialogue which, founded on the Gospels and on the ancient common traditions, may lead to that unity in truth, for which Christ prayed." This dialogue, they declared, was to include "not only theological matters such as Scripture, Tradition and Liturgy, but also matters of practical difficulty felt on either side."

It was as a result of this Declaration that a Joint Preparatory Commission was set up; and the Section received with gratitude the report issued as a result of the three meetings of that Commission.

Essential to such meetings is the spirit in which they are undertaken. For our part we recognize in penitence that many of our past attitudes and actions have contributed to our unhappy divisions and that there are still many things in us for which we must ask the forgiveness of God and of our fellow Christians. Yet we are thankful for the many signs of renewal of the spirit of unity in ourselves and in others.

Together with the Roman Catholic Church we confess our faith in God, Father, Son, and Holy Spirit, as witnessed by the holy Scriptures, the Apostles' and Nicene Creeds, and by the teaching of the Fathers of the early Church. We have one baptism and recognize many common features in our heritage. At the same time substantial divergences exist, many of which have arisen since the sixteenth century, in such matters as the unity and indefectibility of the Church and its teaching authority, the Petrine primacy, infallibility, and Mariological definitions, as well as in some moral problems. These matters will require serious study so that they may be carefully identified and, under the guidance of the Spirit, resolved. This task must be undertaken in the light of the challenge to the whole Church of God presented by the modern world, and in the context of the mission of the Church throughout the world and to all sorts and conditions of men.

SIGNS OF PROGRESS

Relations between Anglicans and Roman Catholics are progressing in various ways and to varying degrees in many places. Examples include common services of prayer and thanksgiving, the joint use of churches, the exchange of preachers, co-operation in theological education, and meetings of official commissions and informal groups. With due regard to individual consciences, we endorse and encourage these developments where local circumstances permit the avoidance of misunderstanding.

We rejoice that the new attitude towards Scripture, expressed in the Constitution on Divine Revelation, has led to co-operation in biblical studies and in the work of the United Bible Societies.

Liturgical renewal and reform represent a field where co-operation is urgent. Unilateral action in regard to the liturgical year and the vernacular forms used by our people is to be avoided.

The Christian witness being given by our clergy and laity in many urgent human issues, in many cases in close association with Roman Catholics, claims our support and our prayers. Where such witness may be strengthened by joint or parallel statements by church leaders, these should be issued.

We welcome the increasing signs of mutual recognition, not least in practical acts on both sides, of the reality of Anglican and Roman Catholic ministry in the whole Body of Christ on earth.

81. Lambeth X, 1968: Collegiality

55. The Conference recommends that the principle of collegiality should be a guiding principle in the growth of the relationships between the provinces of the Anglican Communion and those Churches with which we are, or shall be, in full communion, and draws particular attention to that part of the Section III report which underlines this principle.

The report itself said the following:

EPISCOPACY, COLLEGIALITY, PAPACY

The Anglican tradition has always regarded *episcopacy* as an essential part of its Catholic inheritance. We would regard it as an extension of the apostolic office and function both in time and space, and, moreover, we regard the transmission of apostolic power and responsibility as an activity of the college of bishops and never as a result of isolated action by any individual bishop.

In the discharge of his episcopal responsibility, the bishop is the guardian of the faith, the father of his people, and the driving force of mission in his area.

Traditionally the bishop is father in God to the clergy and laity of a territorial diocese, and part of his vocation is to represent the Catholic Church in his diocese and, conversely, to represent his diocese within the councils of the wider Church.

While we have no wish to diminish the importance of this traditional pattern, the demands of a new age suggest the wisdom of also consecrating bishops without territorial jurisdiction but with pastoral responsibility, directly or indirectly, for special groups such as the armed forces, industry, and particular areas of concern within the mission of the Church. This principle would simply be the extension of the widespread current practice of appointing suffragans, auxiliaries, and assistants. We submit that all such bishops, by virtue of their consecration as bishops in the Church of God, should have their due place in episcopal councils throughout the world.

The principle underlying *collegiality* is that the apostolic calling, responsibility, and authority are an inheritance given to the whole body or college of bishops. Every individual bishop has therefore a responsibility both as a member of this college and as chief pastor in his diocese. In the latter capacity he exercises direct oversight over the people committed to his charge. In the former he shares with his brother bishops throughout the world a concern for the wellbeing of the whole Church.

Within the college of bishops it is evident that there must be a president. In the Anglican Communion this position is at present held by the occupant of the historic see of Canterbury, who enjoys a primacy of honour, not of jurisdiction. This primacy is found to involve, in a particular way, that care for all the Churches which is shared by all the bishops.

The renewed sense of the collegiality of the episcopate is especially important at a time when most schemes for unity are being developed at a national level, because the collegiality of the episcopate helps to stress the worldwide and universal character of the Church. This collegiality must be a guiding principle in the growth of the relationships between the provinces of the Anglican Communion and those Churches with which we are, or shall be, in full communion. Within this larger college of bishops, the primacy would take on a new character which would need to be worked out in consultation with the Churches involved.

As a result of the emphasis placed on collegiality at the Second Vatican Council, the status of bishops in the Roman Catholic Church was in great measure enhanced, though the teaching of the First Vatican Council on the infallibility and immediate and universal jurisdiction of the Pope was unaffected. We are unable to accept this teaching as it is commonly understood today. The relationships between the Pope and the episcopal college, of which he is a member, are, however, still being clarified, and are subject to development. We recall the statement in the Lambeth Conference of 1908, and repeated in 1920 and 1930, "that there can be no fulfilment of the Divine purpose in any scheme of reunion which does not ultimately include the great Latin Church of the West, with which our history has been so closely associated in the past, and to which we are still bound by many ties of common faith and tradition." We recognize the Papacy as a historic reality whose developing role requires deep reflection and joint study by all concerned for the unity of the whole Body of Christ.

Although the declaration and guardianship of the faith has traditionally been regarded as belonging fundamentally to the episcopal office, the collegiality of the episcopate must always be seen in the context of the conciliar character of the Church, involving the *consensus fidelium*, in which the episcopate has its place.

82. Special General Convention, 1969: The Bucharest Statement

In response to a resolution of the Lambeth Conference X, 1968, the General Convention passed the following resolution:

Whereas, In the providence of God, the Orthodox Communion and the Anglican Communion are taking up again the work of *rapprochement,* which went forward so hopefully in the 1930's, but which was interrupted by World War II and subsequent political turmoil; and

Whereas, The Bucharest Conference of 1935 made significant statements of agreement between Anglican and Rumanian Orthodox representatives on the Holy Eucharist, Tradition, Sacraments, and Justification, which were accepted and approved by the Convocations of Canterbury and York in the following year, and which the Lambeth

Conference of 1968 has again called to the attention of the Churches of the Anglican Communion; therefore, be it

Resolved, That this Special General Convention endorse the report of the Bucharest Conference of Anglican and Rumanian Orthodox representatives in 1935, as, in the words of the Convocation of Canterbury, "consonant with Anglican formularies and a legitimate interpretation of the faith of the Church as held by the Anglican Communion"; and be it further

Resolved, That this Convention look forward in particular to the growth of a fuller and deeper common understanding between the Anglican Communion and the Orthodox Church on the meaning of the Holy Communion and all other subjects which will contribute to Christian unity.

83. Special General Convention, 1969: Common Liturgical Forms

Resolved, That the Standing Liturgical Commission, having been designated by the 62nd General Convention as its instrument for the revision of the Book of Common Prayer, and being engaged in the prosecution of that task pursuant to a plan approved by said General Convention, be, and the same is hereby, authorized

1. To explore and take advantage of all opportunities for collaboration, on both the national and international levels, by consultations and otherwise, with comparable bodies related to other Christian Communions that are likewise working for liturgical reform; and

2. To seek agreement with the afore-mentioned groups in respect to those essential structures and basic formularies of sacramental and liturgical rites which are shared in common, whether deriving from the Holy Scriptures or from the universal tradition of the Church.

84. General Convention, 1970: Anglican–Roman Catholic Relations

Whereas, Official representatives of this Church and of the Roman Catholic Church in the United States have, in seven sessions of the joint Anglican/Roman-Catholic Commission (ARC), made great progress in mutual understanding and agreement, notably in regard to the nature of Baptism, Holy Communion, and the Church as Eucharistic Community; and

Whereas, The seventh meeting of ARC, held in December, 1969, adopted a significant document which reported the progress to date, defined the goal as "full communion and organic unity," and affirmed that "nothing in the course of this serious enterprise has emerged which would cause us to think that this goal is unattainable"; and

Whereas, The Bishops' Committee on Ecumenical and Interreligious

Affairs of the Roman Catholic Church voted on March 18, 1970, that it "gratefully and enthusiastically accepts the ARC report, considers it to be a significant report, and will give it very serious consideration"; and

Whereas, The Joint Commission on Ecumenical Relations also gives its enthusiastic approval, and asks the General Convention "to endorse the report and to implement it by adopting the recommendations in its final section"; now be it

Resolved, That this 63rd General Convention of the Episcopal Church (1) Gratefully and enthusiastically accept the report of the Anglican/Roman-Catholic Commission, as incorporated in the Report of the Joint Commission on Ecumenical Relations;

(2) Endorse the progress along the lines of the joint Anglican/Roman-Catholic International Commission;

(3) Direct the Joint Commission on Ecumenical Relations to continue its participation in the joint Anglican/Roman-Catholic Commission, looking toward the defined goal of full communion and organic unity between the Churches of the Anglican Communion and the Roman Catholic Church; and

(4) Authorize and direct the Executive Council to co-operate with the Joint Commission on Ecumenical Relations in the implementation of the programs recommended by the Anglican/Roman-Catholic Commission, especially as set forth in paragraphs 4, 5, 6, and 11 of Section D of the report, relating to joint clergy conferences, sharing in theological training, cooperation between staff personnel in the areas of adult education, professional leadership training, education of the young, missions, and other means of diffusing ecumenical knowledge and understanding through our Churches at all levels.

The resolution then describes eleven recommended programs in detail.

85. General Convention, 1970: Search for an Ecumenical Hymnal
Resolved, That the Joint Commission on Church Music be empowered to seek the cooperation of other Christian bodies in the hope of the eventual production of an ecumenical hymnal.

86. General Convention, 1973: ARCIC Agreed Statement on Eucharistic Doctrine
Whereas. The 63rd General Convention of the Episcopal Church [1970] endorsed the progress of the Anglican–Roman Catholic International Commission; and

Whereas, The same General Convention directed the Joint Commission on Ecumenical Relations to continue to work toward "the defined goal of full communion and organic unity between the Churches of the Anglican Communion and the Roman Catholic Church," and

Whereas, The Anglican/Roman Catholic International Commission at its third meeting in Windsor, England, issued an "Agreed Statement on Eucharistic Doctrine," and

Whereas, The House of Bishops of the Episcopal Church, meeting at Pocono Manor, Pa., in October, 1971, welcomed "the substantial agreement and common eucharistic faith it (the Statement) expresses"; stated that "the Statement if agreed upon . . . would remove eucharistic faith as an obstacle to the unity sought by the churches in God's name," and commended the Statement "to the Episcopal Church for study and action at the next General Convention"; now be it

Resolved, That the 64th General Convention of the Episcopal Church affirms the Statement, "Agreed Statement on Eucharistic Doctrine," from the Anglican/Roman Catholic International Commission to be a significant theological description of the ongoing eucharistic lives of the Churches in question, without trying to force that description into the polemical categories of the past; substantial matters have been discussed and substantial agreement has been reached. We welcome the progress made in this Theological Statement, recognizing that a doctrine of Eucharist cannot be considered in isolation from a doctrine of Ministry. We expect the Commission's forthcoming statement on the Doctrine of the Ministry to illuminate further its Agreement on the Eucharist; and be it further

Resolved, That the Bishops, Ecumenical Officers and Diocesan Ecumenical Commissions (Committees) of our several Dioceses be asked to encourage the study of, and have ecumenical dialogue within each Diocese on the "Agreed Statement on the Eucharist" of the Anglican/Roman Catholic International Commission; and that the Dioceses be asked, with the co-operation of the Bishops, Clergy, and Laity, of our sister Church, to encourage the development of covenant relationships between Episcopal and Roman Catholic parishes and missions, that thereby our unity in the Body of Christ may be manifested and strengthened.

87. General Convention, 1973: Communion with North India, Pakistan, and Bangladesh Churches

Resolved, That the Episcopal Church invite the Church of North India, the Church of Pakistan, and the Church of Bangladesh (Diocese of

Dacca) to enter into full communion with it, on the principles of the 1931 Bonn Concordat; namely,

(a) Each Church recognizes the catholicity and independence of the other, and maintains its own.
(b) Each Church agrees to admit members of the other to participate in the sacraments.
(c) Full communion does not require from either Church the acceptance of all doctrinal opinions, sacramental devotion, or liturgical practice characteristic of the other, but implies that each believes the other to hold all the essentials of the Christian faith.

88. General Convention, 1973: Consultation on Church Union

Whereas, There is a general unreadiness to accept organizational structures as formerly proposed by the Consultation on Church Union in "A Plan of Union"; and

Whereas, In that understanding and the desire for unity are reached through the experience of working and worshiping together at all levels of Church life; therefore, be it

Resolved, That the 64th General Convention of this Church authorize the Joint Commission on Ecumenical Relations to continue its participation in the Consultation on Church Union; and be it further

Resolved, That the Joint Commission on Ecumenical Relations be instructed to continue its emphasis on theologically sound approaches to the problems of Faith and Order as a basis for full communion and organic union, working within the guidelines laid down by the Chicago-Lambeth quadrilateral, and attempt to bring other Christian bodies into conversations with the Consultation.

89. General Convention 1973: Common Eucharistic Lectionary

Whereas, Several Christian Churches are in the process of revising lectionaries for the Church Year; and

Whereas, A common set of lections is an aid to Christian unity and an asset in sharing homiletical material; and

Whereas, The new three-year cycle of lessons in use by the Episcopal Church, the Roman Catholic Church, and the Lutheran Churches already agree in many respects; therefore, be it

Resolved, That the 64th General Convention of the Episcopal Church direct the Standing Liturgical Commission to devise a lectionary, in consultation with the liturgical commissions of other

Churches, which will provide for common readings on common Sundays throughout the three-year cycle.

90. General Convention, 1976: ARCIC Agreed Statement on Ministry and Ordination

Whereas, the Anglican–Roman Catholic International Commission is making a significant contribution to the quest for the mutual recognition and reunion of the Anglican Communion and the Roman Catholic Church:

And whereas, that Commission has now issued a consensus statement on Ministry and Ordination:

Therefore, be it resolved, that this General Convention receive with gratitude the Statement, welcoming the substantial agreement it expresses. As did the International Commission and the national Anglican–Roman Catholic Commission in the United States, we see our faith and the faith of our Church in the Statement:

And be it further resolved, that this Convention commend the Statement to our representatives in other unity discussions and to the Church at large for study and evaluation.

91. General Convention, 1976: Authorize Trial Use of COCU Liturgy

Resolved, That this 65th General Convention authorize, subject to the approval of the several diocesan bishops, for trial use in special study sessions, that certain document entitled "An Order of Worship for the Proclamation of the Word of God and the Celebration of the Lord's Supper," published by the Forward Movement Publications and copyright 1968 by the Executive Committee of the Consultation on Church Union; *provided,* that an ordained Priest of this Church is the celebrant, or one of the celebrants at a con-celebrated service; and *provided further,* that the rubric on page 25 of said document concerning the reverent disposition of the blessed Elements be scrupulously observed.

92. General Convention, 1976: Toward a Mutual Recognition of Members: An Affirmation (COCU)

Resolved, that this 65th General Convention receive with gratitude the document transmitted to it by the Consultation on Church Union entitled "Toward a Mutual Recognition of Members: An Affirmation," welcoming the agreement as representing the traditional Anglican teaching that "The Church is the Body of which Jesus Christ is the Head and all baptized persons are the members";

And be it further resolved, that this 65th General Convention hereby in principle endorses the document known as "Toward a Mutual Recognition of Members: An Affirmation" together with the Preamble and footnotes recommended by the Joint Commission on Ecumenical Relations and appended to this resolution, and the revised text of Annex II, as follows . . .

Preamble

We believe that the document, "Toward the Mutual Recognition of Members: An Affirmation" is a promising way of quickening the sense of responsibility among our several churches for all other baptized persons and for the ecclesial bodies in which they live and by which they express their discipleship and obedience to Christ and respond to His summons to witness and mission. Our common baptism by water and in the name of the Father and of the Son and of the Holy Spirit establishes an imperative for ecumenical concern. If beyond all denominational bodies and divisions we are summoned to live in a genuine fellowship with all who share membership in the body of Christ, this gives importance to all our ecumenical activities. By such activities we seek to make manifest the truth of our common membership in Christ which is so often obscured by our narrow denominational loyalties.

Toward the Mutual Recognition of Members: An Affirmation

As witness to the faith that animates our participation in the Consultation of Church Union, we, the Episcopal Church in the United States of America, confess that all who are baptized into Christ are members of His universal Church and belong to and share in His ministry through the People of the One God, Father, Son, and Holy Spirit.[1]

At this time, when we are living our way toward church union, we affirm that membership in a particular church is membership in the whole people of God. As a participating church in the Consultation we intend to work toward removing any impediments in our life which prevent us from receiving into full membership all members so recognized.

In the divided state of our churches the word "membership" is used to refer to enrollment in a particular church.[2] Affirming our oneness in baptism does not abolish membership in all particular churches, nor does it mean plural simultaneous membership in several, nor does it refer merely to the practice of transferring membership from one particular church to another.

Therefore, we covenant with the other participating churches in the Consultation on Church Union to do everything possible[3] to hasten the day when, together with other churches to whom through the Spirit's leading we may yet be joined, we all shall be one in a visible fellowship truly catholic, truly evangelical and truly reformed.

The Joint Commission on Ecumenical Relations, in recommending the Affirmation above to the 1976 General Convention for endorsement, appended the three following footnotes which became part of the Convention's resolution:

1. Since this Affirmation will have to be its own context, it should state its concepts clearly, explicitly and completely. Thus, baptism should be stated as with water in the name of the Father, Son, and Holy Spirit.

2. While welcoming and endorsing the COCU "Toward a Mutual Recognition of Members: An Affirmation" as an expression of the historic position of this Church that "the Church is the Body of which Jesus Christ is the Head and all baptized persons are the members," the Joint Commission on Ecumenical Relations wishes to call attention to the first sentence of the third paragraph of the Affirmation which acknowledges that the word "membership" often means primarily enrollment in a particular church or congregation. In the divided and separated state of our churches, we believe, however, that each of the differing ecclesial traditions provides a distinctive kind of nurturing and shaping of the spiritual life of those who share in the tradition and that such membership, therefore, is a relationship far more pervasive and internal than the mere enrollment of a name on a roster of church members. In our Anglican tradition an example is our emphasis on a mature commitment in the life of the believer involving confirmation by a bishop. What is more, we believe some of these ecclesial bodies have preserved important elements in the Christian experience which need to be identified and taken up into the life of a united Church. In our opinion a more widespread and frank discussion of and living with these distinctive elements in our several traditions needs to take place before we can make wise and appropriate decisions about the character of a united Church.

3. We understand this sentence as a promise to do everything that accords with Scripture and Tradition (as defined in previous COCU statements) to arrive at the goal of union.

93. General Convention, 1976: Reaffirmation of the Lund Principle

Resolved, and in the spirit of the "Lund Principle" approved by our church's delegates and others attending the World Conference on Faith and Order in 1952 and affirmed by the 1968 Lambeth Conference, that the Episcopal Church at every level of its life be urged to act together and in concert with other churches of Jesus Christ in all matters except those in which deep differences of conviction of church order compel us to act separately;

And be it further resolved, that in all future presentations of budget and program to this General Convention, consideration be given to what efforts have been expended to secure data ecumenically and to plan ecumenically;

And be it further resolved, that the dioceses be urged to establish a similar policy of ecumenical review and planning.

94. General Convention, 1976: Communion with the Church of South India

Resolved, that this Church enter into communion with the Church of South India and instructs the Secretary of Convention to communicate this action to the proper authorities in the Church of South India.

95. General Convention, 1976: Communion with the Mar Thoma Church

Resolved, that this Church, noting that the Mar Thoma Syrian Church of Malabar is a true part of the Church Universal, holding the catholic faith and possessing the apostolic ministry of bishops, priests and deacons, enter into communion with that Church, and instructs the Secretary to communicate this action to the Metropolitan, Juhanon Mar Thoma, informing him that we would be grateful for similar action on the part of the Mar Thoma Church.

96. General Convention, 1976: Conversations with Baptists

Resolved, that the Joint Commission on Ecumenical Relations establish ongoing conversations with the several Baptist associations, churches and conventions through those agencies which are appropriate in order to create better understanding and communication, and to foster where possible, local cooperation in ministry.

97. General Convention, 1976: Interim Eucharistic Fellowship Events (COCU)

Resolved, That this 65th General Convention commend to the consideration of the several diocesan bishops the authorization of Interim

Eucharistic Fellowship events in their dioceses, conforming to the guidelines appended hereto.

ANNEX I
Guidelines for Interim Eucharistic Fellowship

(*Adopted by the House of Bishops, Oaxtepec, Mexico, October 1974*)

Whereas, A responsible consequence of our Church's commitment to the Unity of Christ's Church requires experience in eucharistic fellowship with others who seek this same unity with us, and

Whereas, The churches participating in the Consultation on Church Union have recommended a program for local eucharistic celebration involving churches whose common commitment provides a community base for that program known as "Interim Eucharistic Fellowship" and

Whereas, The Joint Commission on Ecumenical Relations has prepared suggested guidelines to assist Episcopal congregations in a responsible participation in Interim Eucharistic Fellowship,

Therefore be it resolved, That the House of Bishops commend to the several dioceses of this Church participation in local expressions of Interim Eucharistic Fellowship in accordance with the guidelines proposed by the Joint Commission on Ecumenical Relations as follows:

1. Participation by any Episcopal congregation must be authorized by the Bishop after he has determined that the program conforms to the "Guidelines for Interim Eucharistic Fellowship."

2. The COCU liturgy, approved by the General Convention, will be used for the Eucharist.

3. The elements of bread and wine ordained by Christ shall be used for the Holy Communion and provision will be made for the reverent disposal of that which remains after the Communion.

4. An Episcopal priest will be involved as a con-celebrant at the Holy Table at each of the Eucharists.

5. A program involving an agreed upon number of eucharists within a specific period should involve the congregations of the participating churches. These should be preceded by appropriate gatherings for joint study and worship.

6. An evaluation of the program approved initially by the Bishop be made with the Bishop involved, or one he has designated, before Interim Eucharistic Fellowship extends beyond the plan initially approved by the Bishop.

98. Lambeth XI, 1978: The Wider Episcopal Fellowship

14. The Conference requests the Archbishop of Canterbury:

1. in consultation with the primates, to convene a meeting of Anglican bishops with bishops of Churches in which Anglicans have united with other Christians, and bishops from those Churches which are in full communion with Anglican Churches; and to discuss with them how bishops from these Churches could best play their part in future Lambeth Conferences;
2. to recognize the deep conviction of this Lambeth Conference that the expressed desire of both the Lusitanian and Spanish Reformed Churches to become fully integrated members of the Anglican Communion should receive both a warm and a positive response.

99. Lambeth XI, 1978: Relations with Lutheran Churches

The Conference encourages Anglican churches together with Lutheran churches in their area:

1. to study the report entitled 'Anglican-Lutheran International Conversations' (the Pullach Report, 1972), resolution 2 of the second meeting (Dublin, 1973) and resolution 5 of the third meeting (Trinidad, 1976) of the Anglican Consultative Council;
2. to give special attention to our ecclesial recognition of the Lutheran Church on the basis of these reports and resolutions; and
3. to seek ways of extending hospitality and of engaging in joint mission.

100. Lambeth XI, 1978: Ecumenical Relationships

28. The Conference:

1. re-affirms the readiness of the Anglican Communion as already expressed in resolution 44(c) of the Lambeth Conference of 1968 (with reference to the Uppsala Assembly of the World Council of Churches), to 'work for the time when a genuinely universal council may once more speak for all Christians';
2. acknowledges the pressing need stated by the Nairobi Assembly of the WCC that we should develop more truly sustained and sustaining relationships among the Churches, as we look toward the time when we can enjoy full conciliar fellowship (see *Breaking Barriers: Nairobi 1975*, p. 60);

3. encourages the member Churches of the Anglican Communion to pursue with perseverance and hopefulness the search for full communion and mutual recognition of ministries between themselves and other World Confessional Families and the Methodist and Baptist Churches both internationally and locally, on the basis of the Lambeth Quadrilateral and the counsel offered by successive meetings of the Anglican Consultative Council;

4. calls on member Churches of the Anglican Communion to review their commitment to ecumenical structure as well as bilateral conversations at various levels with a view to strengthening the common advance by all Churches to the goal of visible unity;

5. notes that many Christians belong to Churches not members of the World Council of Churches and wishes to develop the opportunities for dialogue and common action with these Churches when appropriate. In particular, the Conference welcomes the participation of Anglican lay persons, priests, and bishops in the Lausanne Congress on World Evangelism of 1974 and subsequent meetings, in which many of these Churches are represented.

101. Lambeth XI, 1978: World Council of Churches

29. The Conference urges that, in this thirtieth anniversary year of the World Council of Churches, all Churches of the Anglican Communion re-affirm their support and strengthen their understanding of this body, which is not only the most comprehensive expression of the ecumenical movement, but also the chief vehicle of world-wide ecumenical co-operation and service. It also asks the World Council of Churches to accept the guidance given through Section 3 of the Conference, considering war and violence;

(a) to re-examine our complicity with violence in its many forms;
(b) to take with the utmost seriousness the question which the teaching of Jesus places against *all* violence in human relationships.

102. Lambeth XI, 1978: Relations with United Churches

32. The Conference requests that those member Churches that have placed limitations on the ministry among them of episcopally ordained clergy from united Churches with which they are in communion be asked to reconsider these restrictions so that the same courtesy might be accorded to the clergy of those Churches as to those of other Churches in communion with us.

103. Lambeth XI, 1978: The Anglican–Roman Catholic International Commission

33. The Conference:

1. welcomes the work of the Anglican–Roman Catholic International Commission which was set up jointly by the Lambeth Conference of 1968 and by the Vatican Secretariat for Promoting Christian Unity;
2. recognizes in the three Agreed Statements of this Commission* a solid achievement, one in which we can recognize the faith of our Church, and hopes that they will provide a basis for sacramental sharing between our two Communions if and when the finished Statements are approved by the respective authorities of our Communions;
3. invites the ARCIC to provide further explication of the Agreed Statements in consideration of responses received by them;
4. commends to the appropriate authorities in each Communion further consideration of the implications of the Agreed Statements in the light of the report of the Joint Preparatory Commission (the Malta Report received by the Lambeth Conference 1968—see p. 134 of its report), with a view to bringing about a closer sharing between our two communions in life, worship, and mission;
5. asks the Secretary General of the Anglican Consultative Council to bring this resolution to the attention of the various synods of the Anglican Communion for discussion and action;
6. asks that in any continuing Commission, the Church of the South and the East be adequately represented.

104. Lambeth XI, 1978: Anglican–Roman Catholic Marriages

34. The Conference welcomes the report of the Anglican–Roman Catholic Commission on 'The Theology of Marriage and its Application to Mixed Marriages' (1975).

In particular we record our gratitude for the general agreement on the theology of Christian marriage where outlined and especially for the affirmation of the 'first order principle'† of life-long union (i.e. in the case of a break-down of a marriage). We also welcome the recognition that the differing pastoral practices of our two traditions do in

* Eucharistic Doctrine (*the Windsor statement, 1971*); Ministry and Ordination (*Canterbury, 1973*), *and* Authority in the Church (*Venice, 1976*).

† *See* Anglican–Roman Catholic Marriages (*London, CIO, 1975*), *p. 21, para. 49.*

fact recognize and seek to share a common responsibility for those for whom '*no* course *absolutely* consonant with the first order principle of marriage as a life-long union may be available.'

We also endorse the recommendations of the Commission in respect of inter-Church marriages:

1. that, after joint preparation and pastoral care given by both the Anglican and Roman Catholic counsellors concerned, a marriage may validly and lawfully take place before the duly authorized minister of either party, without the necessity of Roman Catholic dispensation;
2. that, as an alternative to an affirmation or promise by the Roman Catholic party in respect of the baptism and upbringing of any children, the Roman Catholic parish priest may give a written assurance to his bishop that he has put the Roman Catholic partner in mind of his or her obligations and that the other spouse knows what these are.

We note that there are some variations in different regions in the provisions of Roman Catholic Directories on inter-Church marriages. We nevertheless warmly welcome the real attempts of many Roman Catholic Episcopal Conferences to be pastorally sensitive to those problems arising out of their regulations, which remain an obstacle to the continued growth of fraternal relations between us. In particular, we note a growing Roman Catholic understanding that a decision as to the baptism and upbringing of any children should be made within the unity of the marriage, in which the Christian conscience of both partners must be respected. We urge that this last development be encouraged.

The problems associated with marriage between members of our two Communions continue to hinder inter-Church relations and progress towards unity. While we recognize that there has been an improved situation in some places as a result of the *Motu Proprio,* the general principles underlying the Roman Catholic position are unacceptable to Anglicans. Equality of conscience as between partners in respect of all aspects of their marriage (and in particular with regard to the baptism and religious upbringing of children) is something to be affirmed both for its own sake and for the sake of an improved relationship between the Churches.

105. Lambeth XI, 1978: Anglican-Orthodox Theological Dialogue
35. The Conference:

1. welcomes the achievement of the Anglican-Orthodox Joint Doctrinal Commission as expressed in the Moscow Agreed Statement of 1976, and believes that this goes far to realize the hopes about Anglican-Orthodox dialogue expressed at Lambeth 1968;
2. requests the Anglican-Orthodox Joint Doctrinal Commission to explore the fundamental questions of doctrinal agreement and disagreement in our Churches; and to promote regional groups for theological dialogue which would bring to the Commission not only reactions to their work, but also theological issues arising out of local experience;
3. requests that all member Churches of the Anglican Communion should consider omitting the *Filioque* from the Nicene Creed, and that the Anglican-Orthodox Joint Doctrinal Commission through the Anglican Consultative Council should assist them in presenting the theological issues to their appropriate synodical bodies and should be responsible for any necessary consultation with other Churches of the Western tradition.

Index to Documents

Friends of Peter Day

George M. Alexander
John M. Allin
Paul B. and
Margaret H. Anderson
Robert M. Anderson
Robert B. Appleyard
Robert P. Atkinson
John A. Baden
Scott Field Bailey
Hubert D. Barnes
Ruth Tiffany
  Barnhouse
Dupuy Bateman, Jr.
William Cardinal Baum
Frederick H. Belden
Lee A. Belford
V. Nelle Bellamy
Charles Bennison
Harold J. Berman
Page E. S. Bigelow
Matthew P. Bigliardi
Marion B. Bingley
Roger Blanchard
J. R. Bolger
John H. Bonner, Jr.
James B. Boyles
Allen Brown, Jr.
Elwyn Brown
Isis Brown
James B. Brown
Edmond L. Browning
William G. Burrill
Robert V. Burrows
John H. Burt
Sister Sara Butler
Chester J. Byrns
Isabel M. Calkins
James E. Carroll
Pamela P. Chinnis
William H. Clark
Robert L. Clayton
John B. Coburn
Robert H. Cochrane
Ned Cole

Kenneth R. Coleman
Robert P. Coval
William J. Cox
James L. Cummings
A. Donald Davies
Donald Davis
Graham R. Delbridge
William A. Dimmick
William E. Dornemann
F. Patricia Drapes
James L. Duncan
Eva Elder
Hunley A. Elebash
William H. Folwell
William C. Frey
Stanley P. Gasek
Charles T. Gaskell
W. Fred Gates
Robert Gibson, Jr.
Judy Gillespie
Jackson E. Gilliam
Helen S. Glantz
Margaret R. Grant
Duncan M. Gray, Jr.
William B. Green
Lloyd E. Gressle
James Griffiss
John S. Groenfeldt
Hal R. Gross
George T. Guernsey,
  III
Don M. Gury
Samir Habiby
Donald H. V. and
Ruth G. Hallock
E. R. Hardy
Joseph L. Hargrove
Joseph M. Harte
E. Paul Haynes
Hobart H. Heistand
C. H. Helmsing
W. E. Hobbs
Phebe M. Hoff
Wilbur E. Hogg

Urban T. Holmes
Robert W. Huston
Jean C. Jackson
Frederick M. Jelly
Evelyn B. Jenisch
David E. Johnson
Jean H. Johnson
Edward W. Jones
William A. Jones, Jr.
Frederick D. Jordan
Christoph Keller, Jr.
Marion M. Kelleran
James W. Kennedy
Hanford L. King, Jr.
John E. Kitagawa
Franklin J. Klohn
John M. Krumm
Lewis H. Lancaster, Jr.
John A. Langfeldt
Charles R. Lawrence
William B. Lawson
David K. Leighton, Sr.
George Leisenring
Raymond W. Lessard
Charles H. Long
Gerald N. McAllister
H. Coleman McGehee
George L. McGonigle
Leo Malania
Henry A. Male, Jr.
William H. Marmion
Robert J. Marshall
Nancy L. Marvel
George T. Masuda
DeWitt L. Miller
Gerald F. Moede
Albert T. Mollegen
James W. Montgomery
M. M. Hamond Moore
Paul Moore, Jr.
Marion E. Morey
James F. Morse
Mother Mary Grace
George M. Murray

Kilmer· Myers
Paul Neuhauser
Richard C. Nevius
William A. Norgren
Lyman C. Ogilby
Robert Ray Parks
Donald J. Parsons
William H. and
Priscilla E. Petersen
Morgan Porteus
John R. Portman
Chilton Powell
Jeanne Audrey Powers
David Preus
Charles P. Price
Quintin E. Primo, Jr.
H. Boone Porter
Frederick W. Putnam
Anna L. Quillen
David B. Reed
Douglas E. Remer
R. E. Richardson
Roddey Reid, Jr.
Victor M. Rivera
Harold B. Robinson
G. Charles Rowe
Herbert J. Ryan
John S. Sammond
William E. Sanders
Eric G. Scharf
David W. Schmidt
Oma H. Schmidt
Wayne Schwab
Edward W. Scott
W. Herbert Scott
Massey H. Shepherd,
Jr.
W. Bry Shields, Jr.

George A. Shipman
Elton O. Smith, Jr.
Philip A. Smith
Robert R. Spears, Jr.
John S. Spong
Sara Duff Steptoe
Alexander D. Stewart
Furman C. Stough
Gray Temple
Fredrica Harris
Thompsett
Thomas E. Tiller, Jr.
Robert G. Torbet
Richard M. Trelease,
Jr.
Edward C. Turner
Warren H. Turner, Jr.
Robert L. Turnipseed
C. Charles Vaché
Samuel Van Culin
Albert W. Van Duzer
Henry B. Veatch
David L. Vikner
Arthur A. Vogel
James D. Warner
Cynthia C. Wedel
William L. Weiler
William G. Weinhauer
Edward R. Welles
Edward N. West
Paul Moore Wheeler
Robert H. Whitaker
Harry B. Whitley
Frederick P. Williams
Bette T. Winchester
Robert C. Witcher
Fergus With
William J. Wolf

Robert M. Wolterstorff
Robert L. Woodbury
J. Robert Wright
Frances M. Young
Bishops' Committee on
Ecumenical and
Interreligious
Affairs—National
Conference of
Catholic Bishops
Convention of the Dio-
cese of Washington
Council on Christian
Unity, Christian
Church (Disciples of
Christ)
Diocese of
Eastern Oregon
Diocese of Virginia
Ecumenical
Committee
Episcopal
Churchwomen of the
Diocese of Newark
Episcopal Divinity
School
Greek Orthodox
Archdiocese of North
and South America
J. Ogden Hoffman, Jr.
and the People of
Trinity Church,
Folsom, CA
Southwest Florida
Committee on
Ecumenical Relations